Two of Us

Two of Us

.

John Lennon & Paul McCartney
Behind the Myth

GEOFFREY GIULIANO

PENGUIN STUDIO

PENGUIN STUDIO
Published by the Penguin Group
Penguin Putnam Inc., 375 Hudson Street,
New York, New York 10014, U.S.A.
Penguin Books Ltd, 27 Wrights Lane,
London W8 5TZ, England
Penguin Books Australia Ltd, Ringwood,
Victoria, Australia
Penguin Books Canada Ltd, 10 Alcorn Avenue,
Toronto, Ontario, Canada M4V 3B2
Penguin Books (N.Z.) Ltd, 182–190 Wairau Road,
Auckland 10, New Zealand

Penguin Books Ltd, Registered Offices:
Harmondsworth, Middlesex, England

First published by Penguin Studio 1999

1 3 5 7 9 10 8 6 4 2

Frontispiece: Lennon and McCartney in Liverpool, circa 1960.
Photo © Gina Delponio

LIBRARY OF CONGRESS CATALOGING IN PUBLICATION DATA
Giuliano, Geoffrey.
Two of us : John Lennon & Paul McCartney behind the myth /
Geoffrey Giuliano.
p.   cm.
ISBN 0-14-023460-8
1. Lennon, John, 1940–1980.   2. McCartney, Paul.
3. Rock musicians—Biography.
ML420.L38   G59   1999
782.42166'092'2—ddc21
[B]
96-50894
MN r97

Printed in the United States of America
Set in Simoncini Garamond
Designed by Kathryn Parise

*O*nce a lovely little black-and-white holstein calf named Pishima came to live in the country with a family that loved animals very much. Pishima was quite small and seemed frail, which made the family love her even more. After only a few days the baby calf laid down in her stall and went to sleep forever. The family was heartbroken.

Meanwhile, in homes on just about every street in the free world, innocent animals like Pishima were being cooked up and served to people without anyone ever thinking a thing about it. Back in the country, however, the family remembered Pishima and mourned her passing. This book is dedicated to Pishima and the many people around the world who care enough to love and protect all life. Om Tat Sat.

They did love each other very much throughout the time I knew them in the studio. But the tension was there mostly because they never really collaborated. They were never Rodgers and Hart. They were always songwriters who helped each other with little bits and pieces. One would have most of a song finished, play it to the other, and he'd say, "Well, why don't you do this?" That was just about the way their collaboration worked.

—GEORGE MARTIN

Well, first, I started off on my own. Very early on I met John, and we then, gradually, started to write stuff together.

There's a lot of random in our songs . . . writing, thinking, letting others think of bits—then bang, you have the jigsaw puzzle.

—PAUL McCARTNEY

We wrote together because we enjoyed it a lot sometimes, and also because they would say well, you're going to make an album, get together and knock off a few songs, just like a job.

—JOHN LENNON

The priority was always the song. The song is what remains. It's not how you've done it. I honestly believe in the song more than the music. It's the song people whistle. You don't whistle my drum part. And John and Paul wrote some amazing songs.

—RINGO STARR

I would especially like to thank Deborah Lynn Black for her editorial assistance.

Immensely helpful in the production of this work were: Avalon and India, Stefano Castino, Michael Dor, Devin Giuliano, Sesa Giuliano, Robin Scott Giuliano, His Divine Grace A. C. Bhaktivedanta Swami Prabhupada, Joseph and Myrna Juliana, PETA, Charles F. Rosenay!!!, Marty Schiffert, SRI, Vrndarani Devi, and Dr. Ronald Zuker. Special thanks to my long-suffering editors at Penguin.

In discussions of the various Beatles' recording sessions chronicled throughout this book, only those compositions written by John Lennon and Paul McCartney (jointly or separately) are given real emphasis. The works of George Harrison and Ringo Starr may be mentioned in passing, with no strict analysis as to the particulars of their creation or eventual release.

Further, when a date is given for the taping of a particular song, this represents only the time of the work's initial recording. As many readers know, the Beatles worked on their compositions over several days or even weeks, sometimes rerecording the same track over and over again (as in the case of the *Let It Be* album).

Standing Room Only /
Touched by Genius

*T*hat we have enjoyed the magical music of John Lennon and Paul McCartney for so long now speaks well for the complicated twosome's phenomenal talent and staying power. Many important artists blossomed in the sixties and early seventies: Jimi Hendrix, Bob Dylan, the Doors, the Incredible String Band, the Who, the Moody Blues, the Bonzo Dog Doo-Dah Band, Led Zeppelin, and Pink Floyd, to name a few. Still, great as they were, few, if any, matched Liverpool lads John and Paul for sheer originality and off-the-cuff charisma.

It's one thing for an artist to create a body of work that carries the power to inspire a legion of questioning youth on the weary trail to adulthood, but quite another to produce something so opalescent and innocently ingenious as to permanently transform the very culture that bore it in the first place.

This author, for one, first experienced an array of compelling new notions and aspirations on the receiving end of Lennon and McCartney's masterful collective musical visions. Consciousness expansion, women's issues, emotional isolation, political activism, irrational violence, interpersonal relationships, human and animal rights, spiritual transcendence, ecological concerns, social responsibility, high art, and low fashion all ran through the daring duo's voluminous Beatles and post-Beatles works. Experiencing, it seemed, along with the listener, such life-sculpting imperatives for the very first time, John and Paul had a unique way of melding their high-flown ideals into such alluring musical forms as to completely disarm even the most hardened and opinionated critics.

"Tell the truth and make it rhyme," John Lennon once advised colleague David Bowie back in the machinelike mid-seventies, when asked his primary musical proviso. "I like to think anybody with an open mind can do this," he quipped to me even earlier in the crowded hallway of a Syracuse art museum way back when.

Such mystical openness, one assumes, while philosophically available to all, surely roots itself in only the most finely tuned and accepting of vessels. All told, the musical maelstrom of Lennon and McCartney remains unequaled in its sincerity, breadth of vision, and unfettered, everyday tunefulness. That we will not soon see their like again is reaffirmed daily with each pathetic twist of the holy FM dial.

When at last it was finally over in April 1970, John Lennon stood on a rainy, windswept London corner and growled into a battery of faceless microphones, "It's nothing important, you know. The Beatles are just a bastard pop group that broke up, that's all."

I shuddered along with millions of other turned-on teens who had, perhaps irrationally, invested too many hopes in the all too human foursome from suburban Liverpool. Despite Lennon's nay-saying, however, the Beatles were hugely important. Natural leaders, without ever wanting to be. Mystical poets laying down their simple truth through the timeless medium of popular (or people's) music. Enlightened harbingers of a higher voice, once heard never forgotten. The Beatles were easily all this and more.

Lennon and McCartney always actively disdained such sentiments, insisting instead that they were probably more lucky than talented. Just two vaguely inspired young guys who demanded a bit more than life had originally offered. Two sparsely trained musicians wildly in love with their convoluted art. "We're here to try and explode the talent myth," Paul McCartney casually announced in an interview soon after the Beatles' flying carpet first took off. "If we can do it *anybody* can." It was a message we most definitely needed to hear.

Obeisance to the double-headed dream Phoenix of long ago.

—GEOFFREY GIULIANO
(*Jagannatha Dasa*)
Western New York
September 11, 1998

Two of Us

Footprints /
Getting Together

For all the world knows, the Beatles sprang fully grown from the dank Liverpool earth, drawing their undoubted creative brilliance from the unhappy facts of life that now define the once-prosperous seaport city. The actual fact, however, while significantly less dramatic, is far more human. That the Fab Four changed the world is without question. That they changed it for the better, too, is now almost universally understood. With more than thirty years of masterful publicity, calculated misinformation, and legend, however, the question of *who* this quartet of roving twentieth-century minstrels really was remains. And who, in particular, were John Lennon and Paul McCartney.

It's easy, of course, to imagine how the seemingly unknowing fate that first brought them together touched down and carried them off to meet their destiny as the pied pipers of the Love Generation. Such simple strategies, however, fall short of the convoluted series of chance encounters, frustrated relationships, and winsome ironies that ultimately conjured the Beatles we so fondly remember.

The seed that would one day blossom into the songwriting collective known as Lennon and McCartney was sown when they greeted each other in passing outside a local suburban chippy late in the spring of 1957. Following that first brief encounter Paul recalls seeing John climbing aboard the number 86 bus bound for town a couple of uneventful weeks later. The "official" meeting place of these two potential musical titans, however, took place at St. Peter's Parish Church in blustery Woolton Village. The date was Saturday, July 6, 1957, sometime in the early afternoon, with Lennon and his ragtag skiffle group, the Quarry Men, emphatically busking away on a makeshift stage to the delight of the tiny hamlet's perky youth.

In October 1986 Paul McCartney sat down for a rare interview responding to my questions regarding his fortuitous first meeting with the famous front end of the Lennon-McCartney juggernaut and his extravagant life and times. "As it turned out, John and I were mates with a fellow from Woolton, Ivan Vaughn," he rolled off casually.

One summer's day, he invited me to come along to a fête in Woolton. At the time John was about sixteen, so I was maybe fourteen or fifteen. I remember coming across the field hearing all this great music, which turned out to be from the Quarry Men's little Tanoy system. I thought, "Oh great, I'll go listen to the band," because I was very much into the music. . . .

I remember John singing a lovely tune by the Del Vikings he'd heard on the radio called "Come Go with Me." He didn't really know all the words, so he made up his own. Good bluesy stuff like, "Come go with me down to the penitentiary." He was playing banjo chords on his guitar, which only had about four strings at the time.

After it was over, I met the lads in the church hall. They were having a beer, I think. . . . In those days, the lineup of the band was Len Garry, Pete Shotton, Colin Hanton on drums, Eric Griffiths on guitar, and Nigel Whalley who acted as their manager.

We all used to think John was pretty cool. I mean, he was a bit older and would therefore do a little more greased-back hair and things than we were allowed. He had nice big sideboards and with his drake and all, he did look a bit of a Ted. That particular day I happened to pick up an old guitar that was laying around and started to play "Twenty Flight Rock." I knew a lot of the words, which was very good currency in those days.

Paul again picks up the story. "Later, we all went down to the pub, and I had to try and kid the barman I was really eighteen. As I recall, there was a bit of a panic on, because suddenly word went round a vicious mob was forming up the street considering whether or not to invade the pub! Thankfully, that blew over and in the end we had a very nice evening.

"There was this beery old man getting nearer and breathing down my neck as I was playing. What's this drunk doing? I thought. . . . It was John."

Lennon's recollection of their historic meeting was one of begrudging respect. "He could obviously play guitar," he later admitted. "I half thought to myself, 'He's as good as me.' I'd been kingpin up to then. It went through my head that I'd have to keep him in line if I let him join. But he was good, so he was worth having."

A week later, Paul was in the Quarry Men, merging two divergent personalities and talents that would indelibly change the path of popular music forever. As *Village Voice* reporters Robert Christgau and John Piccarrella later wrote, "For the next decade plus, Paul's unreconstructed boyishness, snazzy melodic ideas, transcendent harmonies, and insufferable pop treacle would clutter and inestimably enrich John's passion, calling, and way of life. That's why it's important to remember that John *chose* Paul, deliberately encouraging this alien alter ego to modify and distort his forceful music."

One need only to peer into their backgrounds to note their dramatic differences. The son of a cotton salesman, Paul, along with his younger brother, Mike, spent much of his youth living in subsidized housing in exchange for his mother Mary's services as a midwife. Recalling those days, Paul has said, "All I wanted out of life was a hundred pounds. I thought with that I could have a house, a guitar, and a car."

Though money was often scarce, Jim McCartney was determined to give his boys a dignified rearing. "I was always very well-mannered and polite," remembers Paul. "My dad brought me up to always tip my cap to my elders." Jim's golden words of "toleration and moderation" would later figure in Paul's lighter, gentler, at times even saccharine, lyrical content acting as the earthy equalizer to John's more biting critical edge. As *Mersey Beat* editor Bill Harry confirmed, "I'm sure it was his father's influence that was behind Paul always liking ballads and soft songs and numbers from musicals."

In school, the ambitious, upwardly mobile McCartney manifested his eagerness to please by being voted "head boy" of his form several times, which allowed him extra privileges. His fellow students at the Liverpool Institute remember him as an exceptional class organizer, a skill he would later exploit to the fullest as a Beatle.

By contrast, Lennon was raised by his Uncle George and Aunt Mary "Mimi" Smith in a roomy, well-ordered, semidetached home known as Mendips at 251 Menlove Avenue, just outside Woolton Village. John's doting uncle, a gentleman farmer with a lucrative interest in a family dairy, scattered to the winds the nonsensical notion that John Lennon somehow emerged from the squalid slums of inner city Liverpool.

Unlike McCartney's compact nuclear family, Lennon was surrounded by an extended clan of five strong women he termed his "Amazon aunties." "My early feminist education," John termed the experience. "It was scary as a child because there was nobody I could relate to," Lennon later remembered. "Neither my auntie, friends, or anybody, could ever see what I did. It was very, very frightening and many times the only contact I had was reading about people like Oscar Wilde, Dylan Thomas, or Van Gogh in all those old books Mimi had. They talked about all the suffering they went through because of their visions. They were tortured by society for trying to express themselves. All I ever saw was loneliness."

A precocious child with a talent for drawing and writing, by the age of seven he was even penning his own little books. One of them, "Sport Speed and Illustration by J. W. Lennon," contained a witty collection of poems, caricatures, and short stories with a keen sense of the absurd. McCartney recalls the literary Lennon: "Inside the house he'd often be busy at the typewriter writing in his famous *In His Own Write* style. I never actually knew anyone who personally owned a typewriter before!"

Interestingly, both McCartney and Lennon claim their earliest musical influence was a parent. With Paul it was his gregarious father, Jim. "If anyone was my big inspiration it was him," he stated unequivocally. "I used to like the radio a lot. Fred Astaire I loved. From a very early age I was interested in singing tunes. My dad used to play a lot of music and even had his own little group called Jim Mac's Band, so I suppose I was quite influenced by him. He had to give it up eventually because he got false teeth and couldn't play the trumpet properly anymore."

Paul took up the trumpet himself at thirteen and quickly discovered he could pick out such tunes as "When the Saints Go Marching In" by ear. His musical tastes swung over an eclectic mix from Pat Boone to Ray Charles. When Lonnie Donegan spearheaded Britain's skiffle craze in the mid-fifties, McCartney was instantly hooked. "You only had to know a couple of chords. Somebody had to get a washboard to do the rhythm so you'd have to go to your mum and say 'Have you got any washboards?'"

If Paul's inspiration was his dad, then Lennon's was definitely his whimsical, fun-loving mother, Julia. His absentee father, Alfred "Freddie" Lennon (having long since deserted the family), left Julia ill-equipped to provide a stable home for her son, so John was placed in the custody of Mimi at age five. It wasn't until his teens that Lennon became reacquainted with the spirited woman whose talents ranged from juggling to picking the banjo and who opened up the world of music to her son.

"The first tune I ever learned to play was 'That'll Be the Day,'" John told an interviewer years later. "My mother taught it to me on the banjo, sitting there with endless patience until I managed to work out all the chords. I remember her slowing down the record so that I could scribble out the words. First hearing Buddy absolutely knocked me for a loop. And to think it was my own mother who was turning me on to it all."

It was Julia who bought John his first guitar and taught him twelve-bar boogies. Fueled by her encouragement and Mimi's disdain, John began to take seriously both the brave new sounds of rock and roll and the ground-breaking artists who were making them. "Before Elvis," Lennon was once quoted as saying, "there was nothing. It was Elvis who really got me buying records. I thought his early stuff was great. The whole Bill Haley era kind of passed me by. When his records came on the wireless, my mother used to like them okay, but they didn't really do anything for me."

McCartney, too, remembers a pair of tunes Julia taught them. "Oddly, one of them was 'Wedding Bells Are Breaking Up That Old Gang of Mine' while another was definitely 'Ramona.' Much later during the Beatle years John and I attempted to write a few songs with a similar feel, with 'Here, There and Everywhere' coming immediately to mind."

In fact, it was the bathroom at Julia's place on Blomfield Road, a fifteen-minute walk from Mendips, that became the popular site of early jam sessions with John and his pals. Perched precariously atop the commode, tucked like sardines into the bathtub or tentatively saddling up on the sink, they somehow managed not only to fit, but actually to play! The door shut securely behind them, they enthusiastically tucked into a bevy of now-classic tunes such as "Maggie Mae," "Besame Mucho," "Alleycat," or the sneaky theme from *The Third Man.*

McCartney remembers, "It was the best room in the house, hands down! Quite crowded too. Don't forget it wasn't only us in there but also our instruments, as well as a tiny pignose amp we used to carry around. Many a fine tune has been composed in that little room, let me tell you. In fact, at home I used to not only stand around with one leg on the toilet, but, if perchance I had to actually go, I would lug my guitar in with me instead of a book. I remember me dad used to say, 'Paul, what are you doing playing guitar in the toilet?' And I'd say, 'Well . . . what's wrong with that, then?'"

Besides their well-defined differences, Lennon and McCartney shared the tragic loss of their mothers. Paul was just fourteen when Mary McCartney succumbed to invasive breast cancer on October 31, 1956, at the age of forty-seven. Paul later admitted blaming his mother's untimely death for turning him off religion: he had prayed for days for her to return home.

"Daft prayers, you know; if you bring her back I'll be very, very good for always. I thought it just shows how stupid religion is. See the prayers didn't work when I really needed them to as well."

"Lose a mother and find a guitar," goes Mike McCartney's memorable line regarding his elder brother's resulting obsession with music. Jim scraped up enough money to buy his son a £15 Zenith guitar, which immediately became the overriding force in his life. "He was lost," said Mike. "He didn't have time to eat or think about anything else. He played it on the lavatory, in the bath, everywhere."

Channeling his pain into his music, always keeping his emotions locked away, Paul's stiff upper lip was a frustrating enigma to John. "How can you sit there and act normal with your mother dead? If anything like that happened to me I'd go off me head."

The irony of that statement became a shattering reality over the fateful summer of 1958. On July 15, Julia, on her way home from Mendips following a visit with Mimi, was fatally hit by a car as she crossed Menlove Avenue for the bus stop. It was rumored that the driver, an off-duty policeman, was under the influence of alcohol. For the seventeen-year-old Lennon, the loss was devastating.

An hour or so after it happened, a copper came to the door to let us know. It was awful, like some dreadful film where they ask you if you're the victim's son and all that. It was absolutely the worst night of my life. I lost me mother twice. Once as a child of five, and then again at seventeen. It made me very, very bitter. I was just trying to reestablish a relationship with her when she was killed. We'd caught up on so much, Julia and I, in just a few short years. We could communicate. We got on. Deep inside, I thought, "Sod it, I've got no real responsibilities to anyone now." Anyway, Twitchy [Lennon's ruthless nickname for his mother's common-law husband, John "Bobby" Dykins] and I got a cab over to Sefton General where she was lying dead. There was no way I could ever bear to look at her. I remember rabbiting on hysterically to the driver all the way there. Twitchy went in to see her for a few minutes, but it turned out to be too much for the poor sod, and he broke down in my arms out in the lobby. I couldn't seem to cry, however; not then anyway. I suppose I was frozen inside.

McCartney remembers how the tragedy united them, as they struggled to cope with their mutual loss.

When I look back on Julia's death, all I see is the word T-R-A-G-E-D-Y in big, black letters. The only way I could help was to empathize, as I'd had the same thing happen to me. I mean, there wasn't anything I could say that would just sort of magically patch him up. That kind of hurt goes far too deep. There was, however, one rather funny incident that happened a year or so after Julia had gone. John was just beginning to get his act together again, you know. That is, he could bluff it out a bit better. I remember us meeting up with someone who happened to ask how my mother was getting on. "Well, actually, she died a few years ago," I replied. "Oh, I'm awfully sorry, son." Turning to John, they asked him the same question, only to be told precisely the exact thing. We somehow found their deep embarrassment rather amusing. Actually, it was a wonderful way of masking our true feelings, and it gave us both a bit more of a bond.

According to Lennon, the impact of the losses could not be understated. "We all want our mummies," he said in 1971. "I don't think there's any of us that don't. Paul lost his mother, so did I. That doesn't make womanizers of us, but we all want our mummies because I don't think we got enough of them."

Both Paul and John would later write and record tributes to their mothers in song (McCartney with "Let It Be" and Lennon "Julia"). Lennon, of course, repeatedly poured out his anguish throughout his musical career.

Both now firmly committed to their blossoming art, Lennon and McCartney were above all a solid team. While a round of faceless Quarry Men came and went, the undisputed nucleus of John and Paul provided the glue that held the group together. Deeply drawn in by the charismatic spell cast by the masterful Lennon, Paul reveled in his role as John's on-stage foil and steady street-corner accomplice. The burgeoning pop titans experienced their first power struggle over the choice of a solid lead guitarist upon which to hang their funky, back-street skiffle sound. For Paul, the obvious candidate was his longtime friend, the young but undeniably talented George Harrison.

"He was always my little mate," observed McCartney. "Nonetheless, he could really play guitar, particularly this piece called 'Raunchy,' which we all used to love. If anyone could do something like that it was generally enough to get them in the group. Of course, I knew George long before any of the others, as they were all from Woolton and we hung out with the Allerton set. I can tell you we both learned guitar from the same book, and that despite his tender years, we were chums."

Lennon, however, was somewhat skeptical about admitting a veritable baby into the group. "He used to follow me around like a bloody kid and I couldn't be bothered. He was a kid who played guitar and he was a friend of Paul's which made it all easier. It took me years to come round to him, to start considering him as an equal or anything."

The story goes that Harrison played "Raunchy" for them in a cellar club called the Morgue, then hung around the band until he was invited to play. He was formally accepted, at age fourteen, as a member on February 6, 1958.

McCartney, however, maintains that George's audition took place on a Liverpool-bound bus: "George slipped quietly into one of the seats aboard this largely deserted bus we were riding, took out his guitar and went right into 'Raunchy.' A few days later I said to John, 'Well, what do you think?' And he finally said, 'Yeah, man, he'd be great!' And that was simply that. George was in."

Despite their improved lineup, the Quarry Men were hardly in demand. Playing mostly private parties and shoddy clubs throughout suburban Liverpool, they struggled to maintain even the most modest playing schedule.

■

THE QUARRY MEN'S 1958/59 ITINERARY

FRIDAY 10 JANUARY 1958
New Clubmoor Hall, Norris Green, Liverpool

FRIDAY 24 JANUARY
Cavern Club, Liverpool

THURSDAY 6 FEBRUARY
Wilson Hall, Garston, Liverpool

THURSDAY 13 MARCH
The Morgue Skiffle Cellar, 'Balgownie', Oakhill Park, Broadgreen, Liverpool

SATURDAY 20 DECEMBER
Upton Green, Speke, Liverpool

THURSDAY 1 JANUARY 1959
Wilson Hall, Garston, Liverpool

SATURDAY 24 JANUARY
Woolton Village Club, Allerton Road, Woolton, Liverpool

SATURDAY 29 AUGUST
Casbah Coffee Club, Hayman's Green, West Derby, Liverpool

SATURDAY 5 SEPTEMBER
Casbah Coffee Club, West Derby, Liverpool

SATURDAY 12 SEPTEMBER
Casbah Coffee Club, West Derby, Liverpool

SATURDAY 19 SEPTEMBER
Casbah Coffee Club, West Derby, Liverpool

SATURDAY 26 SEPTEMBER
Casbah Coffee Club, West Derby, Liverpool

SATURDAY 3 OCTOBER
Casbah Coffee Club, West Derby, Liverpool

SATURDAY 10 OCTOBER
Casbah Coffee Club, West Derby, Liverpool

SUNDAY 11, 18 OR 25 OCTOBER
Empire Theatre, Liverpool

MONDAY 26–SATURDAY 31 OCTOBER
Empire Theatre, Liverpool

■

Following McCartney's first public performance with the Quarry Men (at the New Clubmoor Hall in Broadway), Paul played John a couple of throwaway numbers he'd written himself. Not to be outdone, John soon started thinking up his own tunes and bouncing them off Paul. It was during this period that the Lennon-McCartney songwriting partnership truly began in earnest. Basking in the fervor of the neophyte, they enjoyed what was, in many ways, one of their most prolific periods. Though most of these early works have gone unrecorded, many were later copyrighted and even cataloged. Among these first compositions were: "Hello Little Girl," "Winston's Walk," "Hot as Sun" (eventually released on Paul's *McCartney* LP of 1970), "Years Roll Along," "That's My Woman," "Too Bad About Sorrows," "Catswalk," "I Lost My Little Girl," "Looking Glass," "Thinking of Linking," "Keep Looking That Way," "One After 909" (which ultimately turned up on the *Let It Be* album), "Just Fun," and "When I'm Sixty-four" (which later appeared, of course, on *Sgt. Pepper's Lonely Hearts Club Band*).

Commenting on the absurdly titled "Thinking of Linking," Paul later complained, "It was terrible! I thought it up in the pictures, someone in a film mentioned it, 'We're thinking of linking,' and I came out of there thinking 'That should be a song, "Thinking of Linking," people are gonna get married, gotta write that!' Pretty corny stuff!"

Generally, these impromptu composing sessions took place after school (or even during, if they decided to skip) at Paul's while everyone was still out. After the obligatory fried egg, toast, and tea, the boys would settle back to work in the McCartneys' cluttered front room, all the while puffing away on old Jim's Meerschaum pipe filled not with tobacco but Typhoo tea!

"When we started off," said John, "we were uncertain as to exactly where our writing would take us. Paul was a rocker with one eye on Broadway musicals, vaudeville, and shit like that. I, on the other hand, was inspired by Buddy Holly's songwriting and was determined to show I was as capable as any Yank. To me Buddy was the first to click as a singer-songwriter. His music really moved and his lyrics spoke to us kids in a way no one ever bothered before. It was youth speaking to youth. Which was exactly what people said about the Beatles years later."

Even early on, a spirited sense of competition arose between the fledgling composers. Paul would play John a song he'd written and Lennon would quickly respond by making up his own right on the spot in an effort to "do one better."

"Which didn't mean we wrote everything together," says McCartney. "We'd kind of write 80 percent together and 20 percent was stuff on our own."

Unlike the heralded songwriting teams of the thirties and forties, where one partner exclusively wrote lyrics and the other music, here these roles were not so stringently defined. Lennon's strength lay in composing the initial melody, while Paul generally added the middle eight. Conceded Lennon, "Paul was always more advanced than I was. He was always a couple of chords ahead and his songs usually had more chords in them. When we first started playing together I learned some chords from Paul and of course he taught me left-handed shapes, so I was playing a sort of upside down version of the correct thing if you can work that one out!"

In his book *Lennon and McCartney,* Malcolm Doney further defines their early composing process: "The two would sit with their guitars near enough to hear what each other was playing but far enough away to concentrate on their own sequence of chords. Separately they would chug away, trying out melody lines and chord changes until one would suddenly take an interest in the embryonic tune emerging from the other. When one realized the other had got that indefinable something, they would join forces, pushing the melody, making changes and putting odd phrases to the emerging tune."

"Paul and I made a deal when we were fifteen," revealed Lennon in 1980. "There was never a legal deal between us, just a deal we made when we decided to write together that we put both our names on it, no matter what."

The two eager young boys penned more than one hundred tunes together over the next year or so, which they carefully collected in an old school notebook. Across the top of each Paul would optimistically scrawl, "Another Lennon and McCartney Original."

"Which didn't mean we wrote everything together," says Paul. "When I first began writing songs I started using a guitar. 'I Lost My Little Girl' . . . is a funny little song, a nice song, a corny little song based on three chords: G, G7, and C. Later on we had a piano and I used to bang around on that. I wrote 'When I'm Sixty-four' when I was about sixteen. I was vaguely thinking it might come in handy in a musical comedy or something. I didn't know what kind of career I was going to take." Unfortunately, many of these early works were lost in the mid-sixties when Paul's girlfriend, Jane Asher, inadvertently tossed away several dozen while clearing out a cupboard in McCartney's London home.

The Quarry Men's first recording session, in the summer of 1958, was viewed by the lads themselves as something of a lark. The band (which at this stage included pianist John "Duff" Lowe) showed up at the home of one Percy Phillips, a retired rail worker, to lay down a demo in his makeshift studio at 53 Kensington, Liverpool. Duff later recalled the afternoon in a rare 1993 interview:

"To this day I can't remember who organized it. I've a feeling it was John who'd heard of this little recording studio in Kensington. It was a Saturday afternoon and we waited in an anteroom; it was someone's lounge, I think, whilst somebody was finishing off. Then we all went in and ran through two numbers: 'That'll Be the Day' and 'In Spite of All Danger.'"

The latter, a rare, one-off McCartney-Harrison collaboration, was a spirited late-fifties "doo-wop" that held the distinction of being the first original song recorded by three members of the band that would become the Beatles.

According to Quarry Men pianist Lowe, the actual recording process left much to be desired.

The guy did a sound check, such as it was, as there was only one microphone hanging in the middle of the room. Then he said, "Right lads, you can go onto tape and then I'll do the record off the tape, or you can go straight onto the record. It's an extra 2/6 (12p) if you want to go on tape." And we said, "Oh no, we can't afford that; we'll go straight on record." "In Spite of All Danger" was getting a bit long and he started to wave his hands to bring us to a finish, as we were getting pretty near the hole in the middle of the record. It was just a shellac demo disc; the more you played it, the worse the quality was. Paul wrote on the label, "That'll Be the Day" (Holly-Petty) and "In Spite of All Danger" (McCartney-Harrison).

It was just done for a giggle. It was passed around. Anyone who was a friend could borrow it for a couple of days. In fact, when I spoke to Paul in 1981 he said, "I could say, 'Oh, come on Duff, you're not supposed to hold onto it. You're supposed to pass it on.'" How I ended up with it, I don't know. It must have come to me at the end of the term or something. No one asked me to lend it; so it must have come to me after everyone else had a go. And at the time, who was interested? We'd all listened to it. It was a bit rough; everyone was out buying the new forty-fives. So people forgot about it and it was at the bottom of a linen drawer at my house. I didn't particularly look after it. It had a Parlophone seventy-eight sleeve that someone had put around it.

Ever intent upon cultivating their blossoming image, the group tried on several new names over the following year, including the Beatles, the Silver Beats, the Silver Beetles, the Silver Beatles; by August of 1960, though, they had settled on the Beatles. Earlier that year, in January, Lennon invited his art-school friend, Stuart Fergusson Victor Sutcliffe, known as "Stu," to join the band. The pair had been sharing a dingy flat at Number 3, Gambier Terrace near the grand cathedral in Liverpool, where their sensitive natures and philosophical views drew them ever closer.

Although a brilliant painter and designer, Sutcliffe made no pretense about being any sort of musician and was obliged to learn the bass as he went along. Needless to say, this learning experience certainly didn't endear him to the ever-perfectionist McCartney.

By April 1960, things were finally beginning to perk up for the band. At this point still the Silver Beatles, the boys snagged a solid two weeks of work backing balladeer Johnny Gentle on a ballroom tour of Scotland. Encouraged by what for them was at least a taste of real work, they came home just as empty as ever. "Someone actually asked for my autograph," Paul wrote to his dad from Inverness. "I signed for them too, three times!"

"From that day onwards," Jim McCartney later remarked, "things were never really quite the same."

Contrary to popular belief, the Beatles' initial trek to Germany in August 1960 came about more as a result of a lack of alternatives than of any great success in England. Thinking they had been booked at Hamburg's popular Kaiserkeller through small-time Liverpool promoter Allan Williams, they later discovered they were actually slated to appear as the new house band at the Indra, a seedy former strip club at 34 Grosse Freiheit. Just prior to setting off, Paul McCartney rang up local drummer Pete Best on the spur of the moment and invited him to join the group as a quick fix to the Beatles' ongoing percussion problems. Best, eager to escape the hopeless tedium of attending teacher's training college the following autumn, immediately said yes.

Sutcliffe's influence over Lennon, meanwhile, was rather a double-edged sword. An extremely talented and dedicated artist, he encouraged John to explore his own innate ability as a painter, yet his presence in the Beatles engendered more than a little controversy.

McCartney explains, "I did have problems with Stu, I'll admit. The main thing was he couldn't really play his bass very well in the beginning. So when we did photos and things it was a bit embarrassing. We had to ask him to turn away from the camera, because if people saw his fingers they'd realize he wasn't in the same key as the rest of us."

Bowing to McCartney's pressure and the undeniable reality of his own deficient musical skills, Sutcliffe left the band in June 1961. Just ten months later, his tragic, sudden death from a brain hemorrhage on April 10, 1962, became another bitter blow for the group.

For Lennon and McCartney in particular, the many insights Germany offered, however new and alluring, were not really channeled into their compositions. Sitting alone in their tatty digs, they would scribble away chord changes in an old notebook, busking loudly in a directionless barrage of half-thought-out ideas and images. Although they tried hard to compose amid the incessant clatter of the naughty Reeperbahn, Germany only presented them with but a few, vaguely unfinished possibilities.

If the Hamburg experience didn't exactly inspire their songwriting, it certainly honed and polished their musical skills—and more importantly, shaped their identity. Out of those raucous, seedy basement clubs the Beatles sound was born. As Lennon later explained, "We got better and more confident. We couldn't help it with all the experience, playing all night long. It was handy being foreign. We had to try even harder, put our heart and soul into it, to get ourselves over. In Hamburg we had to play for eight hours so we really had to find a new way of playing."

"In my opinion our peak for playing live was Hamburg," recalls George. "At the time we weren't so famous, and people who came to see us were drawn in simply by our music and whatever atmosphere we managed to create. We got *very* tight as a band there. We were at four different clubs altogether in Germany. Originally we played the Indra, and when that shut, we went over to the Kaiserkeller and then, later on, the Top Ten. Back in England, all the bands were getting into wearing matching ties and handkerchiefs, and were doing little dance routines like the Shadows. We were definitely not into that, so we just kept doing whatever we felt like."

In June 1961, during their second trip to Hamburg, Tony Sheridan, a popular transplanted English club singer, invited the Beatles to play with him on a Polydor recording session that German orchestra leader Bert Kaempfert produced. Although Lennon and Co. had recorded before, these were their first really "professional" sessions. And so it was on the morning of June 22 that they climbed into a taxi (followed by another piled high with their gear) and made their way through Hamburg's sleepy side streets to a shoddy grade school on the outskirts of the city. Setting up on the tiny stage in the gymnasium, they recorded eight tunes, six backing Tony and two others, "My Bonnie" and "Cry for a Shadow."

The latter, a parody of the Shadows' "Frightened City," was penned under the working title of "Beatle Bop." It earned a pair of lofty distinctions: It was the only song ever written by the team of Lennon-Harrison, and it became the Beatles' first original song to appear on record.

Returning home to Liverpool on July 2, they granted themselves a brief holiday and then dove right in, playing the Cavern on July 14, Holyoake Hall (near Penny Lane) the evening of July 15, Blair Hall in Walton that Sunday, and then straight back to the Cavern for a lunchtime session on Monday, July 17, before roaring up to the Litherland Town Hall that night for yet another grueling gig. Thereafter, the new, improved Beatles maintained a gut-wrenching schedule of virtually nonstop performances throughout the North for the remainder of the year.

Things were now rapidly moving ahead for the Beatles, but the most auspicious development was the entrance into their lives of businessman Brian Epstein. Epstein's interest was piqued initially when a young man named Raymond Jones walked into Epstein's parents' record store NEMS (or North East Music Stores) and requested a German import called "My Bonnie" by the Beatles. Epstein promised he would try to track it down, and he eventually did. Ordering a cautious twenty-five copies, he sold out almost immediately. He then repeated the process several more times until he became curious and decided to check out for himself what all the fuss was about.

Somewhat against his better judgment, on Thursday, November 9, 1961, the dapper twenty-seven-year-old bachelor carefully descended the famous eighteen stone steps of the Cavern Club on Matthew Street to witness first-hand this up-and-coming beat group he had heard so much about. Alistair Taylor, Brian's longtime personal assistant, remembers the grand occasion.

As for their act, I don't think they'd go down very well at the Royal Variety Performance. It seems like they've got a permanent long-running set of private jokes which they share as they play. They crack one-liners to each other and from time to time let the front row of the audience in on it. When the girls shouted requests, the Beatles shouted back, adding their own suggestions and comments. Brian and I gave a discouraged look at each other and settled down to pay attention to the music. This isn't much, I thought. For a start, it's too damned loud and from what I heard as we crossed the dance-floor the Beatles are a bunch of five-chord merchants.

We sat through five numbers, four of them standard beat songs: "Money," "Till There Was You," "A Taste of Honey," and "Twist and Shout." I never heard standards like that played with the sort of raw excitement the Beatles put into them. Then Paul came to the microphone and announced that they were going to play a song that he had written with John Lennon: "Hello Little Girl." Brian and I exchanged a glance. "So they write their own songs too."

"The Beatles were on stage raving it up," remembered Eppy (as Brian was affectionately known). "I sensed that something was happening, something terribly exciting, although I didn't know what it was. There was this amazingly direct communication with the audience and this absolutely marvelous humor. There was something about it that was totally of today. I knew they could be one of the biggest theatrical attractions in the world."

Brian returned to the "vile and smelly" club several more times, and in a December 3 meeting at NEMS suggested to the boys that he become their manager. For some years, the introverted homosexual young man had felt bottled up, merely retracing his father's footsteps by running the family business. As it happened, the Beatles were quietly despairing of ever breaking out of Liverpool's obviously limited beat scene. Impressed by Epstein's prominent standing in the musical community, they quickly accepted. For Brian, life looked up immediately: "They represented the direct, uninhibited relationships which I had never found and felt deprived of. And my own sense of inferiority and frustration evaporated because I knew I could help them and they wanted and trusted me to."

Although Brian felt he had finally connected with something solid in his uneventful life, the fact that he was a so-called rough-trade homosexual was not lost on the often cynical, verbally abusive Lennon. McCartney, ever the grinning diplomat, was more than willing to get what he could from Epstein, but the outwardly homophobic Lennon was still cautious.

Further on down the road, in a brief, recently discovered track recorded on July 19, 1968, John sang a sarcastic ode to his mentor entitled "Brian Epstein Blues." After going on about the Beatles manager laboring in a mine, he says that Brian is a dirty old man, and that his mother, Queenie, is "the biggest queen of them all."

Lennon's acerbic wit aside, the Beatles now had both an actual record and a well-to-do manager to boot. It looked like they might finally be on their way.

Notably, the Beatles performed their first gig in London on Saturday, December 9, 1961, at the seedy Blue Gardenia Club on St. Anne's Court off Wardour Street in Soho. In town visiting an old friend, the boys somewhat reluctantly agreed to get up on stage and make a bit of noise for the late-night contingent of hustlers, harlots, and drunkards that lined the bar. They must have felt right back home in Hamburg. Ironically, the next time the Beatles ventured south was the very next month to lay down tracks at Decca Studios in West Hampstead, North London, for their first really big-time audition.

Arriving in London on Monday, January 1, 1962, John, Paul, George, and Pete shook hands with Decca A&R man Mike Smith and went to work, nervously running through some fifteen tunes picked out by Brian as most representative of their sound. Recorded straight on two-track mono, the session began at around 11:00 A.M. and ended a scant one hour later.

Much bootlegged today, the audition saw the boys performing three original numbers, "Like Dreamers Do," "Love of the Loved," and "Hello Little Girl," as well as several well-worn cover versions of various standards: "Money," "Crying Waiting Hoping," "Till There Was You," "Take Good Care of My Baby," "September in the Rain," "The Sheik of Araby," "Sure to Fall," "To Know Her Is to Love Her," "Besame Mucho," "Memphis, Tennessee," "Three Cool Cats," and "Searchin'."

As to the genesis of the trio of tunes penned by Lennon and McCartney, John has confirmed that "Hello Little Girl" was perhaps his personal best from that period. "This was one of the first songs I ever finished. I was then about eighteen and we gave it to the Fourmost."

Lennon's inspiration came from the Cole Porter tune "It's De-lovely," a favorite of his mother's. "It's all very Freudian," he quipped. "She used to sing that one. So I made 'Hello Little Girl' out of it."

"Love of the Loved" claims its creation to a teenage McCartney who graciously donated the song to Epstein charge Cilla Black in 1963. Interestingly, the Beatles themselves recorded the track that same year under George Martin at EMI (along with "Hello Little Girl"). To date, both tracks have yet to be properly released.

As the boys wordlessly packed away their instruments after the session,

Brian stepped forward and wondered out loud if they had, in fact, passed the audition. Smith smiled politely and extended his hand. "We'll let you know, chaps," he offered quietly. "Thanks very much for coming down."

As almost every card-carrying Beatles fan knows, the boys did not pass the audition that windy afternoon, giving rise to Decca recording manager Dick Rowe's famous prediction to Eppy that "Groups with guitars are on the way out."

Down but not yet out, Epstein carefully filled out a taxing three-page application at the BBC in Manchester requesting an audition from the Variety Department, hoping that Auntie Beeb might elect to feature his young charges on one of the many teen radio shows that proliferated within her hallowed halls. Brian's carefully worded request apparently did the trick and on Monday, February 12, 1962, the boys arrived at Broadcasting House off Piccadilly and played four songs for producer Peter Pilbeam.

This time their delivery was significantly more convincing, as evidenced by the bureaucrat's gentle toe-tapping as they ran through "Till There Was You," "Like Dreamers Do" (with Paul on lead vocals), followed by "Memphis" and "Hello Little Girl." The boys passed the musical trial and were subsequently booked for their initial radio appearance on the show *Teenagers' Turn,* to be broadcast later in the month.

By this time, word had gotten round among the teen population of Liverpool that their beloved Beatles had not only made a record while they were away in Germany, but that it was soon to be made available at home. In a local newspaper article entitled "They're Hoping for a Hit Record," the boys received some of their first ever publicity. "Three local guitarists, who are members of Merseyside's most popular beat group, are to have their first record released tomorrow (Friday)."

> The guitarists, all members of "the Beatles" group, together with twenty-year-old drummer Pete Best, 8 Haymans Green, West Derby, are John Lennon, 251 Menlove Avenue, Woolton, George Harrison, 25 Upton Green, Speke, and Paul McCartney, who lives at 20 Forthlin Road, Allerton.
>
> The record was recorded in Germany while they were appearing at a Hamburg club, and their manager, Mr. Brian Epstein, believes that it made a showing in the German popularity charts.
>
> Now the record, backing singer Tony Sheridan, is to be released in En-

gland, and it is their hope that their own records will make the British charts later next year.

Twenty-one-year-old John Lennon plays the guitar and sings, and writes articles in "beat" language, while 19-year-old Paul plays the guitar, sings and writes songs in conjunction with John.

The boys have always been full-time musicians, ever since they left school, and are making quite a name for themselves locally. Who knows it might not be long before they achieve nationwide acclaim.

The Beatles first began to make great strides nationally during the sweltering summer of 1962. Finally against all odds, Brian landed them a modest recording contract with Parlophone Records (a small subsidiary of the gigantic EMI) and they began working with the immensely talented and versatile George Martin. Their first formal session took place on Wednesday, June 6, at EMI Studios in the willowy suburbs of central London.

Contrary to popular myth, this historic session was *not* simply another audition, but rather a proper recording date with the Beatles cutting demonstration lacquers of "Besame Mucho," "Ask Me Why," "Love Me Do," and "P.S. I Love You," which were never commercially released.

"Love Me Do" and "P.S. I Love You" would, of course, go on to become big Beatle hits. Although generally considered to be a "John" song, Lennon himself—who later dubbed "Love Me Do" as "pretty funky"—conceded, "Paul wrote the main structure of this when he was sixteen or even earlier. I think I had something to do with the middle."

"I slagged off school to write that one with John when we first started," said Paul. "You get to the bit where you think, if we're going to write great philosophy it isn't worth it. 'Love Me Do' was our greatest philosophical song. That's what we want to get back to—simplicity. You can't have anything simpler yet more meaningful than 'love, love me do.'"

The Hamburg-period ballad, "P.S. I Love You," was written in the form of a letter and has "McCartney" stamped all over it. Soppy and decidedly middle of the road, this was one of the many occasions someone should have asked George Harrison if he had anything lying around he might like to record.

Lennon later commented that this one used to make him cringe from the moment they struck the first note. Although some music critics draw comparisons to Lennon's own teen love call, "Ask Me Why," with its similar slow

Latin swing, John told interviewers toward the end of his life, "It was shit. Paul was trying to write a 'Soldier Boy' like the Shirelles. He wrote it in Germany or when we were going to and from Hamburg."

In mid-August, on the eve of the group's stellar breakthrough, there emerged a great controversy within the Beatles' camp. Popular drummer Pete Best was sacked in favor of Rory Storm and the Hurricanes' Ringo Starr. Starr had sat in with the band on several occasions. In yet another recently discovered document, the old idea that it was Paul alone who wanted Best out of the group was refuted by Brian Epstein in a letter to a friend.

"[Pete was too] conventional," he wrote. "Didn't fit well as a drummer or a man. Beat too slow, or George thought so. I liked him though he could be moody. Friendly with John, but Paul and George didn't like him. . . . I wasn't too happy about Ringo. I didn't want him, but then as now I trusted the Beatles' judgement."

With the eventual inclusion of Starr in the group on August 18, the Beatles' indestructible outer shell was complete. The songwriting collective of Lennon and McCartney, however, was only just coming up to speed.

By the autumn of 1962, the Beatles, while definitely up and away, were not out of danger. Undeniably the biggest thing ever to hail from the North, the powers that be down in London still considered them a ha'penny outfit of untrained wannabes.

At this early stage, however, right up until around mid-1965, Lennon and McCartney's lyrics were unquestionably derivative of their boyhood heroes, Buddy Holly, Little Richard, Bill Haley, skiffle king Lonnie Donegan, and the like. Later, of course, the Beatles became hugely important for their introspective, heartfelt lyrics, but not yet.

As John Jones writes in *The Lennon Companion,* "Lennon and McCartney's early lyrics were thin and conventional. There was rain in the heart, there were stars in the sky, birds were always threatening not to sing. The tunes were good, some as good as those of Rodgers or Leonard Bernstein. But the gap between words and music in pieces like 'If I Fell,' 'And I Love Her,' 'Ask Me Why,' and 'Not a Second Time' was embarrassing for anyone who wanted to take the songs seriously."

Surprising to many, Lennon's lampooning literary side did not, at this stage, translate into his musical compositions. Many would pin the blame on Paul for reining his partner in, but in fact Jones suggests such experimental, often irreverent lyrics simply wouldn't have been acceptable to a mass audience. "More likely they are being tactful towards their public. They know that people are offended by nonsense, by things they can't understand; they know that people tend to take jokes that baffle them as a personal insult, a calculated exclusion. And their songs are, after all, a commercial enterprise, recorded by almost anyone you can think of."

And so it was on the afternoon of Tuesday, September 4, that John, Paul, George, and now Ringo ducked into the bureaucratic maze of EMI Studios for an ambitious session. It began when the foursome balked at recording "How Do You Do It," a number by fledgling songwriter Mitch Murray. George Martin decided the tune was perfect and proclaimed it would place the band on the map.

"When I played them the tune they were not very impressed," remembers Martin. "They said they wanted to record their own material and I read them the riot act. 'When you can write material as good as this I'll record it,' I told them. 'But right now we're going to record this.' And record it we did, with John doing the solo part. It was a very good record indeed, and it is still in the archives of EMI. I heard it recently and it sounds quite good even today. But it was never issued. The boys came back to me and said, 'We've nothing against that song, George, and you're probably right. But we want to record our own material.'"

The real gem of the day was the haunting "Love Me Do," on which Paul and John shared lead vocals. Engineer Norman Smith recalls the genesis of the now-legendary track. "After the first take we listened to the tape. It was horrible. Their equipment wasn't good enough. We hooked Paul's guitar up to our own bass amplifier and had to tie John's amplifier together because it was rattling so loud.

"They were very much in awe of the studio. They didn't realize the disparity between what they could play on the studio floor and how it would come out sounding in the control room. They refused to wear headphones, I remember. In fact, they hardly ever wore them."

Things got a bit shaky when John had to pull together the song's distinctive harmonica solo literally on the spot. The style was heavily borrowed from Delbert McClinton's intro on the Bruce Channel hit "Hey Baby." A few months earlier McClinton had appeared on the same bill with the Beatles, and a highly impressed Lennon prodded the harmonica player to give him a fifteen-minute lesson. He utilized what he had learned to give "Love Me Do" its resulting bluesy edge.

John's ad libbed instrumental left McCartney to pitch in on the lead vocal. "I was very nervous," says McCartney. "John was supposed to sing lead, but they changed their minds and asked me at the last minute, because they wanted John to play harmonica. Until then, we hadn't rehearsed with a harmonica; George Martin started arranging it on the spot. It was very nerve-wracking."

Following the session, Martin confessed he wasn't all that thrilled with the trite, sophomoric lyrics of "Love Me Do." "That was the best of the stuff they had, and I thought it pretty poor."

Nevertheless, the tune was released on Friday, October 5, 1962, and peaked at number 17 two days after Christmas. The record's modest success represented a milestone to the group. Paul McCartney remembers, "In Hamburg we clicked, at the Cavern we clicked, but if you want to know when we knew we'd arrived, it was getting in the charts with 'Love Me Do.' That was the one, it gave us somewhere to go."

Even as the group was basking in its early success there were problems. A paternity action was brought against Paul by Erika Heubers, a buxom Hamburg waitress whom Paul had dated for a short time. Although McCartney denied he was the proud papa of little Bettina, born December 18, 1962 (Beatles personal assistant Peter Brown, however, insists the allegation is true), that didn't stop him from paying out some £2,700 in 1966 toward her support. A subsequent German legal action commenced in the early eighties was, however, ultimately unsuccessful in proving the Heubers's claims.

A second unfortunate episode took place when a Liverpool woman, Anita Cochrane, claimed her son, Philip, was fathered by McCartney. Counsel David Jacobs was forced to arrange a hush-hush £3,000 payment prohibiting Anita from going public with the claim that McCartney was the boy's father.

Paul's romantic imbroglios apparently didn't faze John, who'd himself stepped out a time or two on wife Cynthia Powell, whom he had married on August 23, 1962. As Lennon's personal assistant Fred Seaman put it, "John had had great difficulty in keeping his pants zippered in the early days."

In a humorous sidelight to the paternity suits, Seaman revealed how, during the seventies, letters from alleged mothers of McCartney offspring would regularly come to John and Yoko's Dakota apartment in New York asking for Paul's address. Yoko even kept a special file on hand labeled "Paul's Wives."

These incidents, however, did not sit well with Brian Epstein. McCartney had a habit of overstepping boundaries by interfering with tour itineraries and release dates of records—which, needless to say, Eppy resented. Epstein noted in Ray Coleman's biography *Lennon* how Paul's mercurial nature often made him difficult to handle. The Beatles' manager related McCartney's habit of "switching off" when things didn't go his way: "He settles down in a chair, puts one booted foot across his knee and pretends to read a newspaper, having consciously made his face an impassive mask."

"Paul was the only one who ever gave him any little worries," NEMS secretary Joanne Newfield remembered some years later. "When he rang to complain about something or ask things. The others might ask exactly the same, but he always worried more about pleasing Paul. He could be upset by talking to Paul on the phone, but never any of the others."

Feeling the near-constant need to ingratiate himself to the often petulant, self-involved McCartney, Eppy went well out of his way. Lavishing the young man with expensive presents, poor Epstein often got no more than an off-hand "Yeah, thanks Bri" from Paul before he shuffled soundlessly out of the room.

"With Paul I had to really try," Epstein worried to friends. "I don't know what it is. He won't look me in the eye."

"Never mind, Brian," music publisher Dick James once quipped. "The bastard won't look *anyone* in the eye."

That is not to say, however, that Paul was moody or uncooperative. The fact is the ambitious McCartney was fervently dedicated to success at any cost. Early on, when Brian insisted that the boys lose their scruffy black-leather look and trim their hair, it was Paul who convinced the rebellious Lennon (and to a lesser extent, Harrison) to go along at least until they got what they wanted.

The Beatles returned to the studio on Monday, November 26, and reaped substantial benefits. The centerpiece of the session featured a souped-up remake of "Please Please Me." The initial recording of the tune featured a slow, tepid tempo that Martin found unsatisfactory.

Written entirely by Lennon at Mendips, he later recalled the inspiration behind the song. "It was my attempt at writing a Roy Orbison–type song. . . . I remember the day and the pink eyelet on the bed [in Aunt Mimi's bedroom] I heard Orbison doing 'Only the Lonely' or something. . . . I was always fascinated by the words 'Please, please lend your little ears to my pleas,' a Bing Crosby song. I was intrigued by the double use of the word 'please.' So it was a combination of Bing Crosby and Roy Orbison."

"Martin's contribution was a big one," confirms Paul. "The first time he ever really showed me he could see beyond what we were offering him was

'Please Please Me.' He said, 'Well, we'll put the tempo up.' George lifted the tempo and we all thought that was much better and it was ultimately a big hit."

Ever the perfectionist, Martin was so impressed that he allowed a mistake to remain in the final version where Paul and John sing different lyrics on one line of the last verse. He admitted in his book *All You Need Is Ears,* "It went beautifully. I told them what beginning and what ending to put on it and they went into number two studio to record. The whole session was a joy. At the end of it I pressed the intercom button in the control room and said, 'Gentlemen, you've just made your first number-one record.'"

True to Martin's prognostications, "Please Please Me," officially released on January 11, 1963, shot to number one in both the *New Musical Express* and *Melody Maker* charts. After nearly seven years of backbreaking, largely unrewarded, nonstop work, the Beatles were finally an "overnight success."

Silver Horses /
Early Work

It was the song "Please Please Me" that first attracted the attention of music publisher Dick James. A former singer himself (he belted out the macho theme to the popular *Robin Hood* TV series from the early fifties), James saw that rare mix of personal charisma and sheer talent in the boys. Besides, the canny businessman figured, unlike most other homegrown groups of the era they had an honest to goodness record deal.

"I was in my office at ten-thirty one morning when Brian walked in, half an hour earlier than arranged," James later remembered. "He said he'd been to this other music publisher's. He'd waited twenty-five minutes but only an office boy turned up. So he said I could have first option instead. He played it to me and I told him it was the most exciting song I'd heard in years."

After a respectable bit of dickering, a deal was struck and Dick James Music Ltd. became Lennon and McCartney's exclusive music publisher. It was a move the eager duo would eventually live to regret.

Heretofore, the Beatles would generally work on two or three tracks per session, but in the wake of their stunning success with "Please Please Me" the tide swiftly turned. The public demanded more Beatles music and George Martin was quick to catch the wave.

A complete album had to be readied as quickly as possible. With that in mind, the boys settled in for a mammoth thirteen-hour session on Monday, February 11, 1963.

Recorded on that memorable occasion was the material that would encompass the debut album *Please Please Me—With Love Me Do and 12 Other Songs*. Six of the fourteen tunes were covers; the remainder comprised some early Beatle classics.

One of the best was surely "I Saw Her Standing There," which owed 80 percent of its creation to Paul. Written in the McCartneys' front parlor while the boys were skipping school, the runaway rocker became one of Paul's trademark tunes. Interestingly, John himself performed the song with Elton John at New York's Madison Square Garden in 1974; it was the only time he ever sang lead on that particular song.

"Misery" was basically a fifty-fifty proposition, written originally for teen queen Helen Shapiro while the Fabs were on tour with the sixteen-year-old sensation. Her management later turned down the work, reasoning that young Helen had no business glorifying the messy downside of love. It was her loss.

Interestingly, Lennon's first serious ballad was penned on his honeymoon. "I was in the first apartment I'd ever had that wasn't shared by fourteen other students. I'd just married Cyn and Brian Epstein gave us his secret flat he kept in Liverpool to keep his sexual liaisons separate from his home life." With its breathy lyrics entreating the imaginary young woman to come "closer" and inquiring seductively "do you promise not to tell," this became the tantalizing "Do You Want to Know a Secret?"

John's marriage had little, if any, effect on his relationship with McCartney. John and Cynthia had been going together since art school, and Paul was extremely fond of the kind-hearted and down-to-earth Cyn, Lennon's answer to his favorite pinup, Brigitte Bardot. Far from envying his partner's state, McCartney, for his part, didn't seem in any hurry to tie the knot.

John remembered yet more on his first postnuptial composition: "My mother was a comedienne and a singer. Not professional, but she used to get up in pubs and things like that. She had a good voice. She could do Kay Starr. She used to do this little tune when I was just a one or two year old, yes, she was still living with me. The tune was from a Disney film, 'Want to know a secret? Promise not to tell. You are standing by a wishing well.' So I had this in my head, I wrote it and gave it to George to sing."

"There's a Place" was also written totally by John. Author Jeff Russell commented on the mature construction of this slightly obscure number in his excellent book, *The Beatles On Record:* "The tight harmony of John and Paul, with John singing solo at times, combine perfectly with the wailing soulful harmonica on this fine example of John's early ballad writing."

Please Please Me—With Love Me Do and 12 Other Songs was released in the States on the Vee Jay label under the title of *Introducing the Beatles* on July 22, 1963, and proved once and for all that Lennon and McCartney had what it took both as performers and composers. Still, the ever-cynical Lennon remained skeptical of their success.

"*Everyone* can be a success," declared John in the early seventies. "If you keep saying that to yourself, you can be. We aren't any better than anybody else. What's talent? I don't know. Are you born with it? Do you discover it later on?

"Up until the age of fifteen I was no different from any other cunt of fifteen. Then I decided I'd write a little song and I did. But it didn't make any difference. It's a load of crap that I discovered a talent. I just *did* it. I've no talent except a talent for being happy or a talent for skiving [getting by on one's wits]." It was just this very disarming and unusual penchant for speaking his mind no matter the cost that gave John so much credibility among the world's youth. He might have played the game all right, but deep inside he was as true to himself as when he first picked up the guitar. It was a quality he carried with him throughout his life. He might have been a millionaire pop star composer, but he never *really* sold out, not completely. Not in the obvious way McCartney ultimately did.

That John Lennon was always very much his own man even during the early sixties, a time when conformity was still the rule, is to his eternal credit. A case in point was his reaction to Epstein's sophomoric dress code.

"In the beginning it was a constant fight between Brian and Paul on one side and me and George on the other," he later remarked. "Brian put us in neat suits and shirts and Paul was right behind him. I didn't dig that and I used to try and get George to rebel with me. I'd say to him, 'Look, we don't need these fucking suits. Let's chuck them out of the window.' My little rebellion was to have my tie loose, with the top button of my shirt undone, but Paul'd always come up and put it straight."

McCartney, on the other hand, ever the diplomat, stated in the seventies,

It does seem to have fallen in my role to be a bit kinder than the others. I was always known in the Beatles as the one who would sit the press down and say, "Hello, how are you? Do you want a drink?" and make them comfortable. My family loop was like that. So I used to do that. . . . You're aware you're talking to the press. You want a good article, don't you, so you don't want to go slaggin' the guy off.

I'm not ashamed of anything I've been, you know. I kind of like the idea of doing that sometimes and if it turns out in a few years to look a bit soppy I say, "So what?" I think most people dig it. . . . Once you get into the critical bit, people analyzing you and then you start to look at yourself and think, "Oh Christ, you got me," and things start to rebound on you, why didn't I put on a smarter image . . . you know, why wasn't I tougher? I'm not really tough. I'm not really lovable either, but I don't mind falling somewhere in the middle.

Of course, if Lennon's bravado had been allowed to hold sway totally, the Beatles might never have made it. John would have probably stayed right there in Liverpool, playing it the way *he* wanted for the next forty years. The simple fact is, Lennon needed McCartney as much as Paul needed him. Their fates were intertwined. In all honesty, George and Ringo were basically peripheral. From almost the very beginning, the writing was on the wall for the Beatles: Divergent energies like John and Paul may travel together for a while, but eventually they must, by definition, blow apart.

"We reckoned we could make it because there were four of us," Lennon remembered. "None of us would've done it alone because Paul wasn't quite strong enough, I didn't have enough girl-appeal, George was too quiet, and Ringo was the drummer. But we thought everyone would be able to dig at least one of us and that's how it turned out."

Along with the prestige and money that came from being Britain's top group, there was also increased opportunity. That was no more evident than on Thursday, April 18, 1963, when, realizing a rather significant showbiz dream, the Beatles played the Royal Albert Hall in London. That show, which was broadcast over radio by the BBC, was called the "Swinging Sounds '63" and featured several top acts.

The Beatles performed four songs altogether ("Please Please Me," "Misery," "Twist and Shout," and "From Me to You") and joined in on the grand finale with the entire company busking through a rowdy rendition of "Mack the Knife."

Even more important to Paul McCartney than this high-rent gig was meeting a young lady who would change his life, lovely teen actress Jane Asher.

For the upwardly mobile bachelor, Asher was as close to perfect as it gets. Born in London on April 5, 1946, she was the daughter of prominent physician Richard Asher and his wife, Margaret, a professor at the Guildhall School of Music. Jane herself had been a professional actress since the age of five.

The beautiful redhead was everything McCartney envisioned in a woman, and was certainly worlds apart from the numerous other ladies he had known.

Lovely, talented, gracious, and refined, Jane was the perfect royal consort to this lanky prince of rock 'n' roll. From almost the moment they met, they began dating regularly. Jim McCartney was thrilled with what he considered his son's first official girlfriend. Nothing would have made him happier, he said, than to see them wed. Even brother Mike was smitten.

Remembering their first meeting, Paul later recalled, "We [the Beatles] all said, 'Will you marry me?' which was what we said to every girl at the time. [She was a] rare bird, the sort we'd always heard about. We thought we were set."

Over the next few weeks they became inseparable, roaming the streets of Mayfair arm in arm. Ironically, in those days it was the radiant actress people tended to recognize, not Beatle Paul, which caused a few ripples that would help slowly erode the ill-fated relationship over the next five years. For the moment, however, they were head over heels, so much so that, unknown to his many female fans, McCartney soon accepted an invitation from Jane's mother to move into the Ashers' smart family home at 57 Wimpole Street in central London.

Not surprisingly, Epstein was less than thrilled that the group's number-one heartthrob was making himself psychologically off-limits to a generation of nubile ingenues. "A Beatle must not marry," declared Brian in his book, *A Cellarful of Noise.* He'd even gone to lengths to keep John's marriage a secret until word got out and he was forced to revise his edict, "It is all very well if one is married before one is a fully-grown Beatle."

Love lives aside, by mid-1963 the songwriting aspect of Lennon and McCartney's relationship had made considerable inroads, and was now firmly imbued with the Midas touch. Their April 11 release, "From Me to You" (with the flip side, "Thank You Girl"), sailed triumphantly to number one. The bouncy ditty, whose title originated from the *New Musical Express'* letters column, "From Us to You," had been written just a month earlier on a bus outside Shrewsbury while the Beatles were touring with Helen Shapiro.

"We nearly didn't record it," revealed John. "We thought it was too bluesy at first, but when we'd finished it and George Martin scored it with harmonica it was all right."

The song marked the debut of the vocal trademark "woooo." Lennon told Helen Shapiro that he rendered the falsetto, bragging, "I can do the high stuff better than Paul." It was a statement he would contradict just a year later.

As for the flipside, "Thank You Girl," Lennon brushed it off, having remarked, "It was just a silly song we knocked off. It was one of our efforts at writing a single that didn't work. So it became a B-side."

June saw the group's fortunes increase considerably with the hastily dashed off "She Loves You." Composed in a tatty hotel room following a gig in Newcastle on April 26, this was a true joint effort. McCartney came up with the original idea for the spirited rocker. "I thought of it first and thought of doing it as one of those answering songs, the sort of thing the American singing groups keep doing. A couple of us would sing 'she loves you' and the others would do the 'yeah, yeah, yeah' ones. The one would be answering everything the other two sang. John and I agreed it was a pretty crummy idea as it stood and since we were borrowing an American thing, I suppose it was crummy. But at least we had the basic idea of writing the song."

Lennon's recollection of the tune, meanwhile, went like this: "I remember it was Paul's idea. Instead of singing 'I love you' again, we'd have a third party. . . . He'll write a story about someone and I'm more inclined to just write about myself. The 'woo woo' was taken from the Isley Brothers' 'Twist and Shout,' which we stuck into everything then."

Singer Kenny Lynch, who toured with the group in 1963, remembers John and Paul discussing how they intended to run up to the microphone together and shake their hair and sing "woooo." "They'll think you're a bunch of poofs!" cried Lynch, falling into hysterics along with everyone on the bus.

"What do you mean?" countered Lennon. "It sounds great. We're puttin' it into the act."

If Jim McCartney had had his way, however, the Beatles' trademark "yeah yeah yeah" would have been "yes, yes, yes," to retain, he said, a modicum of British dignity.

On the production side, it was producer Martin who suggested that John and Paul launch right into the chorus of the song, instead of the first verse. "Occasionally," recalls McCartney, "we'd overrule him. On 'She Loves You' we'd end on a sixth chord [George Harrison's suggestion], a very jazzy sort of thing, and he said 'Oh! You can't do that! A sixth chord? It's too jazzy.' We just said, 'No, it's a great hook, we've got to do it.'"

Back in the studio on July 18, the Beatles began recording material for their second album, a process that would take three months. The plan was to cut two albums and four singles each year, an ambitious schedule they successfully maintained through 1965.

The resulting *With the Beatles* featured John and Paul paying tribute to a number of influential black artists: Chuck Berry's "Roll Over Beethoven,"

Smokey Robinson's "You Really Got a Hold on Me," Berry Gordy's "Money," the Marvellettes' "Please Mr. Postman," plus "Anna" by Lennon's early idol Arthur Alexander. Even their own compositions reflected the R&B style. "That's me trying to do Smokey Robinson again," said John of "All I've Gotta Do," while Paul conceded that his "Hold Me Tight" "was a bit Shirelles."

The departure from the trend included McCartney's borrowing from the Broadway stage. His rendition of the romantic "Till There Was You," from *The Music Man,* was backed by Lennon and Harrison on acoustic guitar. Brian Epstein, on hand for the song's recording, told Martin he thought he detected a flaw in Paul's vocal rendition, to which the often caustic Lennon replied into the microphone, "We'll make the fuckin' records, Brian. You just go on counting the percentages!"

The album as a whole represented the Beatles' commitment to their on-going musical evolution. There was much experimentation with the double tracking of vocals, which John later contended was overused. Lennon's harmonica solos, so prominent on the first album, were, with the exception of "Little Child," notably absent.

George Martin got into the act playing piano on three tracks: "You Really Got a Hold on Me," "Money," and "Not a Second Time." The last, another Lennon effort, was unique in that neither Harrison nor McCartney was present for the recording. Only Lennon's acoustic guitar plus Ringo's drumming, along with Martin's piano, comprised the backing track.

Oddly, this clearly Smokey Robinson–influenced number was the first to attract the attention of the high-brow music critics. William Mann of the London *Times* began to speak to the Lennon and McCartney use of harmonics and key switches. "So natural is the Aeonian cadence at the end of 'Not a Second Time' (the chord progression which ends Mahler's *Song of the Earth*)," he wrote. To which the quick-witted Lennon retorted, "I don't have *any* idea what Aeonian cadences are. Really, it was just chords like any other. That was the first time anyone had written anything like that about us."

The album's anchor, though, was the infectious, toe-tapping "All My Loving." Paul revealed in 1984 that it was the first song he'd ever written where the lyrics came before the music. "I wrote it like a piece of poetry and then, I think, I put a song to it later."

McCartney's lead vocal made good use of double tracking and yet another Beatles trademark, a second or so break of silence.

Even Lennon begrudgingly admitted this one was a keeper. "'All My Loving' is Paul, I regret to say . . . because it's a damn good piece of work."

The frantic "I Wanna Be Your Man," penned entirely by McCartney, was the only song released by both the Beatles and the Rolling Stones (who recorded it the following month). "It was a throwaway," Lennon said of the tune. "The only two versions were by Ringo and the Stones. That shows how much importance we put on it, we weren't going to give them anything great, right?"

Sometime later, "I Wanna Be Your Man" would be answered by Bob Dylan with his "I Wanna Be Your Lover," which remained unreleased until his 1985 *Biograph* LP.

It was during this period that John and Paul truly worked together as a team. Selflessly toiling on behalf of the group, the two young men sat together hour after hour and wrote their music, Beatles music.

Their close collaboration was based on record company pressures to issue a single every three months. "So the cooperation was functional as well as musical," noted Lennon.

Purely, simply, and without a lot of fuss, they offhandedly molded the consciousness of an entire generation with only a handful of elementary chords and a savvy talent for rendering heartfelt lyrics and tuneful melodies wrought from their day-to-day lives.

Lennon admitted, however, that at this early stage their musical loves were not influenced by specific relationships. "We were just writing songs à la Everly Brothers, à la Buddy Holly, pop songs with no more thought to them than that, to create a sound. The words were almost irrelevant. She loves you, he loves her, and they love each other. It was the hook and the line and the sound we were going for."

That was disputed, in at least one case by Iris Caldwell, the comely sister of Rory Storm, whom Paul dated for about a year. Caldwell commented years later, "The first song they recorded together, 'Love Me Do,' was a tune Paul had written for me. When the record entered the *New Musical Express* chart at number twenty-seven I was over the moon going 'round saying, 'Wow, jeez,' because a song written for me was in the charts."

On their second major project, the indelible Lennon-McCartney hallmarks were already beginning to show up: their clever use of octave ascents as exemplified in "Please Please Me" and "I Wanna Be Your Man"; the unique key switches, most notably from C major to A-flat major, as well as their exquisite harmonies.

William Mann in the London *Times* reported, "One gets the impression they think simultaneously of harmony and melody, so firmly are the major tonic sevenths and ninths built into their tunes."

Lennon added that early on he and Paul composed in the key of A believing that was the key in which Buddy Holly wrote. Later, however, they discovered that Holly generally played in the key of C. Undaunted, Lennon shrugged it off, saying: "It all sounded okay in A so that's the way we played our stuff."

Beyond that, earmarking their unique sound was Paul's purposeful bass line, "with a musical life of its own," as one critic put it.

George Martin hailed McCartney "probably the best bass player there is, a first class drummer, brilliant guitarist and competent piano player."

That neither could read music was, in fact, a blessing in disguise. After neatly scrawling out the words in order and perhaps placing a few chord notations over certain words, they were finished. Anything more would be left to the capable hands of George Martin.

According to the Beatles' producer, formal training might have actually inhibited their inventiveness. "Once you're being taught things, your mind is channeled in a particular way. Paul didn't have that channeling, so he had freedom and could think of things I would have considered outrageous. The ability to write good tunes often comes when someone is not fettered by the rules and regulations of harmony and counterpoint. A tune is a one-fingered thing, something you can whistle in the street; it doesn't depend upon great harmonies. The ability to create them is simply a gift."

Martin's fatherly guiding hand was as important as their raw, emerging talent. Often omitted from the accolades showered on the Beatles' music (and certainly deprived of the fortune that followed), the kindly, ceaselessly perfectionist producer contributed (in this author's opinion anyway) *at least* as much as any Beatle and very often more. For all the millions of words spoken about Lennon and McCartney's prolific output, it was very often Martin who organized, streamlined, and focused the work.

It was now all coming together, what they'd been working toward year after thankless year: the chance to really say something with their music, to make an impact. Sure, they were in it for the money, but Lennon and McCartney had great integrity, refusing to turn out substandard work simply for a quick buck.

"John and I used to have this joke about sitting down to 'write' a speed boat or a sports car," says Paul. "Not because we were greedy, but simply out of sheer fucking working-class glee that we could."

John Lennon, so long the unquestioned philosopher of the group, tried to come to grips with the intricacies of the creative process during a 1966 interview.

As kids, we were all opposed to folk songs because they were so middle class. It was all the college students with big scarves and a pint of beer in their hands singing folk songs in what we call la-di-da voices, "I worked in a mine in New-cast-le" and all that shit. It's all a bit boring like ballet, a minority thing kept going by a minority. Today's folk music is rock and roll. Although it happened to emanate from America, that's not really important in the end, because we wrote our own music and that changed everything.

When I started rock 'n' roll, it was the basic revolution to people of my age and situation. We needed something loud and clear to break through all the unfeeling and repression that had been coming down on us kids. We were a bit conscious to begin with of being imitation Americans. But we delved into music and found it was half white country-and-western and half black rhythm and blues. Most of the songs came from Europe and Africa and now they were coming back to us.

Though I must say the more interesting songs to me were the black ones because they were more simple. They sort of said shake your arse or your prick which was an innovation really. And then there were the "field songs" [those that evolved from the African-American slaves], mainly expressing the pain they were in. They couldn't express themselves intellectually so they had to say in a very few words what was happening to them. And then there was the city blues and lot of that was about sex and fighting. But right through the blacks were singing about their pain and also about sex, which is why I like it.

A man of deep conviction and emotion, Lennon brought to his work with McCartney an innate honesty and level of perception previously unknown in popular music. Only occasionally could Paul tap into the deep waters that readily flowed from his introspective partner. Even in these early days when McCartney sang "Close your eyes and I'll kiss you," Lennon was already tearing his guts out crying, "The world is treating me bad, misery."

On Sunday, August 3, 1963, following some 292 appearances, the Beatles played the Cavern for the very last time. According to John, it was more than an end of an era, it was the end of the Beatles. "We were performers in Liverpool, Hamburg and other dance halls. What we generated was fantastic, when we played straight rock there was nobody to touch us in Britain. As soon as we made it the edges were knocked off. The Beatles music died then."

Although Brian Epstein promised the fans that they would soon return, they never did. The fact is, John, Paul, George, and Ringo were squired away by the freight train that was Beatlemania, only just then rounding the bend.

By this time, virtually every day brought with it something exciting for these four provincial lads and for their growing legion of fans. A case in point was the Beatles' appearance at the London Palladium on Sunday, October 13, 1963. This, legend has it, was the official beginning of Beatlemania, with Fleet Street reporting hordes of out-of-control fans phoning the upmarket Argyll Street theater screaming for their shaggy-haired idols. The national media had at last caught up with what every kid in Britain already knew: The Beatles were the newly crowned kings of popular music.

It is important to remember that from the day they met, John and Paul had been close friends who became partners. This, of course, is one of the reasons they meshed so well. Together they were not only a formidable song-writing team, but a hilarious, irreverent comedy duo as well. Deeply inspired by *The Goon Show* as kids, they both grew up readily imitating all manner of silly voices and accents à la Peter Sellers and Spike Milligan.

Mike McCartney recalls the delightful ruckus. "John was a great comedian all right, a natural. He was the heavy one, and Paul was a very good feed. Two good comedians. But then again, Ringo's a very funny guy as well. Liverpool life is the best apprenticeship in the world because our families are virtual gold mines of upbringing. Without that grounding I doubt very much whether the Beatles would have stayed on top for so long or kept their sanity when all about them so many died. Of course, an enormous contribution to that longevity was their wicked sense of humor. They always say in Liverpool, 'You've got to have a sense of humor to survive.'"

To ignore the element of humor in Lennon and McCartney's work is to miss a critical element of their great achievement. "I was twelve when 'The Goon Show' first hit," John wrote in the early seventies,

sixteen when they finished with me. Their humor was the only proof that the *world* was insane. . . . The Goons influenced the Beatles as did Lewis Carroll and Elvis Presley. Before becoming the Beatles' producer, George Martin, who had never recorded rock 'n' roll, previously recorded with Milligan and Sellers, which made him all the more acceptable. Our studio sessions were full of the cries of Neddie Seagoon, etc., etc., as were most places in Britain. . . . One of my earlier efforts at writing was a "news-paper" called *The Daily Howl.* I would write it at night, then take it to school and read it aloud to my friends. Looking at it now seems strangely similar to "The Goon Show"! Even the title had "highly esteemed" before it! . . . Spike Milligan's a genius and Peter Sellers made all the money! (Harry Secombe got *show biz.*) I love all three of them dearly, but Spike was extra. His appearances on TV as "himself" were something to behold. He always "freaked out" the cameramen/directors by refusing to *fit the pattern.*

Influential, too, for John and Paul were several latter-day saints of the absurd, including Peter Cook and Dudley Moore, Vivian Stanshall and his loony Bonzo Dog Doo-Dah Band, and, of course, the inimitable *Monty Python's Flying Circus.* When the now-classic show came on the telly, the Beatles often cut short their sessions to rush home and howl at the inside-out antics of future chums John Cleese, Eric Idle, and Michael Palin.

Practically all of the Beatles' music and much of Lennon and McCartney's solo work was wrought with one eye on this type of crazy, borderless humor. If not readily apparent in the finished version (and many times it is) then it's there somewhere in the miles of zany outtakes that seem to follow these two monumentally silly gentlemen.

An example of their humor is the Beatles' legendary annual Christmas records. Their first effort (written by Beatles press officer Tony Barrow) was recorded on Thursday, October 17, 1963, and highlighted the boys' unrestrained penchant for blatantly taking the piss out of virtually every sacred cow that came their way, including the Beatles themselves. Never officially released to the public, these seven-inch flexi-discs were mailed out only to members of the Beatles Fan Club. Beautifully packaged in specially designed picture covers (often with club inserts), these saucy little records provided John and Paul with the chance to break out as the frustrated vaudeville comedians they were.

Altogether there were seven singles from 1963 through 1969, with a limited-edition album pressed in 1970 comprising all the various forty-fives. One of the most alluring features of this timely collection was the brilliantly conceived jacket art showing the Fabs' radical change of appearance from 1963 to 1969. Once again, sent only to fan clubbers as a parting gift, this too was never widely available except as a bootleg. Apple, one would think, should consider putting the album out properly now that so many years have passed.

By October 1963, with Britain still firmly in the grip of Beatlemania, Brian Epstein was already thinking farther afield. Thus far, Capitol Records had inexplicably refused to release Beatles singles in the United States. Following several unsuccessful attempts to convince the company otherwise, Epstein had another strategy in mind. He told the Capitol brass that the Fabs were about to release a new single produced specifically with the "American sound." Once the single hit in Britain, it was clear that Epstein's tactics had worked. Capitol not only agreed to release the record but was launching a $50,000 advertising campaign beginning January 1 to break the Beatles in America.

That single, the Beatles' calling card to the American market, was, of course, "I Want to Hold Your Hand." Not appearing on *With the Beatles,* but rather its American equivalent, *Meet the Beatles,* this was the mega-worldwide breakout hit. A strict fifty-fifty effort, Lennon recalled that the duo wrote the tune "eyeball to eyeball. I remember when we got the chord that made the song. We were in Jane Asher's house, downstairs in the cellar playing on the piano at the same time. And we had 'oh, you-u-u . . . got that something. . . .' And Paul hits this chord and I turn to him and say 'That's it!' I said, 'Do that again!' In those days we really used to absolutely write like that, both playing into each other's noses."

The Beatles Illustrated Lyrics deemed the musical structure "full of subtle tricks and adventurous ploys that reveal a rapidly growing maturity in their work. From the deliberate stumble of the opening time-signature to the calculated dissonances of the chorus, the whole conception of this song was unlike anything attempted before, and owed little or nothing to their well-publicized tap-root American influences."

Inevitably the song made an impact in circles everywhere. On first hearing the tune in a New York nightclub, poet Allen Ginsberg was so carried away that he leapt from his table and danced exuberantly, something he had never done before in public.

Soul crooner Teddy Pendergrass, then a junior high school student, remembered the tune had an altogether different impact, bringing the Beatles into the black community. Pendergrass lauds the group for its originality and for inspiring his own musical pursuits.

On Friday, November 22, 1963—the day President John F. Kennedy was assassinated on a Dallas street—the Beatles' second album, *With the Beatles,* was released in Britain. As a giant shadow descended on a stricken America, felling Camelot and signaling the end of an era, just across the water an album cover depicted four heads emerging from the shadows, ready to usher in another era very much their own.

With the Beatles scored an immediate impression on several rising young artists. "It Won't Be Long" and "Money" were the first two songs that Canadian rocker Neil Young performed for a high school cafeteria concert. Pete Thomas, drummer for Elvis Costello, was also heavily influenced by the album.

"When I was nine I got *With the Beatles* and my grandma bought me a honky old drum and an old cymbal. That's it, isn't it? What more is there? A drum, a cymbal, and *With the Beatles.* Has the world really come much further?"

With orders of more than 300,000, *With the Beatles* swiftly became a huge hit, charting at number one only five days after its release. One week later, Parlophone single R 5084, "I Want to Hold Your Hand" (backed by the melancholy "This Boy") reached the $9 million mark from advance sales alone. All this time, of course, the Beatles were still very much a live act, playing top venues from Glasgow to Wimbledon.

With the coming of 1964, the Beatles were at the very brink of their massive international, mind-bending success. On January 29, the boys hunkered down in EMI Pathé Marconi Studios in the heart of Paris for a session not in French, but in German. In an effort to appease the group's Euro fans, they would, under mild protest, record "I Want to Hold Your Hand" ("Komm, Gib Mir Deine Hand") and "She Loves You" ("Sie Liebt Dich") along with "Can't Buy Me Love."

George Martin remembers the grand occasion.

I fixed the session for late morning. Norman Smith, myself, and the translator, a chap named Nicholas, all got to the studio on time, but there was no sign of the Beatles. We waited an hour before I telephoned their suite at the George V Hotel. Neil Aspinall answered, "They're in bed, they've decided not to go to the studio." I went crazy, it was the first time they had refused to do anything for me. "You tell them they've got to come, otherwise I shall be so angry it isn't true! I'm coming over right now."

So the German and I jumped into a taxi, we got to the hotel and I barged into their suite, to be met by this incredible sight right out of the

Mad Hatter's tea party. Jane, Paul's girlfriend, with her long red hair, was pouring tea from a china pot, and the others were sitting around like her March Hares. They took one look at me and *exploded,* like in a schoolroom where the headmaster enters. Some dived onto the sofa and hid behind cushions, others dashed behind curtains. "You bastards!" I screamed, to which they responded with impish grins and roguish apologies. Within minutes we were on our way to the studio.

The next great chapter in Lennon-McCartney's legacy was now at hand. Britain and Europe had fallen, and now Brian and the boys had their eyes set on the ultimate prize: America.

Epstein had already made a short exploratory trip to New York in November 1963. Accompanied by NEMS artist Billy J. Kramer, he met with television pioneer Ed Sullivan to discuss plans for the Beatles' appearance on his "really big shew." After a bit of a tussle over the billing, a deal was finally struck for two appearances, on February 9 and 16, 1964, and a subsequent taped appearance all for a fee of about $10,000. Later, New York promoter Sid Bernstein persuaded Brian to allow him to book the boys into Carnegie Hall for two shows on February 12.

"I Want to Hold Your Hand" was sizzling on the *American Cashbox* charts as the four anxious pop stars boarded a flight from London's Heathrow to New York's Idlewild Airport. "America's got everything," thought Lennon out loud, "why should they fuckin' want us?"

John later recalled his precarious state of mind on that momentous day. "When we arrived we knew how to handle the media. The British press are the toughest in the world; we could handle anything. I know on the plane over I was thinking, 'Oh, we won't make it,' or I said it on a film or something, but that's that side of me. We knew we would wipe you out if we could just get a grip on you [Americans]. We were new.

"When we got here you were all walkin' around in fuckin' Bermuda shorts with Boston crew cuts and stuff on your teeth. The chicks looked like 1940s horses. There was no conception of dress or any of that jazz. We just thought, 'What an ugly race.' It looked just disgusting and we thought how hip we were. But, of course, we weren't. We used to really laugh at America, except for the music. It was black music we dug, but the blacks were laughin' at people like Chuck Berry and the blues singers. They thought it wasn't sharp to dig the really funky black music and the whites only listened to Jan and Dean and all that."

Lennon and his cohorts needn't have worried about their New York reception. From the mass hysteria that greeted them upon landing to the bizarre, anything-goes airport press conference to their landmark debut performance on *The Ed Sullivan* Show (viewed by some 73 million), fears about the impending invasion proved moot. The Americans were already well and truly conquered.

On February 11, the boys headed out to Washington, D.C., for two dates, never dreaming they were about to become movie stars. The previous fall, Bud Orenstein, production chief for United Artists film division, offered the group a three-picture deal in order to obtain the Beatles' soundtracks. Orenstein, only interested in snagging the surging Fabs on record, had no idea the gold mine he was unearthing.

With production on the first movie slated to begin on March 2, there was no time to lose. On the heels of their whirlwind minitour, the Beatles went back to Abbey Road to lay down tracks for their new venture.

The resulting album, *A Hard Day's Night,* was filled with milestones. First, Lennon and McCartney were put to the test, commissioned to write specifically for the project. This was also the initial album that exclusively featured Lennon and McCartney originals and highlighted Harrison's 12-string Rickenbacker 360 guitar, revolutionary in its day. This session also inaugurated George Martin's tenure as arranger in addition to producer.

Eclipsing these landmarks, however, *A Hard Day's Night* was John Lennon's coming-out party. He penned most of the material, and the album showcased his growing confidence in writing melodies. Critic Malcolm Doney writes in his insightful book, *Lennon and McCartney,* "In 1964 pop songs remained only vague expressions of feeling, the lyrics provided a useful catch phrase here and there, but were more a vehicle for voice than meaning. But the music was improving; the melody lines, the sense of rhythm and pace was altogether sharper. *A Hard Day's Night* marked the change. The variations of tempo and direction are masterly."

The title track was a crackling Lennon tour de force rocker. Of the tune's genesis John explained, "I was going home in the car and Dick Lester suggested the title 'Hard Day's Night' from something Ringo'd said. I'd used it in *In His Own Write,* but it was actually an off-the-cuff remark by Ringo."

As Ringo explained to one puzzled Japanese interviewer, "Roughly it means it's been a helluva day and it's going to be a helluva night."

The next morning Lennon brought in the song. Written, arranged, and recorded in a scant twenty-four hours, the track features George Martin on piano doubling the guitar solo line and Paul sharing vocals. "The only reason he sang on 'Hard Day's Night' was because I couldn't reach the [high] notes," John said—contradicting his earlier statement to Helen Shapiro.

"Happy Just to Dance with You" (noted for Ringo's tasteful use of Arabian-style bongos) was written by John specifically for George to sing in the movie. "To give him a piece of the action," explained Lennon. "That's another reason I was a bit hurt by his book [*I Me Mine*], because I even went to the trouble of making sure he got the B-side of a Beatles single. He hadn't gotten one because Paul and I always wrote both sides. . . . We weren't deliberately keeping him out; his material just wasn't up to scratch."

"Tell Me Why," another first-class rocker, was also generally dismissed by John. "I just knocked it off. It was like a black New York girl group song."

When McCartney finally contributed to the mix, he did so in grand style. "And I Love Her," generally considered Paul's best ballad to date, came with, as one critic put it, "a high haunt count." Unlike previous compositions with their anonymous loves, this one took its inspiration from Jane Asher— although Paul, in typical give-nothing-away fashion, refuted the allegation in a 1984 *Playboy* interview: "It's just a love song; no, it wasn't for anyone. Having the title start in mid-sentence, I thought that was clever. Well, Perry Como did 'And I Love You So' many years later. Tried to nick the idea. I like that, it was a nice tune, one I still like."

The two final new cuts used in the film were "If I Fell" and "I Should Have Known Better." The former, whose authorship was 100 percent Lennon, has been described as the precursor to "In My Life." "It's semi-autobiographical, but not consciously. It shows that I wrote sentimental love ballads, silly love songs way back when."

The superior vocals that hallmark the tune captured the lilting romantic feel and proved that the caustic tough guy certainly had a softer side as well. "This was our close-harmony period," noted McCartney. "We did a few songs, 'This Boy,' 'If I Fell,' 'Yes It Is,' all in the same vein."

Some twenty-four years later, Lennon's original rendering of the lyrics was auctioned for £7,800 at Sotheby's in London.

"I Should Have Known Better," meanwhile, was a definite variation on "A Hard Day's Night," so similar was its structure and feel. The song, too, marks a memorable sequence in the film. It was shot with the boys sitting in a van amidst crates of live chickens, with the crew outside gently rocking it back and forth to mimic the movements of a speeding train.

The final cut used in the movie was the pulsating McCartney classic "Can't

Buy Me Love," which was written in Miami and actually released as a single on March 16. Some critics suggested the title referred to "love for sale," which drew immediate ire from its author.

"Personally, I think you can put any interpretation you want on anything," said Paul, "but when someone suggests that 'Can't Buy Me Love' is about a prostitute I draw the line. That's going too far."

Once again, as with "She Loves You," George Martin suggested they begin the tune with the chorus. "I said, 'We've got to have an introduction, something that catches the ear immediately, a hook. So let's start off with the chorus.'"

Jazz legend Ella Fitzgerald's recording of the song just a few months later not only scored a minor hit, but opened the floodgates of artists clamoring to cover a Beatles tune. Suddenly everyone from Joe Cocker to Herb Alpert— even the cartoon Chipmunks—was recording Lennon-McCartney compositions, and all were having hits.

Throughout the album's making, a power struggle with enormous future ramifications was beginning to grow. According to George Martin, the friendly, almost-sibling rivalry between pop's premier tunesmiths was escalating. "The truth is deep down they were very, very similar indeed. Each had a soft underbelly, each was very much hurt by certain things. John had a very soft side to him. But you see, each had a bitter turn of phrase and could be quite nasty to the other.

"It was like a tug of war. Imagine two people pulling on a rope, smiling at each other and pulling all the time with all their might. The tension between the two of them made for the bond."

At this point Lennon had the upper hand, admitting he'd dashed off the title song, "A Hard Day's Night," on a matchcover to beat Paul to the punch. "There was a little competition between Paul and I as to who got the singles. If you notice, in the early days the majority of singles, in the movies and everything, were mine. And then only when I became self-conscious and inhibited did Paul start dominating the group a little too much for my liking."

Lennon's domination was apparent even away from the studio. Singer Kenny Lynch recalled the scene backstage while on tour with the Beatles as Paul would attempt to rule the roost, saying, "Now listen, we're going to do it this way."

Lennon inevitably would abruptly step in and bark, "Fuck it, we're not!"

And Lennon's word, according to Lynch, was law.

Adds Beatles personal assistant Peter Brown, "It was not a dominant-supplicant relationship, but if Lennon didn't like something he would tell McCartney."

Paul, for his part, seldom challenged his partner's final word, but rather conveyed his disagreements through a telling gesture or an offhand suggestion. "I believe, keep cool and that sort of thing and it passes over," he reasoned at the time.

McCartney was simply biding his time. Little by little the power balance shifted and thereby dramatically changed the fortunes of everyone in the Beatles camp.

For the moment, however, the pair had other things on their minds. The album tracks laid down, the Fabs went straight to work at London's Twickenham Film Studios on their second career, as actors.

A Hard Day's Night owes as much to the remarkable blend of talent behind the camera as to the Beatles themselves. Walter Shenson, a former Hollywood publicist with a decided taste for the offbeat, was brought on board to produce.

On the suggestion of McCartney, scriptwriting duties went to playwright Alun Owen, a burly down-to-earth Liverpudlian who'd come up the hard way via Dublin's renowned Gate Theater. It was Owen who developed the concept, a thirty-six-hour slice of the group's lives, and whose harsh sense of humor gave the film its quirky edge.

The real stroke of brilliance, however, was engaging Richard Lester to direct. He'd done some stellar work on Shenson's *The Mouse on the Moon,* the renowned follow-up to *The Mouse That Roared,* as well as an early Peter Sellers classic, *The Running, Jumping and Standing Still Film.*

Gilbert Taylor, one of Britain's finest cameramen, signed on to shoot the film in black and white. Like Lester, he was devoted to the verité style of film making, but little did anyone know just how "verité" it was actually to be.

When the production moved to London's Scala Theater for filming of the musical numbers, Lester hadn't counted on raging Beatlemania. As fans were storming the Charlotte Street venue the director had an inspiration. After a word with the police he filmed the chaos in the auditorium with all six cameras. The damage to the sets and equipment was negligible with that suffered by the budget, for it took the police quite some time to round up the near-hysterical intruders before normal filming could be resumed.

Explained one tearful fan on her way out: "Hearing all the screaming inside was just too much!"

Just prior to the end of shooting at the Scala, a freckled thirteen-year-old collided with a lamppost hard and square. Hoping to find the address of the unconscious girl, the police opened her school bag to find a complete set of housebreaking tools that the enterprising fan must have intended to apply to the locked doors of the Scala.

Toward the end of March 1964, John Lennon realized a very personal ambition that had been with him even longer than his profound love of music. A clever, highly original poet since childhood, John finally published his first book, *In His Own Write,* a witty collection of cheeky vignettes and caricatures that immediately hit the best-seller lists on both sides of the Atlantic.

"I put things down on sheets of paper and stuff them in my pockets," John said in 1980. "When I have enough, I have a book. I suppose they were all manifestations of hidden cruelties. They were very *Alice in Wonderland* and *Winnie the Pooh.* I was very hung-up then. . . . If I wrote in normal spelling there would be no point in writing."

To many people's surprise, the critics, for the most part, genuinely enjoyed the lauded Lennon wit. On Thursday, March 26, 1964, the London *Times Literary Supplement* had this to say about the chief Beatle's second career:

> His writings are remarkable; they are a world away from the underdeveloped language of his songs. It's a linguistic never never land somewhere between Joyce, Lewis Carroll and Thurber. They are also very funny . . . the nonsense runs on, words and images prompting one another in a chain of pure fantasy.
>
> The book is beautifully designed . . . it is worth the attention of anyone who fears for the impoverishment of the English language and British imagination . . . humorists have done more to preserve and enrich these assets than most serious critics allow. Theirs is arguably our liveliest stream of "experimental writing" and Mr. Lennon shows himself well equipped to take it farther. He must write a great deal more.

Contemporary novelist Tom Wolfe added: "This is nonsense writing, but one has only to review the literature of nonsense to see how well Lennon has brought it off."

That is not to say, however, that the critics were unanimous in their kudos.

Christopher Ricks of the *New Statesman,* for one, saw things a little differently: "It's hard to see how anyone unaware that John Lennon is a Beatle could get much pleasure out of *In His Own Write.* A few expressive drawings, and one or two nice puns, but most of the time it is feeble. Nonsense-punning needs a nightmarish logic or else it becomes mere wool-gathering."

Incredibly, Lennon's literary talents were also fodder for a full-fledged debate in the House of Commons! On June 19, 1964, at exactly 12:48, Uxbridge Conservative Charles Curran delivered an impassioned plea for improved education for the mass of British youth based on the appalling state of literacy as highlighted by Beatle Lennon's wholesale slaughter of the mother tongue.

> The book contains a number of poems and fairy stories written by Lennon. These tell a great deal about the education he received in Liverpool. He explains that he was born there in 1940 and attended various schools, where he could not pass the examinations.
>
> Two things about John Lennon: He has a feeling for words and story-telling and he is in a state of pathetic near-literacy. He seems to have picked up bits of Tennyson, Browning, and Robert Louis Stevenson while listening with one ear to the football results on the wireless.
>
> The book suggests to me a boy who, on the evidence of these writings, should have been given an education which would have enabled him to develop the literary talent that he appears to have. I do not know whether my Honorable Friend, the Joint Under-Secretary of State can tell us anything about what kind of school this Beatle went to. The volume from which I have quoted strikes me as singularly pathetic and touching.

In reply, Norman Miscampbell, a fellow Conservative from Blackpool, North, countered eloquently, begging to take issue:

> I was interested in my Honorable Friend's mention of the Beatles. It is unfair to say that Lennon was not well educated. I cannot say which, but three of the four went to grammar school and as a group are highly intelligent, highly articulate, and highly engaging.
>
> I think we would draw the wrong conclusions if we thought that the success which they are having came from anything other than great skill. They provide an outlet for many people who find it difficult to integrate themselves into society when they move into adolescence. The Beatles and

groups like them are giving such people an outlet, and are taking up the slack which ought to have been provided by a deeper education.

Slow day in the Empire? Not a bit. The fact is the Beatles were gradually becoming the popular icons we view them as today, and Lennon was very much their fearless leader. As nascent legends, it's not really surprising how far they'd managed to work themselves up the ladder or how consistently the older generation missed the point.

On June 4, 1964, the group jetted off for two appearances in Denmark, followed by a fifteen-date tour of the Pacific rim. Touching down in Sydney on June 11, they were greeted by zealous Australian fans. To the eager Aussies the saucy Beatles were indeed big news.

"Nearly 250,000 people lined the Anzac Highway in Adelaide, from the charming airport to the city center," recalls Beatles PR man Derek Taylor. "I told journalist Al Aronowitz all about it for the *Saturday Evening Post* a few weeks later. 'It was like the Messiah come to Australia,' I said, understating as best I could. 'Cripples threw away their sticks and blind men leapt for you.' The only thing left for the boys after this tour, I told him, would be a 'healing tour' of the world. It *was* like that."

The Beatles arrived home in London on July 2. The royal premiere of *A Hard Day's Night* was on July 6, 1964, at the London Pavilion—with much attendant hoopla and glitterati. After returning from the receiving line where the boys exchanged pleasantries with a radiant Princess Margaret and Lord Snowdon, Lennon cornered press liaison Taylor, inquiring brusquely, "Right, who was better in the film, me or Paul? No fuckin' bullshit now. I want to know."

"Paul," the dapper Brit answered slyly.

"Bollocks!" Lennon growled, edging closer to the vaguely bemused PR man. "For real, man!"

"You were, John, of course," Taylor came back, slapping him smartly on the back.

"Of course," Lennon whispered under his breath as he made his way to the open bar.

A few days later, on the tenth, the film opened at Liverpool's Odeon Cinema to rave reviews from the international press. Writing in New York's *Village Voice,* Andrew Sarris dubbed the film "The *Citizen Kane* of jukebox musicals. To watch the Beatles in action with their constituents is to watch the kind of direct theater that went out with Aristophanes. There is an empathy here that a million Lincoln Center Repertory companies cannot duplicate. It is in the beat that the passion and togetherness is most movingly expressed and it is the beat that the kids in the audience pick up with their shrieks as they drown out the words they have already heard a thousand times."

John Lennon later remarked on his feelings for the now famous flick. "I dug *A Hard Day's Night,* although Alun Owen only came with us for two days before he wrote the script. He invented that word 'grotty,' did you know that?

"We thought the word was really weird. George curled with embarrassment every time he had to say it. But it's part of the language now, you hear society people using it. Amazing."

"What we liked about it," commented Paul in 1989, "was it was a film, not just a vehicle for a rock 'n' roll act; it captured our personalities. We were glad it was in black and white. It just seemed harder, more artsy."

To its credit, the film received two Academy Award nominations and raked in some $14 million in its initial run, not a bad return on its dime-store budget of only $200,000. Add another notch on the glistening solid gold Lennon-McCartney belt: film composers.

The soundtrack for *A Hard Day's Night* was released in Britain on July 10, 1964, and became the number-one-selling album in the country less than a week later. Side two of the record contains six songs that weren't used in the movie, including two songs Lennon dubbed "Wilson Pickett rip-offs": "When I Get Home" and "You Can't Do That." The latter, which initially went public as the flip side to "Can't Buy Me Love," has Lennon playing lead guitar on his highly treasured Rickenbacker Slimline 1966 with Ringo backing him up on cowbells. "I'd find it a drag to play rhythm [guitar] all the time so I always work myself out something interesting to play," he said. "The best example I can think of is what I did on 'You Can't Do That.' There wasn't really a lead guitarist and a rhythm guitarist on that because I feel the rhythm guitarist role sounds too thin for records."

"Things We Said Today" is a prime example of McCartney at his rocking best. A solo effort written in May while vacationing in the Bahamas with Jane and Ringo and his wife, Maureen, the tune captured an appealing nostalgic edge that even moved Lennon to dub it "a good song."

Yet beneath the surface of the album's seemingly carefree mood there are disturbing undertones in several of John's contributions. "Tell Me Why" levels charges of dishonesty; "When I Get Home" hints at marital discontent. Particularly revealing is "I'll Cry Instead," where we see the first public chink in John's armor, a hint that all was not quite right with the quirky urban poet. Fame, with its resulting madness and pressures, was beginning to take a toll on the sensitive Beatle. His oft-repeated phrase in "I'll Cry Instead," "I've got a chip on my shoulder that's bigger than my feet" was an accurate description, Lennon admitted, of his state of mind.

Yet he and Paul were poised on an unprecedented brink of fame and outrageous fortune. From the cluttered parlor of McCartney's Forthlin Row council house to the ivy-covered walls of St. John's Wood and beyond, they had come a hell of a long way. Hailed as the greatest composers since Beethoven, they earned five prestigious Ivor Novello Awards from the British music industry and had become movie stars and millionaires, all well before the age of thirty—not bad for a couple of suburban roustabouts from the seamy north.

Their best days still lay ahead, yet the suffocating swirl of Beatlemania had already begun to take its toll. *A Hard Day's Night,* however, signaled the end of the days of innocence for John and Paul.

Giants / The Impossible
Heyday of Beatlemania

By the dawn of 1965, Lennon and McCartney were moving swiftly away from cuddly pop idols to mature musical artists, painting on vinyl a reflection of the mood, attitudes, and climate of their extraordinary times.

The transformation had already begun at the tail end of 1964 with the release of Lennon's progressive "I Feel Fine," the Beatles' sixth consecutive number-one single. The song was written at a session around the opening riff. John was quick to exude, "I defy anyone to find an earlier record, unless it's some old blues number from the twenties, with feedback on it."

Everything about the piece is groundbreaking, from Harrison's challenging guitar work to the double lead guitar "solo" by John and George. The noticeable buzz coming from the amplifier was accidental, but Martin left it in, as well as what sounds like barking dogs. Actually, it was Paul just fooling around, as he did later on "Hey Bulldog."

The B-side to the release, "She's a Woman," wasn't exactly a throwaway either. Written in the studio and recorded the same day, this was McCartney proving he could also create syncopated rock 'n' roll. The song was noted for the Fabs' first hallucinogenic reference.

Explained John, "We put in the words 'turn me on.' We were so excited to say 'turn me on,' you know, about marijuana and all that. . . ."

The reference probably would have not been made if not for their meeting with pop's reigning icon, Bob Dylan, who first turned them on to marijuana. Following the Beatles' gig on August 28, 1964, at Forest Hills, they locked themselves up in New York's ritzy Delmonico Hotel in anticipation of the great man's arrival.

Driving in from Woodstock with minder Vic Mamoudas and pop journalist Al Aronowitz, Dylan parked around the corner from the hotel in a futile effort to avoid the fans. Once on the Beatles' private floor, Dylan was a little taken aback to see not only several of New York's finest hanging out with drinks in their hands, but also a celebrity retinue that included fabled folkies Peter, Paul, and Mary and the unbearable Kingston Trio.

Having only just choked down a quartet of aptly named Delmonico steaks, the boys looked up to see Dylan cautiously sidestepping into their inner sanctum. Following Eppy's slightly intoxicated introductions, Bob was asked what he was drinking.

"Cheap wine," he shot back sarcastically, to the great delight of John Lennon. Both the evening and the relationship had gotten off to a brilliant start.

With that, roadie Mal Evans was packed off to the nearest liquor store to fetch Mr. Zimmerman his favorite poison. In the interim, someone suggested that the party might like to do up a little speed. Dylan was shocked.

"No, man," he countered. "That shit is nowhere. How about a smoke?"

Looking around the room, Lennon finally piped up, "We've never actually smoked before. How 'bout it, lads?"

Virtually every one of the Brit contingent nodded in silent agreement, then an immediate flurry exploded with people double-locking doors, lighting incense, and otherwise pot-proofing the luxury suite. As Dylan rolled the first of several large joints in his lap he wondered out loud how it was that the Beatles had never toked; after all, in "I Want to Hold Your Hand" they so clearly sing "I get high."

"No, man," Lennon corrected him, "that was 'I can't *hide.*'" Just like that, the ultracool Beatles had been effortlessly outhipped by a lanky Jewish kid from small-town Minnesota.

As the evening wore on, Paul, in particular, seemed mightily impressed with the acute effect of cannabis on the old brain stem. With a flick of the wrist he ordered Mal to follow him around everywhere so that Mal might write down the sage wisdom that uttered from the severely compromised Beatle's famous oval. The others, fortunately, just sat back and laughed like the stoned-out sods they were.

"Come back and see us, Bob!" Lennon erupted, when at last the party was over. And he did, the very next time the circus pulled into town.

That landmark occasion led to further meetings between the two composing giants, setting up an on-and-off friendship that endured until Lennon's death in 1980.

As Lennon explained: "Whenever we used to meet, it was always under the most nerve-wracking circumstances. I was always uptight and I know Bobby was. People like Al Aronowitz would try and bring us together. We'd spend time together, but I always used to be too paranoid or I'd be aggressive or something and vice versa. He'd come to my house, can you believe it? this bourgeois life I was leading, and I used to go to his hotel."

Initially Lennon vehemently denounced the folk singer–composer. At London's Ad Lib Club, just before the first American tour, John had confided to journalist Pete Hamill, "To hell with Dylan. We play rock 'n' roll. Give me Chuck Berry. Give me Little Richard. Don't give me fancy crap, American folky intellectual crap."

Lennon was won over by Dylan's dramatic, trail-blazing 1965 LPs *Bringing It All Back Home* and *Highway 61 Revisited.* Ironically, it was "I Want to Hold Your Hand" that first inspired Dylan to lay down his acoustic guitar and take off in the revolutionary new direction of electric folk rock.

"They [Lennon and McCartney] were doing things nobody else was doing," he praised. "Their chords were outrageous and their harmonies made it all valid. I knew they were pointing the direction of where music had to go. I was not about to put up with other musicians, but in my head the Beatles were it."

The raspy-voiced singer impressed all the Beatles, most notably George, who said in 1987, "He's fantastic, you know. There's not a lot of people in the world who I see from a historical point of view. Five hundred years from now, looking back in history, I think he will still be the man. Bobby just takes the cake."

Added Paul, "John was probably the most influenced, but George is one of the guys who can quote all of Dylan's lyrics. . . . George goes, 'Oh, well! Remember! The pumps don't work 'cos the vandals took the handles.' "

Lennon himself would never forget the advice his Minnesotan friend gave him. "I remember the early meetings with Dylan, he was always saying, 'Listen to the words, man' and I said 'I can't be bothered. I listen to the sound of it, the overall sound.' Then I reversed that and started being a word man. I naturally play with words anyway, so I made a conscious effort to be wordy à la Dylan after that."

Dylan's influence first showed up on *Beatles For Sale,* released in December 1964, and on its American equivalent, *Beatles '65,* later that month. "I'm a Loser," a down-to-the-bone Lennon original, was the first Beatles tune directly inspired by the incomparable artist.

John remembered, "Part of me suspects I'm a loser and part of me thinks I'm God Almighty."

Purportedly written on a plane somewhere over the United States during the summer tour of 1964, John always considered it one of his best early compositions. "I always was a rebel because of whatever sociological thing gave me a chip on the shoulder. On the other hand, I want to be loved and accepted. That's why I'm on stage, like a performing flea. It's because I want to belong. Part of me would like to be accepted by all facets of society and not be this loudmouth, lunatic, poet-musician. But I cannot be what I am not."

With the release of *Beatles For Sale* and its obvious morose overtones, hints of Lennon's growing personal unrest could no longer be denied. Consider the bleak triad that opens the album: "No Reply," "I'm a Loser," and "Baby's in Black"—images of isolation, rejection, and love gone wrong.

Yet, as the songs dug deeper, so did they become more sophisticated, like "No Reply," a 100-percent Lennon undertaking. "That's the one," remembered John in 1972, "where Dick James, the publisher, said, 'That's the first complete song you've written where it resolves itself.' Apparently, before that, he thought my songs tended to sort of wander off.

"It was my version of the Silhouettes. I had that image of walking down the street and seeing her silhouetted in the window and not answering the phone, although I never called a girl on the phone in my life. Because phones weren't part of the English child's life."

"Baby's in Black" turned out to be one of those increasingly rare incidences when John and Paul enjoyed a true fifty-fifty collaboration. As Lennon put it, "We wrote it together in the same room."

Its lyrics belie the surface nursery-rhyme melody, exposing the moody magnificence of the duo at their most compelling. Speculation had it that the tune's central character, the "baby in black," was none other than Astrid Kirchherr, photographer girlfriend of bassist Stuart Sutcliffe. Astrid, who was responsible for the Beatles' moptop haircuts, was believed to be portrayed in the song as mourning Stu's death.

Two additional top-notch songs came off that album. McCartney's "I'll Follow the Sun," an early pre-Beatles composition, took some friendly jibes from Lennon: "That's Paul, can't you tell?" This acoustic ballad, however, accented by Ringo on bongos, once again boasted the trademark McCartney easy melody, which prompted John to inevitably concede, "a nice one."

The snappy "Eight Days a Week" represented a departure from the usual

Lennon-McCartney songwriting routine. Heretofore John and Paul had normally brought in their songs pretty much completely finished off. "Eight Days a Week," however, was still basically just an undeveloped idea Paul had from hearing Ringo fooling around one day.

Notes McCartney: "He said it as though he were an overworked chauffeur: [heavy accent] 'Eight days a week.' When we heard it we said, 'Really? Bing! Got it!'"

"We struggled to record it and to make it into a song," Lennon later complained. "It was Paul's initial effort, but we both worked on it."

Despite such naysaying, "Eight Days" was significant in that it was the first Beatles tune to be faded up at the beginning, a technique widely copied to this day. Also, for a song that credits 70 percent authorship to McCartney, it is Lennon—in a substantial break from tradition—who takes the lead vocals. Said to be written about Brian Epstein and his overburdened professional life, the simple fact is the Fabs were scheduled to star in another film tentatively entitled *Eight Arms to Hold You,* and here was an attempt to tuck one of the needed musical numbers under their belts. The movie, of course, would later become *Help!* and the song would be released as another giant hit single.

Meanwhile, a complex series of factors revealed that Lennon was clearly in a crisis. On the home front, Lennon's exhaustive commitments to touring, recording, and film making were slowly eroding his marriage.

Observed Cynthia, "John spent weeks and months away from home; there seemed to be very little time for us to be as close as we were in the early days. We seemed to be pulling in opposite directions. We never rowed; we just rubbed along together without fireworks. Our bond was Julian, but even the simple pleasures of fatherhood were denied him due to the pressure of work and lack of time."

As the relationship was unraveling, John tried desperately to live up to the image expected of the nouveau-riche Beatles. He purchased a castlelike Tudor in the stockbroker belt of Weybridge, complete with a sunken Italian marble bathtub, a sumptuous Oriental lounge, a dining room with purple velvet walls, and a spectacular near-Olympic-sized swimming pool with an elaborate "psychedelic eye" set in mosaic tile at the bottom.* Playing the part of the rich

---

*The individual tiles that made up the "eye" were carefully removed in the 1980s and sold to fans, complete with a certificate of authenticity from the new owner.

and famous pop star to the hilt, he filled his garage with a Ferrari, a Rolls, and even a customized Mini Cooper before he even had a driver's license.

Even back in 1965, Lennon was painfully aware of his superficial lifestyle. "Weybridge won't do at all. I'm just stopping there, like a bus stop. Bankers and stockbrokers live there; they can add figures and Weybridge is what they live in and they think it's the end. I think of it every day, me in my Hansel and Gretel house. I'll take my time; I'll get my real house when I know what I want. You see there's something else I'm going to do, something I must do, only I don't know what it is. That's why I go round painting, taping, drawing and writing and that, because it may be one of them. All I know is, this isn't it for me."

Lennon tried desperately to drown his sorrows not only with overt materialism, but increasingly with drugs and alcohol. Although he had been drinking since he was fifteen, often heavily, it soon escalated into amphetamine abuse. "*A Hard Day's Night* I was on pills, and that's drugs, that's bigger drugs than pot," Lennon stated. "I started on pills when I was fifteen, no seventeen, after I became a musician. The only way to survive in Hamburg—to play eight hours a night—was to take pills. The waiters gave you them, the pills and drink. I was a fucking dropped-down drunk in art school. *Help!* was where we turned to pot and dropped drink, simple as that. . . . The others [needed drugs] too, but I always had more, more pills, more of everything because I'm probably more crazy."

Harrison recalls how uppers circulated among all the Fabs. "The best flight I remember was the one to Hong Kong [in 1964]," says George. "It took several hours and I remember them saying, 'Return to your seats because we're approaching Hong Kong,' and I thought, 'We can't be there already.' We'd been sitting on the floor drinking and taking Preludins for about thirty hours so it seemed like a ten-minute flight.

"On all those flights we were on uppers and that's what helped us get through because we'd drink a whiskey and Coke with anyone, even if he were the devil, and charm the pants off him."

Alistair Taylor, personal assistant to Brian Epstein, maintains the four young musicians were living under incredible stress.

If you weren't there, you can't begin to understand the pressures they were under and their way of life. I don't give a damn how many books you've read or how many people you interview, even I can't convey to you what it was like! I was very close to them, and I was under a lot of pressure. But I was not even remotely in their league. It was getting pretty unbearable and they had to do something.

Imagine not being able to walk down the street. You can't go out in a car, you can't do anything without literally being torn to shreds, day in, day out, night in, night out, for years!

In the early days, possibly even before I knew them very well, they were on pills, but that was just youngsters experimenting. We've all done it, but lately I think it was an escape. It was fun and they could afford it and they mixed with people who said, "Hey try this, man." Recently I've heard the statement that John Lennon was high almost every single day of the sixties! Well, when did he find time to compose songs, make movies, go on tour, do interviews, appear on television shows, or write books?

Ironically, as Lennon was floundering, the ever-together McCartney seemed to be thriving. The status-seeking Paul clearly enjoyed the limelight and the fulfillment of his boyhood goals of a car, house, and one hundred pounds, although on a slightly grander scale!

Jane Asher proved a formidable influence, introducing her ambitious steady to the cultural stratosphere of ballet, opera, art, and theater. "She gave Paul's ego an enormous boost," confirmed Cynthia Lennon.

McCartney said at the time, "I'm trying to cram everything in, all the things I've missed. People are saying things and painting things and writing and composing things that are great and I must know what people are doing."

Jane's paramount contribution to Paul's cultural education, however, was introducing him to classical music. McCartney began to assemble an admirable collection of Brahms, Mozart, and Beethoven that soon made a profound impact on the course of his music.

Jane also helped to broaden his horizons by opening doors to the high-society circles orbited by opera's Joan Sutherland and Irish viscount Lord Nicholas Gormanston. McCartney donned tailored three-piece suits and squired his Lady Jane about London in the most expensive car on the market, a blue Aston Martin DB6. The couple became regulars at exclusive clubs like the Scotch of St. James and Rasputin. Paul even had his own table at the trendy Ad Lib.

As Ray Coleman noted, "Paul McCartney, with his keen eye on being the Beatles' diplomat and self-appointed publicist, was the social climber. He desperately needed self-improvement and he worked towards it."

By the time the group's next album, the soundtrack for their second film *Help!*, was released in August 1965, John and Paul were once again constrained to come up with several new songs to fuel both the sagging, silly script and later the lucrative but undistinguished soundtrack.

The burden of being a two-man hit-record machine, however, was growing difficult. As Lennon once told this author, "In the beginning we wrote because we were in love with the music. After the whole Beatlemania thing though, it became a fucking business, like selling shoes or something. Almost right from the very beginning we wanted out. But there was nowhere to run. By then we were virtually public property anyway. It's the old 'Be careful what you wish for' scenario."

One of the album's most distinctive offerings was "Ticket to Ride," which had already catapulted to number one as a single. John termed its heavy rumbling beat "one of the earliest heavy metal records ever made." The song, which drives the film's spontaneous skiing sequence, featured Paul taking lead guitar for the second time on the album. Just as importantly, McCartney coached Ringo into the most creative and effective drumming of his career, punctuated by hard-hitting machine gun triplets.

According to noted rock journalists Roy Carr and Tony Tyler, "'Ticket to Ride' was unquestionably their most ambitious piece of musical structuring to date. The weightiness of the piece was accentuated by the harshness of the lyrics which reveal Lennon as a misogynistic cynic, a role he was later to have much trouble abandoning."

Two songs off the album, one by McCartney, one by Lennon, make for an interesting comparison as both reflect attempts to adopt a definite Dylanesque style. Paul's "I've Just Seen a Face" was embarrassingly dismissed as having "a slight Dylan influence, but more like an up-tempo 'Rocky Raccoon,'" while Lennon's melancholy "You've Got to Hide Your Love Away" was characterized as "strikingly Dylanesque in its images and vocals with acoustic guitar chords and flute replacing Dylan's harmonica."

From its intriguing lyrics to its plaintive wailing delivery, it was almost more Dylan than the curly-topped icon minstrel himself.

As Lennon himself said in 1980, "This was written in my Dylan days for the film *Help!* I am like a chameleon, influenced by everything that's going."

The song also held the distinction as the first Beatles tune to incorporate session musicians—in this case flutists—paving the way for the addition of outside artists on future projects.

Pete Shotton, Lennon's longtime friend, said in his excellent book *John Lennon: In My Life* that this was the first song to be written in his presence. "I myself contributed the sustained 'hey's' that introduce the main chorus. This Dylan-inspired number originally included the line, 'I can't go on, feeling two-foot tall'; when he first performed it for Paul McCartney, however, John accidentally sang 'two-foot *small*.' He paused to correct himself, then burst into laughter. 'Let's leave that in, actually!' he exclaimed. 'All those pseuds will really love it.'"

If for nothing else, on this largely undistinguished album one tune looms as the definitive Paul McCartney standard. It is, of course, the melancholy "Yesterday." The now legendary tune suffered through monumental indignities including such early lyrics as "Scrambled egg, how I love your legs." After coming up with the title, Paul felt that perhaps it was a little too corny; George Martin, however, assured him that it wasn't.

At one point McCartney actually offered to give the song away to two different artists, thinking this might not be the right vehicle to record with the Beatles. The first was front man Chris Farlow and the second was Billy J. Kramer. Paul had apparently met up with Kramer in Blackpool, and after playing the tune for the singer, McCartney asked him if he might like to record it.

"I'm awfully sorry, Paul," Billy J. replied, "but I really don't think it's right for me. Sorry."

McCartney remembers the unlikely genesis of the song. "I fell out of bed. I had a piano by my bedside and I must have dreamed it, because I tumbled out of bed and put my hands on the piano keys and I had a tune in my head. It was just a complete thing. I couldn't believe it. It came too easy. In fact, I didn't believe I'd written it. I thought maybe I'd heard it before, it was some other tune, and I went round for weeks playing the chords for people and asking them, 'Is this like something? I think I've written it.' And people would say, 'No, it's not like anything else, but it's good.'"

After McCartney played the tune for the rest of the Beatles, who gave their approval, he and Martin cooked up an idea.

I wanted just a small string accompaniment and he said, "Well, how 'bout an actual string quartet?" I said, "It sounds great." I was so proud of it, I felt it was an original tune, it didn't copy off anything and it was a big tune, it was all there and nothing repeated. I got made fun of because of it a bit. I remember George [Harrison] saying, "Blimey, he's always talking about 'Yesterday,' you'd think he was Beethoven or somebody." But it's the one. I reckon it's the most complete thing I've ever written.

It's a very catchy tune without being sickly. When you're trying to write a song, there are certain times when you get the essence. It's like an egg being laid, it's just so there, not a crack or flaw in it.

I remember Mick Jagger saying, "Oh, I wish I could sing like that," because at the time he didn't reckon he could. Later, Mick's voice improved a lot.

I like ballads, and I know people like a love song.

Offering additional insight into the piece, McCartney's childhood neighbor Thomas Gaulle contends that the lyrics, at least in part, refer to the death of Paul's mother, Mary. Apparently, when told of her death, the first thing fourteen-year-old Paul blurted out was, "What are we going to do without her money?" The lines, "I said something wrong/Now I long for yesterday" are a regret for his boyhood insensitivity and longing to go back in time to make it right.

By 1980 more than 2,500 artists, from Sinatra to Tom Jones, Liberace to Marvin Gaye, had covered the tune.

And what did John Lennon have to say about this McCartney tour de force? "That's Paul's baby. . . . Beautiful, and I never wished I'd written it."

As Paul found his fortunes rising considerably, his foundering partner was issuing a desperate public SOS via the album's title track. "When *Help!* came out in 1965 I was actually crying for help," John remembered toward the end of his life. "I just wrote the song because I was commissioned to write it for the movie. But later, I knew I really was crying out for help. It was my fat Elvis period. You see the movie: He—'I'—is very fat, very insecure, and he's completely lost himself. And I am singing about when I was so much younger and all the rest, looking back at how easy it was."

As for the Beatles' second film, despite the scenic Bahamas location and more generous budget, there unfortunately wasn't much to be done about the inane premise: Ringo is pursued by a gang of Hindu thugs out to amputate his hand to obtain a sacrificial ring for their cult ritual.

"*Help!* was a drag," Lennon complained in 1970, "because we didn't know what was happening. In fact, Lester was a bit ahead of his time with the

Batman thing, but we were on pot by then, all the best stuff is on the cutting-room floor with us breaking up and falling about all over the place."

Even McCartney, in his ever diplomatic way, added, "*Help!* for us was a strange film; it wasn't approached as seriously [as *A Hard Day's Night*]. We were a bit blasé at the time. I didn't even look at the script until the first day. We were sort of guest stars."

Reviews were universally abysmal. So turned off by the experience were the lads that a projected third film, *A Talent for Loving,* a cowboy comedy set in Mexico, never got past the discussion stage. As they coldly informed producer Walter Shenson, "We don't want to play the Beatles anymore!"

The entire *Help!* project accentuated Lennon's overwhelming difficulty coping with fame.

It just built up, the bigger we got, the more unreality we had to face. Like sitting with the governor of the Bahamas when we were making *Help!* and being insulted by these junked-up, middle-class bitches and bastards who would be commenting on our working-classness and manners. I couldn't take it, it would hurt me. I would go insane, swearing at them, whatever, I'd always do something. It was a fuckin' humiliation.

One has to completely humiliate oneself to be what the Beatles were, and that's what I resent. I mean, I did it, I didn't know, I didn't foresee; it just happened bit by bit, gradually, until this complete craziness is surrounding you and you're doing exactly what you don't want with people you can't stand. The people you hated when you were ten.

Onetime McCartney girlfriend Iris Caldwell summed up, "I think Paul got a lot of peace by becoming famous—it was a justification of all he had worked for—he was terribly insecure and felt wanted when he became famous. But for John fame brought pain."

Throughout 1965, other exciting things were happening in John and Paul's life. On June 12, the Beatles were named to the Queen's Birthday Honors list and were awarded the prestigious MBE, the Most Excellent Order of the British Empire.

They approached the throne at Buckingham Palace to receive their silver medals, adding a brush of refreshing humor to the proceedings.

"How long have you been together?" asked the Queen.

"Oh, for many years," replied Paul.

"Forty years," added Ringo dryly.

"Oh, are you the one who started it all?" asked Her Majesty.

"No ma'm. I was the last to join. I'm the little fella."

The awards caused considerable controversy as many of the older, less culturally aware recipients (and many in the media) were less than enthused that the Fabs would be so honored.

"I feel that when people like the Beatles are given the MBE the whole thing becomes debased and cheapened," said one. "I hope the Queen's position in this situation can be reinforced so that she can resist and control her Ministers."

Another patriot took exception that his late brother was given the award for his bravery in war and now the government was bestowing it on mere popular entertainers. "He won it for combating three enemy planes at a height of 20,000 feet in 1917. Giving it to the Beatles is an insult to all of us."

"For the next war, do not count on me," cried one retired colonel. "Use the Beatles or the Beatniks!"

Lennon, for one, couldn't have agreed more. "Taking the MBE was a sell-out for me. Before you get an MBE the Palace writes to ask if you're going to accept it because you're not supposed to reject it publicly and they sound you out first. I chucked the letter in with all the fan mail until Brian asked me if I had it. He and a few other people persuaded me that it was in our interest to take it, [but] it was hypocritical of me to accept it."

Even the great Noël Coward seemed grumpy about the appointment. "The Beatles have all four been awarded MBEs, which has caused considerable outcry. Furious war heroes are sending back their bravely won medals by the bushel. It is, of course, a tactless and major blunder on the part of the Prime Minister and I don't think the Queen should have agreed. Some other decoration should have been selected to reward them for their talentless but considerable contributions to the Exchequer."

The discerning Coward, having once attended a Beatles concert, concluded, "It is impossible to judge from their public performance whether they have talent or not. They were professional, had a certain guileless charm, and stayed on mercifully not too long."

That summer, John Lennon's companion book to *In His Own Write* was published. Cleverly titled *A Spaniard in the Works,* it was the concentrated fruit of a year of very pointed work by the "literary Beatle," and a wonderful piece of inspired lunacy. Common among the critics was the charge that

Lennon was heavily influenced by such absurdist heavyweights as James Thurber or Edward Lear.

"I deny it because I'm ignorant of it," John shot back.

> Lear I'd never heard of. Well, I'd heard the name obviously, but we didn't do him at school. The only classic or very highbrow anything I read or knew of is Chaucer. I might have read a bit of Chaucer at school because I think they do that. And so I bought all the books they said it was like. I bought one book on Edward Lear, I bought *Finnegans Wake,* Chaucer, and I couldn't see any resemblance to any of them.

> Charles Dickens I don't like too much. I've got to be in a certain mood. It's too school. I'm too near school to read Dickens or Shakespeare. I hate Shakespeare. I don't care whether you should like him or not. It doesn't mean anything to me.

McCartney, who wrote the introduction to *Spaniard,* was not to be outshone by his partner in the literary department, having contributed along with Lennon to *Mersey Beat* in the early sixties. *Mersey Beat* editor Bill Harry observed that Paul wrote in a style "very similar to John. It was very humorous, tongue in cheek and rather good, a great sense of humor. All the stuff he wrote for me had a very good sense of humor."

Ironically, this work marked a pivotal turning point in Lennon's attitude toward songwriting. "To express myself I would write *A Spaniard in the Works* or *In His Own Write,* the personal stories which were expressive of my personal emotions. I'd have a separate songwriting John Lennon who wrote songs for the sort of meat market and I didn't consider them—the lyrics or anything—to have any depth at all. . . . Then I started being me about the songs, not writing them objectively but subjectively."

This more introspective approach, unveiling a maturing Lennon, was launched in the Beatles' sixth album, the multiplatinum *Rubber Soul.* His growing marital woes, which had been alluded to over the past two albums, were all but spelled out in the haunting composition "Norwegian Wood." Proving a bad union is often fodder for great art, Lennon tilled the fields of Cyn's growing discontent, plowing up the now classic tune.

John later admitted that "Norwegian Wood" was about his own clandestine infidelities. "I was trying to write about an affair without letting my wife know I was writing about an affair so it was very gobbledegook. I was sort of composing from my experiences, girls' flats, things like that."

Although Lennon added, "I can't remember any specific woman it had to do with," several sources close to the Beatles insist that the lady in question was a prominent London journalist. At the time, Maureen Cleave from the London *Evening Standard* was the only female writer known to be traveling in Beatle circles and thus some have suggested that she might be the inspiration behind the work. For his part, though, Lennon always claimed they were just good friends.

Boyhood chum Pete Shotton has said that the lyrical reference to lighting fires comes from Lennon's poverty-stricken days as a student in Liverpool, when he and Stu regularly burned sticks of furniture just to keep warm. To give credit where it's due, however, John has stated that Paul did help out a bit with the lyrics.

Melodically, the song was a stand-out highlighted by George Harrison's sitar. The guitarist, who tuned the Eastern instrument to Western notes, became the first artist to use the sitar on a pop song.

Lennon continued baring his soul in "Nowhere Man," which seemed to take up where "I'm a Loser" left off. Writing at Kenwood, Lennon spent five hours trying to think of a song and nothing came. "I was cheesed off and went for a lie down having given up. Then I thought of myself as a 'nowhere man' and it came, words and music, the whole damn thing as I lay down." Later John confessed he was disappointed in the lyrics, which he thought were too trite.

McCartney, who'd been conspicuously silent regarding the tribulations of his partner during this difficult period, tactfully commented in 1984, "That was John after a night out, with dawn coming up. I think at that point in his life he was wondering where he was going."

Ray Coleman called "Nowhere Man" "a curiously nihilistic pop song, casting Lennon as a monarch of nothingness, without opinion, power or desire. The Nowhere Man is an impotent, hollow symbol of the swinging sixties."

Meanwhile, the invasion of hemp into the lives of the two Fab tunesmiths was boldly reflected in the capsule of sixties philosophy, "The Word." " 'The Word' was written together," acknowledged John. "It's the love-and-peace thing. The word is 'love' right?"

Added Paul, "To write a good song with just one note in it, like 'Long Tall Sally,' is really very hard. It's the kind of thing we've wanted to do for some time. We get near it in 'The Word.' "

Rubber Soul left a dramatic and unprecedented watermark in the evolution of Lennon and McCartney. As George Martin put it, "It was the first album to present a new, growing Beatles to the world. Up till then we had been making albums rather like a collection of singles. Now we were really beginning to think out albums as a bit of art on their own, as entities of their own. And *Rubber Soul* was the first to emerge that way." The album's title belonged to Paul, a droll pun about white artists trying to play soul music. A dozen originals were written over the course of a single month (October–November 1965).

The Beatles were also adding to their instrumental repertoire. Besides Harrison's sitar, the record also featured McCartney's fuzz bass on the Harrison composition "Think for Yourself"; George Martin can be heard playing the harmonium (a small keyboard the sound of which is produced through metal reeds) on "The Word" and "If I Needed Someone." Martin also experimented with a stereo mix that would reproduce for mono. "I put lead voices on the right, bass on the left, and not much in the middle," he revealed.

Although people don't generally think of John Lennon when listening to "Michelle," the fact is, he was intimately involved in its creation. "Paul and I were staying somewhere and he walked in and hummed the first few bars and he says, 'Where do I go from here?' I had been listening to Nina Simone. There was a line in it that went: 'I love you, I love you, I love you.' That's what made me think of the middle eight.

"My contribution to Paul's songs was always to add a little bluesy edge to them."

With the breathtaking "Girl," Lennon, the inveterate rocker, proved he could not only equal but better McCartney's ballad efforts. Calling the tune "one of my best," John admitted, "this was about a dream girl." In its deeper layers Lennon is dealing with Catholicism, in particular, his rejection of the axiom that one must suffer to attain happiness. Explained Lennon, "I was in a way trying to say something or other about Christianity, which I was opposed to at the time."

Speaking to the song's technical side, McCartney adds, "Listen to John's breath on 'Girl.' We asked the engineer to put it on treble, so you get this huge intake of breath and it sounds just like a percussion instrument."

Just as "Yesterday" became McCartney's signature tune, Lennon's intimate and wistfully affecting "In My Life" became his.

"'In My Life' was the first song I wrote that was really consciously about my life," he reflected shortly before his death. "It started out as a bus journey from my house to town, mentioning every place I could remember."

The song's only flaw, according to Pete Shotton, is Lennon's inability to sustain the affecting nostalgic edge. "The second half of the song," he said, "dribbled off into stock romantic cliches."

This was the first of two compositions where Lennon and McCartney disputed authorship. There's no doubt that John penned the lyrics, but there seemed to be a differing opinion regarding the musical contributions. Charged Paul: "John either forgot or didn't think I wrote the tune. I remember he had the words, like a poem sort of about faces he remembered. . . . I recall going off for half an hour and sitting with a Mellotron he had, writing the tune which was Miracles-inspired, as I remember. In fact, a lot of stuff was then."

Lennon, on the other hand, claimed that McCartney only helped with the middle-eight. And so it went for Lennon and McCartney.

Rubber Soul was released on December 6, 1965, in the United States; Beach Boy Brian Wilson later commented, "I was sitting around a table with friends, smoking a joint, when we heard *Rubber Soul* for the very first time; and I'm smoking and getting high and the album blew my mind because it was a whole album with good stuff! It flipped me out so much I said, 'I'm gonna try that, where the whole album becomes a gas.'"

The importance of *Rubber Soul,* besides its obvious musical attributes, was the pivotal rise of Paul McCartney, supplanting John Lennon's eight-year artistic reign. This was no more apparent than in the studio where Martin clearly favored working with Paul.

"I'm a melody man rather than a lyric man, being a musician and not a lyric writer," explains the veteran producer. "My brain accommodates music much more easily than it does words. Paul's melodies and his harmonic structures appealed to me more than John's because John's melodies and music were tailor-made to fit his words rather than the other way round. The lyrics would lead and develop John's songs. He would write one verse and the music was already there once the words told him the way the line would go."

As far as Lennon's musical acumen was concerned, Martin said, "John's concept of music is very interesting. I was once playing Ravel's *Daphnis and Chloe* to him. He said he couldn't follow it because the melodic lines were too long."

The producer further contended that as Lennon wasn't at all technically oriented the studio didn't really interest him. He wanted to progress quickly from song to song; get it over with and move on to the next. Paul, on the other hand, would wring out every last effect and nuance, driving Lennon crazy.

Martin later addressed the differences between the partners in the studio.

Paul would sit down and ask what I planned to do with his songs, every note virtually. "What do you think the cellos should be doing here, George?" Lots of the arrangements to his songs were very much his ideas which I would have to implement.

John would be more vague in what he wanted. He would talk in metaphors about his ideas. I'd have to get inside his brain to find out what he wanted, a more of a psychological approach. Paul would want to know *how* I was going to go about achieving what he wanted. John couldn't care less. He just wanted the result.

Lennon's oft-repeated philosophy of songwriting, as told to fellow rocker David Bowie, "Tell the truth and make it rhyme," belied the painstaking process of pop composition.

"Boil everything down to as few words as you need for the job," he explained back in the late sixties.

It was something I'd been told in the classroom about writing poetry. You had to be ruthless and prune your sentences. It became even more important when there was a musical tune to be brought in as well. Your lyrics couldn't wander. You had to get rid of asides and afterthoughts. You had to list your ideas in a logical order so they'd be easy to follow even in the middle of a lot of music. I used to think kids didn't bother to listen to the words of pop songs, but I was wrong. When we did new things in a club, people would come up afterwards to ask about lines they'd missed. Next time you did the number, the really keen ones would be singing along with you.

Ever the anguished artist, Lennon often felt the need to both rewrite and polish. "I just can't leave lyrics alone," he once commented. In contrast, McCartney generally adhered to the old Allen Ginsberg axiom, "First thought, best thought."

The intensity of John and Paul's relationship was based on a keen sense of the unique abilities of each of the parties. From the very beginning, Lennon was certainly more of a word man, and McCartney excelled at constructing engaging musical frameworks to surround John's introspective lyrics. In that sense, their rivalry spurred one another to sharpen their weak points.

"I've always had an easier time with lyrics," revealed Lennon, "although Paul is quite a capable lyricist who doesn't think he is; therefore, he doesn't try." The problem with McCartney's material, charged John, was a good setup without any real resolution. Citing the example of the dreamy "Yesterday," Lennon pointed out, "if you read the song it doesn't say anything."

How much of this John directly expressed to Paul is uncertain, but McCartney took up the challenge, which, according to George Martin, he met.

> He's the sort of Rodgers and Hart of the two. He can turn out excellent potboilers, I don't think he's particularly proud of this. All the time he's trying to do better, especially trying to equal John's talent for words. Meeting John has made him try for deeper lyrics. But for meeting John, I doubt Paul could have written "Eleanor Rigby."
>
> Paul needs an audience, but John doesn't. John is very lazy, unlike Paul. Without Paul he would often give up. John writes for his own amusement. He would be content to play his tunes to Cyn. Paul likes a public.

Certainly McCartney's seeming ability to dash off a hit melody at will must have unnerved the sensitive and often insecure Lennon. "I've developed a system of how to write 'McCartney kind of stuff,'" Paul coolly asserted. "I just sit down when I'm in the mood, grab a guitar and I get lucky. I'll hit some chord that interests me, and in that, there is the opening chords. . . . I've got a gift. If you said, 'Do a tune now,' I could go off, in five minutes I could guarantee I'd come back with a tune."

Lennon himself conceded as much. "Paul has a special gift when it comes to making up tunes. I find myself using tunes which already exist and fitting my words to them. . . . I realize I'm pinching an old American hit. With me, I have a theme which gets me started on the poetry side of the thing. Then I have to put a tune to it, but that's the part of the job I enjoy least." Although George Martin claimed McCartney was "trying to do better, especially trying to equal John's talent for words," Peter Brown dismisses the effort as not really serious. "Because [Paul] is so prolific, he is not really aware of the quality. It's stream of consciousness. He puts it down, and that's it, he's on to the next project."

Realizing his own shortcomings, Lennon expressed doubts about who was actually the better composer. After listening to a tape of Paul's songs to be included on *Rubber Soul,* John begrudgingly confided to his partner, "I probably like your songs better than mine." Almost defensively, Lennon admitted in 1980 that early on he didn't really consider himself a melody man, that being

Paul's forte. But upon reflection, citing examples of "This Boy" and "In My Life," he changed his tune, saying, "I was writing melody with the best of them."

John was very touchy about any criticism that didn't come from Paul. Critics were a particular bane. "Reviewers are such shit!" he once proclaimed. "They can barely write their fucking names and here they are criticizing my work. How many hit tunes have you heard from a critic?"

So irate was John about the intrusion of so-called critical journalism into his life that he once took a match to a great pile of reviews on Brian Epstein's desk at NEMS. Struck dumb by this display, neither the other Beatles nor Eppy dared say a word. After milking the scene for all it was worth, Lennon dramatically whooshed the fiery mass into a nearby wastebasket.

Paul's growing dominance peeled back another yet Lennon insecurity: Now that the material was moving away from pop-rock to a more artsy, reflective, progressive sound, John grew uneasy about his voice. After all, Lennon's raw, throaty delivery was that of "a rock 'n' roll guitarist who couldn't give a damn," as Ray Coleman pointed out.

"Twist and Shout" had given way to "In My Life," requiring the more melodic qualities McCartney had in spades. Although Martin applauded Lennon's as "one of the best voices I've heard," John would constantly fret, "Do something with my voice. You know, put something on it. Smother it with tomato ketchup. Make it different."

At one point, John charged, "George was always more like a Paul McCartney producer than for my music."

While Martin acknowledged some truth in his allegations, he pointed out that Lennon simply wasn't interested in putting a lot of time into recording. If McCartney's compositions seemed to get preferential treatment, it was because he showed far more interest in the meticulous details of studio production.

There was ample evidence that McCartney was bouncing his newfound weight around, especially at the expense of George Harrison. Harrison, a more than competent soloist, saw his efforts undermined by the often insufferable McCartney.

Engineer Norman Smith observed, "With *Rubber Soul,* the clash between John and Paul was becoming obvious. Mind you, there's no doubt at all that Paul was the main musical force. He was also that in terms of production as well. He could tell an arranger how to do it just by singing a part. Most of the ideas came from Paul."

The escalating power struggle between these two pop dynamos, however, underscored far greater rumblings: an emerging cultural revolution on the brink of global explosion. The world was rapidly changing, and in the vein of all great artists, they would be the first to reflect the change. For these musical pioneers, *Rubber Soul* was merely a bridge to a new frontier of experimentation, endless possibility, and inevitable controversy. Leaving their clean-cut mod image forever behind, they were ready for their next incarnation, led by the controversial mind-altering chemicals that would take them there.

Emperor Gate / LSD and the Sound of Music

Clearly, John Lennon was mired in a deep personal crisis, as exemplified by songs like "I'm a Loser" and "You've Got to Hide Your Love Away." Isolating himself at Weybridge in a near-constant pot-induced stupor, he observed, "It's like black space out there. . . . Being an artist is torture. If I had the capabilities of being something other than I am I would. If I could be a fuckin' fisherman, I would." Writing by himself, for himself, Lennon became so wrapped up in his solitary, brooding existence that even McCartney and the Beatles were rapidly becoming irrelevant.

But in the prepsychedelic dawn of late 1965, something blasted Lennon out of his funk: LSD. His initiation was quite by accident and led by, of all people, the Beatles' London dentist. The good doctor invited the Lennons and George Harrison and his lady, model Pattie Boyd, to his posh Bayswater Road flat. Cythnia Lennon remembers thinking it strange that he had taken the trouble to line up four sugar cubes in a neat row atop his mantel, which he carefully dropped into his guests' after-dinner coffee.

For some reason, Pattie was reluctant to finish hers, but at the polite insistence of her host graciously obliged. Retiring to the drawing room, they were casually informed that the cubes each contained a rather respectable dose of pure, pharmaceutical LSD and were advised to settle back and enjoy the avalanche of distorted sights and sounds that would shortly follow. Cynthia and Pattie were immediately terrified.

"What if this turns out to be some sort of aphrodisiac?" Pattie whispered to George.

"Let's get the hell out of here," he said. "Perhaps he's trying for an orgy."

Excusing themselves, the two couples piled into Harrison's car and were about to speed away when the dentist intercepted them at the curb.

"I would advise you not to leave," he warned sternly. "You don't understand what's about to happen. If you stay here I guarantee you'll be all right. If you go, anything could happen."

"We'll take our chances," yelled Harrison and off they roared. Determined not to allow them to escape, the dentist and his girlfriend jumped into a taxi and took off in hot pursuit. Realizing they were being tailed, George began careening through the rainswept side streets at breakneck speed.

The harried chase set up a night of wild club hopping, with the LSD neophytes sucked into a vacuum of disjointed sensory clutter, tripping out to distorted sights and sounds where time was another dimension.

At one stop, the Ad Lib appeared lit up like a Hollywood premiere, complete with hundreds of screaming fans. As they drew closer, however, they realized it was just the usual lone small light outside the club's entrance.

John remembered,

It was insane going around London. We were cackling in the streets and Pattie was shouting, "Let's break a window!" It was insane. We were just out of our heads. When we finally got on the lift we all thought there was a fire, but it was just a little red light. We were all hot and hysterical and when we arrived on the floor the lift stopped and the door opened and we were all screaming. I had read somebody describing the effects of opium and I thought, "Fuck! It's happening." Then some singer came up to me and said, "Can I sit next to you?" And I said, "Only if you don't talk," because I just couldn't think.

George somehow managed to drive us home in his Mini. We were going about ten miles an hour, but it seemed like a thousand and Pattie was saying, "Let's jump out and play football." It was just terrifying, but it was fantastic. I did some drawings at the time of four faces saying, "We all agree with you!" I did a lot of drawing that night.

"Day Tripper," released in December 1965 simultaneously with *Rubber Soul,* was a direct result of the experience. Lennon cleverly wove the lyrics into a double meaning: "Day Trippers are people who go on a day trip, right? Usually on a ferryboat or something. But it was a kind of, you know, 'you're just a weekend hippie.' Get it?"

The line "She's a big teaser" was originally "She's a prick teaser," reveals Shotton. Lennon enjoyed plays on words, especially where he could slip in a piece of shock or naughtiness.

Cynthia Lennon recalls how the trendy hallucinogen jump-started her floundering husband.

The psychedelic qualities of LSD were quickly absorbed and directed into the Beatles' music. As an artist, John found LSD creative and stimulating, his senses filled with [the] revelations and hallucinations he experienced each time he took it. John was like a little boy again. His enthusiasm for life and love reached a new peak; he opened the floodgates of his mind and escaped from the imprisonment which fame entailed.

In many ways it was a wonderful thing to watch. Tensions, bigotry and bad temper were replaced by understanding and love. The peacock spread its fine feathers and dazzling colors took the place of conservative suits and ties. It was as though the whole youth movement was shedding its skin and throwing away years of inhibitions, rules and regulations. The Beatles and the Rolling Stones led the revolution without even trying.

Perhaps predictably, McCartney didn't trek into the uncharted territories of his mind via LSD until nearly a year later following a Beatles recording session. It all came about when Lennon had taken what he assumed was a handful of uppers, realizing too late he had accidentally ingested several thousand micrograms of powerful White Micro Dot. Teetering precariously close to the edge, Lennon panicked during a vocal overdub and was whisked outside in an effort to calm him.

"I can't remember what album it was," he later recalled. "But I took it and suddenly got so scared on the mike. I thought I was going to crack."

"I think I'd better take John home with me," Paul confided to Harrison as it became clear no work would be accomplished with Lennon in such a hyper, electric state. On their way to Cavendish Avenue in McCartney's purple Mini, Paul decided it was now or never. "You haven't got another hit there, have you?"

"Yeah, sure," croaked Lennon, rustling through his coat pocket for another bright white tab. "I could use the company."

Sitting cross-legged together on the huge oriental rug in the dining room at the rear of McCartney's house, the two men stared intensely into each other's glazed eyes for what seemed an eternity. "I know, man . . ." McCartney trailed off after an hour of this time-honored psychedelic ritual. "I *know*."

Now that Paul had finally entered the doors of perception, he emerged a changed person. "God is in everything," he observed to a journalist friend a couple of weeks later. "God is in the space between us. God is in the table in front of you. It just happens I realize all this through acid. It could have been through anything."

He went even further, telling the press, "It opened my eyes. We only use one-tenth of our brain. Just think what we could accomplish if we could only tap into that hidden part. It would mean a whole new world if the politicians would take LSD. There wouldn't be any more war or poverty or famine." Back home in Liverpool, old Jim McCartney was singularly unimpressed.

By the time the Beatles' hallucinogenic adventures hit the papers, McCartney was convinced that if not an outright psychic panacea, LSD was, at least, a powerful catalyst in the spiritual evolution of the species. With the evangelical zeal of the neophyte, he eagerly discussed his acid-induced insights with both reporters and friends, praising the wonders of this accidental derivative of the humble ergot fungus.

McCartney found himself immediately in hot water over his flagrant, ill-advised public exulting of the hallucinogen. Just days later, in a scathing editorial entitled "*Beatle Paul, MBE, LSD and BF [Bloody Fool]*," the *Daily Mirror* charged that he had behaved "like an irresponsible idiot," and suggested he should see a psychiatrist.

Racing to the aid of his charges, Brian Epstein granted several interviews the following month defending the Beatles' statements about the drug. "Paul rang me to say he had told the press he'd taken LSD," he explained to one reporter. "I was very worried. I came up to London knowing I was going to be asked to comment on Paul's decision. I finally decided I would admit I had taken LSD as well. There were several reasons for this. One was certainly to make things easier for Paul. People don't particularly enjoy being lone wolves. And I didn't feel like being dishonest and covering up, especially as I believe a lot of good has come from hallucinatory drugs."

Toward the end of McCartney's relatively short-lived fascination with acid, he began to think twice about having been so keen to sing its praises and backed off from stirring up any further controversy. "I don't recommend it," he told the papers. "It can open a few doors, but it's not any answer. You get the answers yourself."

Ever the cynic, John Lennon later charged that it was simply McCartney's inbred squareness that led him to recant his earlier position on the unholy sacrament.

"In L.A., the second time we took it, Paul felt very out of it, because we were all a bit slightly cruel, sort of, 'We're taking it and you're not!' But we kept seeing him, you know? Paul is a bit more stable than George and I; we are probably the most cracked. I think LSD profoundly shocked him and Ringo. I think maybe they'll regret it."

McCartney later offered another less critical assessment of his crazy acid days. "Me, I'm a conservative. I feel the need to check things out. I was the last to try pot, LSD, and floral clothes. I'm just slower than John, the least likely to succeed in class."

In 1986, Lennon's prophecy that McCartney might one day regret his flirtation with the drug was realized when he told Britain's *Q Magazine:* "I was given a lot of stick for being the last one to take acid. I wish I'd held out in a way, although it was the times. . . . I remember John going on the 'Old Grey Whistle Test' saying, 'Paul only took it four times! We all took it twenty!' It was as if you scored points."

While McCartney's actual acid experience was short lived, it served another purpose: opening to him the world of the "beautiful people" like Guinness heir Tara Browne and Chelsea photographer Michael Cooper.

The way Paul tells it, it was actually he, not the housebound Lennon, who was the real culture vulture. Having recently purchased a pricey Georgian town house at 7 Cavendish Avenue, St. John's Wood, Paul now hung his hat with central London's jet set. Hanging out with the likes of William Burroughs, Allen Ginsberg, and cutting-edge filmmaker Michelangelo Antonioni, the superstar bachelor flitted from party to party, happening to happening, meeting and greeting the fab and nearly fab.

"He wasn't especially interested in the art scene at first," remembers London gallery owner and longtime McCartney cohort John Dunbar. "He was just generally being turned on to things. Acid had come along by that time and it made a big difference."

Together McCartney and Dunbar began making their own underground films, stalking anything they considered far out. Back in St. John's Wood, the two spaced-out cinematic pioneers would carefully dub in a soundtrack of McCartney's own electronic music, often working late into the night. Although nothing of any great importance surfaced from all this frantic activity, Paul certainly had fun.

McCartney remembers,

The funny thing is, John ended up as the one with the avant-garde [reputation]. . . . Well actually, quite a few years before he'd ever considered it, when he was living out in the suburbs by the golf club with Cynthia, I was getting in with a guy called [Barry] Miles and the people at Indica. . . .

It's something I didn't put around a lot at the time, like I helped start Indica Bookshop and Gallery where John met Yoko. Was big buddies with Robert Fraser and very into Magritte. So I had a rich avant-garde period which was such a buzz, making movies and stuff. Because I was living on my own in London and all the guys were married out in the suburbs. They were very square in my mind. They'd come to my pad where there'd be people hanging out, and weird sculptures, and I'd be piecing together little films and stuff.

It was quite heady and very artistic. Like showing my movies to Antonioni, stuff like that. Dead cool really. And watching movies with Andy Warhol round at my house. My place was almost the center of the social scene at one point because I was on my own. There was nobody to hang anyone up. This big house in St. John's Wood. It was like a salon, almost. Brian Jones, John, Mick, and Marianne were always round there. It was great. Some magic moments. Robert Fraser was this gallery owner, he died a few years ago, he was great. I bought a couple of these Magritte paintings through Robert, dirt cheap. . . .

I used to go to avant-garde music concerts. That was me, all that Stockhausen shit in the Beatles. I went to this guy, Luciano Berio, who's now an electronic classical kind of guy. It was a good crossover. A lot of stimulation for me. . . . I'm not trying to say it was all me, but I do think John's avant-garde period later was really to give himself a go at what he'd seen me having a go at. He didn't dare do it while he was living in suburbia. Couldn't do it because the vibe was wrong. He had to come to my house and sneak his vicarious thrills.

The LSD influence didn't take long to show up once again, this time on their next single, "Paperback Writer," with its freaky four-part harmonies and driving guitar.

Even Lennon admitted, "'Paperback Writer' is son of 'Day Tripper,' meaning a rock 'n' roll song with a guitar lick on a fuzzy loud guitar." The hook included a riff of authorative chords in the style of the Who's "Substitute." "The Who, along with Dylan, [were] our two greatest influences," Paul said at the time.

The song, written on a paper bag, is 80 percent McCartney, taken from his brief experience in early 1966 of helping set up the trendy Indica Bookshop. Apparently Paul wasn't too proud to roll up his sleeves and help decorate the place, shuffling several hundred books around with the help of partners Peter Asher, John Dunbar, and Barry Miles. With books and publishing so much on his mind, it has been suggested that here was the original inspiration behind the electric rocker.

The hypnotic B-side, "Rain," introduced John's fascination with backward tape loops. The story has it that Lennon was tripping out in his Kenwood studio when he put a version of the song on his recorder backward. When he played it the following day, "The fade-in is me actually singing backwards, Sharethsmnowthsmeaness."

George Martin, however, tells a different story. "I was playing around with tapes and thought it might be fun to do something extra with John's voice. So I lifted a bit of his main vocal off the four-track, put it onto another spool, turned it round and then slid it back and forth until it fitted. John was out at the time, but when he came back he was amazed. It was backwards everything after that."

Later Lennon bragged about the big "backwards" innovation, commenting, "That's me again with the first backwards tape on any record anywhere. Before Hendrix, before the Who, before any fucker. Maybe there was that record 'They're Coming to Take Me Away'; maybe that came out before 'Rain,' but it's not the same thing."

Both tunes, written in early 1966, provided a crucial link from *Rubber Soul* to their next major project. The folky essence of "Norwegian Wood" and "In My Life" were now being married to the more aggressive American folk-rock that delineated the Byrds' style. In short, Lennon and McCartney were once again blazing the trail with exciting hybrid sounds.

All this, however, was just a tune-up for the budding flower power manifesto, *Revolver*. Many critics contend that this album represents Lennon and McCartney's finest hour. While the forthcoming *Sgt. Pepper* may have been lauded as the composers' masterwork, many attest that *Revolver* is their most flawless and timeless production.

Critic Peter Clayton points out in *Gramophone* magazine, "Listening to it you realize that the distance these four odd young men have travelled since that first record of 'Love Me Do' in 1962 is musically even greater than it is materially. Much of it involves things which are either new to pop music or which are being properly applied for the first time and which can't be helpfully compared with anything. In fact, the impression you get is not of any one sound or flavor, but simply of smoking hot newness."

About the album, which is packed with an eclectic mix of sitars, tablas, brass and string sections, tape loops, and sound effects, Paul commented, "There are sounds that nobody had done yet, I mean nobody, *ever*."

This album clearly demonstrates how LSD had become very much a third partner in Maclen's creative efforts, drawing from the pair a perspective that surely wouldn't have been there without it. Out rolled a plethora of drug-influenced material, starting with "I'm Only Sleeping," which Pete Shotton says "brilliantly evokes the state of chemically induced lethargy into which John had drifted."

Lennon by now had retreated inside the velvet-lined walls of Kenwood, sleeping all day, often conversing or playing all night, living a life devoid of structure. "I'm Only Sleeping" reflected this somnambulant, drug-induced mood, particularly via the ghostly, backward guitar.

Martin explains the process: "You work out what your chord sequence is and write down the reverse order of the chords—as they are going to come up—so you can recognize them. You then learn to boogie around on that chord sequence, but you don't know what it's going to sound like until it comes out again. It's hit or miss, no doubt about it, but you do it a few times and when you like what you hear you keep it."

Still, acid was affecting Lennon and McCartney's work even more directly. "She Said, She Said" evolved from an incident in which three of the Beatles took their first acid trip together. During their American summer tour of 1965, Brian Epstein rented the boys an extravagant estate deep in the Hollywood Hills. The site in this rarefied air of Tinseltown marked Ringo's first encounter with the drug, and John's and George's second. Paul stubbornly abstained, content to smoke himself into oblivion trying to play catch-up with his three severely compromised comrades.

"They showed us a movie, a drive-in print of *Cat Ballou* with the audience laughing on it," George Harrison recalls. "We were on the height of acid in a room full of starlets which some man had wafted in for us. I'd gone so far from what I thought this life was about that it was a shock to land back in my body and realize I was still there."

Along for the ride that warm blustery afternoon were various members of the Byrds and actor Peter Fonda, who'd rolled up in his Jag and was nearly torn apart by fans. "We dropped acid and began tripping for what would prove to be all night and most of the next day," recalls Fonda, "all of us, in-

cluding the original Byrds, eventually ended up babbling our minds away."
Fonda went on,

> I had the privilege of listening to four of them sing, play around, and
> scheme about what they would compose and achieve. They were so enthu-
> siastic, so full of fun. John was the wittiest and most astute. I enjoyed just
> hearing him speak. There were no pretensions in his manner. He just sat
> around, laying out lines of poetry and thinking, an amazing mind. He
> talked a lot, yet seemed so private.
>
> It was a thoroughly tripped-out atmosphere because they kept finding
> girls hiding under tables and so forth; one snuck into the poolroom
> through a window where an acid-fired Ringo was shooting pool with the
> wrong end of the cue. "Wrong end?" he'd say. "So what fuckin' difference
> does it make?"

As the long, crazy afternoon turned to night, the freaked-out crew set sail
in an empty hot tub tucked away in the lavish master bedroom. It was here
that Fonda began whispering in Lennon's ear that he had almost died during
a recent operation and therefore knew "what it's like to be dead." Over and
over the future "Easy Rider" kept repeating the frightening mantra. Pretty
soon Lennon's fragile psyche had enough and lashed out. "I don't fuckin'
care, man. Shut the hell up about it."
Lennon, too, gave his account of the bizarre day.

> We were on tour in one of those places like Doris Day's house and the
> three of us took it, Ringo, George, and I. As well as Neil [Aspinall], a
> couple of the Byrds, the one in the Stills and Nash thing, [David] Crosby
> and [Roger] McGuinn. There was a [British] reporter, Don Short, when
> we were in the garden. It was only our second trip so we didn't know any-
> thing about doing it in a nice place and cool it, we just took it. Then we
> suddenly saw this journalist behaving extraordinarily, which we weren't.
> We thought surely somebody could see. We were terrified waiting for him
> to go. He wondered why he couldn't come over. And Neil, who never had
> acid either, had taken it and still had to play road manager. We said go and
> get rid of Don Short and he didn't know what to do, he just sort of sat with
> it. And Peter Fonda kept saying in a whisper, "I know what it's like to be
> dead." We said, "What?" and he kept saying it. And that's how I wrote
> ["She Said, She Said"].

It was a sad song. It was an acidy song, I suppose. "When I was a little boy," you see . . . a lot of early childhood was coming out.

Once Lennon wrote the first verse, he tossed away convention and decided to create the middle eight from whatever came to him. This resulted in a beat change in that section that was very unorthodox, but effective nonetheless.

Lennon identified the droning cacophonous "Tomorrow Never Knows" as "my first real psychedelic song." Lennon captured a legion of dope-smoking, questioning youth in one fell swoop and introduced them en masse to not only his own psychedelic vision but the subtle possibility that beyond it lay the indomitable shadow of true spirituality. All in all, a lot more than any other pop song accomplished.

Based on acid guru Timothy Leary's rather liberal interpretation of *The Tibetan Book of the Dead* (entitled *The Psychedelic Experience*), "Tomorrow Never Knows" went a long way toward capturing Lennon's current state of mind, but according to its creator did not go quite far enough.

"With 'Tomorrow Never Knows' I'd imagined in my head that in the background you would hear thousands of monks chanting," John said. "That was impractical, of course, so we did something different. I should have tried to get nearer my original idea, the monks singing."

One amusing incident that took place during the recording of this track has John Lennon begging George Martin to emulate the sound of his vocals processed through the revolving speaker of a Hammond organ by suspending the Beatle upside down from the middle of the ceiling, placing a mike on the floor, and then twirling him around while he squawked out his vocals.

"Don't you think it would be a great effect, George?" he offered enthusiastically.

"We're working on it, John," replied the slyly bemused Martin. "We're working on it."

Although not noticeable at first, Paul's energetic Motownesque "Got to Get You into My Life" also had strong lyrical ties to LSD. A tune McCartney claimed as his property, Lennon has indicated that he and George may have helped a bit on the distinctive lyrics, which describe Paul's experience with acid. John praised the song as one of Paul's best and even had a bit of fun with it in the studio. While rehearsing the high-velocity number, Lennon ribbed on the title, changing it to "Got to Get You into My Wife," much to the amusement of all.

Typical of McCartney was the airy ballad "Here, There and Everywhere," inspired by the Beach Boys' "God Only Knows." Paul commented, "This one was pretty much mine, written sitting by John's pool. Often I would wait half an hour while he would do something, like get up. So I was sitting there tootling around in E on the guitar."

Arguably, Paul's finest composition was the extraordinary life capsule, "Eleanor Rigby." In many ways, the development of this piece is as fascinating as the musical tale itself. Take, for instance, the conflicting accounts of the origins of the song's lovelorn principals. Initially, Paul had come upon the name Daisy Hawkins for the song's central character, picturing her as a young Annabel Lee type. Envisioning her picking up rice in the church, Paul then decided she must be a cleaner.

"She had missed the wedding," he explained, "and she was suddenly lonely. In fact, she missed it all, she was the spinster type."

Shortly afterward, McCartney was wandering the streets of Bristol waiting for Jane Asher to finish a play when he decided the name Daisy Hawkins just wouldn't fly. "I wanted a name that was more real; the thought just came, 'Eleanor Rigby picks up the rice . . . ,' so there she was."

But this self-admitted passing inspiration doesn't jibe with the explanation Paul gave in another interview. "I got the name Rigby from a shop called Rigby. And I think Eleanor was from Eleanor Bron, the actress we worked with in the film [Help!]. But I just like the name. I was looking for a name that sounded natural; Eleanor Rigby sounded natural."

Adding to the confusion is this intriguing tidbit: Back in Liverpool in the small graveyard attached to St. Peter's Parish in Woolton lies buried one Eleanor Rigby. One wonders if Paul, hanging out there as a teenager with John (Lennon's beloved Uncle George is buried nearby), didn't stumble across the grave and file the name away somewhere deep in his subconscious.

The second pivotal character, the parish priest, was originally to be named Father McCartney, which Lennon reportedly favored. "But then I thought that was a bit of a hang-up for my dad," Paul decided, "so we looked through the phone book."

If it was just a name in the phone book, then what about the fellow identified by the *Sun* newspaper in 1984? The tabloid published a story about the song with an accompanying photo of former dance-hall compere Tom McKenzie, posing by the Rigby gravestone. The article reported that the gentleman claimed to be, in fact, the Father McKenzie of the song. McKenzie identified himself as compere for many of the Beatles' early gigs and relayed a story about darning his socks while on sentry duty during World War II, saying he passed it along to Lennon and McCartney.

"They thought it was very funny," McKenzie recalled. "I think when they wrote 'Eleanor Rigby' they had not forgotten me. They always used to say I treated them just like a father when I compered their early shows."

This was the second number whose composition was heatedly disputed by Lennon and McCartney. Officially, Paul is given 80 percent composer's credit, but Lennon insisted he penned more than two-thirds of the lyrics.

> The first verse was his and the rest are basically mine. But the way he did it. . . . He knew he had a song, but by that time he didn't want to ask for my help. We were sitting around with Mal Evans and Neil Aspinall, so he said to us, "Hey, you guys, finish up the lyrics."
>
> Now, there was Mal, a telephone installer, who was our road manager, and Neil, a student accountant, and I was insulted and hurt that Paul had just thrown it out in the air. He actually meant he wanted me to do it, and of course, there isn't a line of theirs in the song because I finally went off to a room with Paul and we finished the song. But that's the kind of insensitivity he would have, which upset me in later years. "Here, finish these lyrics up," like to anybody who was around.

Lennon's account may sound convincing, but other sources suggest that none of the other Beatles were present in the studio during its conception as they didn't contribute instrumental backing to the track. On top of that, as Lennon himself admitted in an interview with *Rolling Stone,* he recalled little of these sessions.

As if all this isn't difficult enough to keep straight, Pete Shotton insists that he was present when the song was written and weaves yet a different story. By his reckoning, the tune was composed at Kenwood during a weekend house party in the presence of the four Beatles and himself.

They had all tramped upstairs to Lennon's modest attic recording studio after dinner. Paul picked up a nearby acoustic and started to strum the first few chords of "Eleanor Rigby." "What do you think of this, fellas?" he called out. "It's a new one I've been working on, but I really don't know where to go with it. Any suggestions?"

Before long, everyone had joined in, tossing out ideas. John, however, didn't really say a word. It was Ringo, maintains Shotton, who thought up the line about old Father McCartney darning his socks in the night all alone.

Next, claims Pete, he mentioned to Paul that his father might somehow be offended at turning up in such a sad song, and thus began thumbing through the phone book searching for a suitable replacement. One amusing candidate was the name "McVicar," but it didn't really fit lyrically. Shotton remembers what happened next.

> Fully caught up in the creative process, I was seized by a brain wave. "Why don't you have Eleanor Rigby dying," I said, "and have Father McKenzie doing the burial service for her? That way you'd have the two lonely people coming together in the end, but too late."
>
> Not a bad suggestion, if I thought so myself, but then John piped in with his first comment of the entire evening, "I don't think you understand what we're trying to get at, Pete."
>
> That little remark proved enough to stop the creative juices dead in their tracks. It was so unlike John to disrupt one of the Beatles' songwriting sessions—let alone insult me in front of Paul, George and Ringo—that all I could think of to say was, "Fuck you, John."

With that, Paul quietly put away his guitar and the impromptu session ended. "Though John was to take credit for most of the lyrics," comments Shotton, "my own recollection is that 'Eleanor Rigby' was one Lennon-McCartney classic in which John's contribution was virtually nil."

Perhaps the fact that so many want to take credit for the song points to its timeless brilliance. McCartney brushes it off with his usual dab of PR modesty: "My Auntie Lil said to me, 'Why do you always write songs about love? Can't you ever write about a horse or a summit conference or something interesting?' So I thought, all right, Auntie Lil."

Looking at *Revolver* as a whole, the farsighted George Martin realized something quite extraordinary was blowing in the changing winds of the mid-sixties. "The indications were already there. 'Eleanor Rigby' and 'Tomorrow Never Knows' had been strong hints of what was to come. They were fore-runners of a complete change of style. Even I didn't realize how significant it was, nor the reasons for it. Flower Power and the hippie drug revolution had been taking place, affecting the boys right in front of my very eyes, yet my own naiveté prevented me from seeing the whole thing for what it was. I hardly knew what pot smelled like, although it was right under my nose! But I did realize something was happening in the music and that excited me. It was time to experiment."

Revolver, like *Rubber Soul* before it, gave indisputable evidence that the Beatles had now grown into a progressive, innovative studio band who'd long ago ceased to reap any creative fulfillment from the road and had only been going through the motions for the better part of two years.

From 1957 to 1966, the Beatles, in their various configurations, played some 1,430 live shows in almost every country on every continent of the free world. They performed for millions of hysterical teenyboppers, were pelted by jelly beans, and were constantly harassed by fans looking for souvenirs—everything from personalized autographs to bits of their hair, clothes, and even fingernails. Airport terminals were continually fouled by young women upon catching up with their favorite Beatle.

Perhaps not surprisingly, Paul found the road experience far from drudgery, and likened the bizarre atmosphere to that of a football match. "People used to say, 'Isn't it a drag, because no one listens to your music?' But some of the time it was good they didn't, because some of the time we were playing rough."

By stark contrast, Lennon despised the experience. "Everybody wants the image to carry on. The press wants you to carry on because they want the free drinks, free whores, and the fun. Everybody wants to keep on the bandwagon. It was like *Satyricon.* We were the Caesar. Who was going to knock us when there's a million pounds to be made? All the handouts, the bribery, the police, all the fucking hype, you know. Everybody wanted in. It was, 'Don't take it away from us, don't take Rome from us. Not a portable Rome where we can all have our houses, our cars, our lovers, our wives and office girls, parties, drink, and drugs. Don't take it from us, you know, otherwise you're mad, John, you're crazy. Silly John wants to take all this away.' "

Indeed, this was all in all quite a lot of madness for four provincial young men from the inherently sensible north of England to endure. And so, when the Beatles laid down their instruments after their final number at Candlestick Park in San Francisco on August 29, 1966, they said good-bye forever to touring. From that point, John and Paul planned to devote themselves exclusively to working their magic only in the sanctity of the recording studio.

That fall, things were stirring at Abbey Road once again. It was clear that Lennon and McCartney wanted to build on the direction of their last two albums, and the two were acutely aware they were not the only artists pushing the limits of musical convention. That year alone they drew influences from three extraordinary albums. One was Dylan's much heralded double LP

Blonde on Blonde, which George Harrison turned them on to. The second, which planted the seed of the concept album, was Frank Zappa and the Mothers of Invention's *Freak Out.* The record was among the first to merge classical influences with rock, and also addressed the state of contemporary America.

But the third, and most influential, was the Beach Boys' *Pet Sounds,* even today noted for its superb arrangement and state-of-the-art production. Paul had already taken inspiration from "God Only Knows" for "Here, There and Everywhere." Then, when the Beach Boys put out "Good Vibrations," which took an unheard-of six months to record, McCartney seized this as a personal challenge to try and top it.

"I'm a competitor, man," said McCartney. "It's never stopped. I will never stop competing with every other artist in this business. *Pet Sounds* kicked me to make *Sgt. Pepper.* It was direct competition with the Beach Boys."

Capitol Records, however, wasn't satisfied to wait half a year for a new album. A single needed to be rush released to the public. Never in the history of the music business have the resulting A- and B-sides been so equally strong.

"Strawberry Fields" was written solely by John with only minor musical help from the rest of the group. Composed in Almeria, Spain, while Lennon was on location for his role in Richard Lester's antiwar flop *How I Won the War,* the song at first carried a softer tone.

John later revealed that something very strange happened with that song, allegedly at the hands of Paul McCartney. "He subconsciously tried to destroy songs, meaning we'd play experimental games with my great pieces like 'Strawberry Fields,' which I always felt was badly recorded. . . . Usually we'd spend hours doing little detailed cleaning-ups of Paul's songs; when it came to mine, . . . somehow this atmosphere of looseness, casualness, and experimentation would creep in."

Tampering aside, the tune remains a lyrical masterpiece. "The awareness trying to be expressed is, let's say in one way I was always hip," revealed Lennon. "I was hip in kindergarten. I was different from the others. I was different all my life! Therefore, I must be crazy or a genius, because I seemed to see things other people didn't." Despite its high-flown connotations, however, Lennon also remembered the psychedelic anthem's more mundane roots.

"Strawberry Fields" is the name of a Salvation Army home for orphans and as a kid I used to go to their garden parties with my friends Ivan,

Nigel, and Pete. We'd all go up there and hang out and sell lemonade bottles for a penny. We always had fun at Strawberry Fields. But I just took the name, nothing to do with the Salvation Army. . . .

The song later helped unleash the infamous "Paul is dead" hysteria due to Lennon whispering what to fans and DJs sounded like "I buried Paul."

"That was actually John saying 'cranberry sauce,'" Paul explained. "That's John's humor. If you don't realize John's apt to say 'cranberry sauce' when he feels like it then you start to hear a funny little word there and you think, 'Aha!'"

The B-side, "Penny Lane," as well-known and beloved a Beatles song as exists, may have been sparked after McCartney read the Dylan Thomas poem *Fern Hill*, which reflects on the poet's childhood in rural Wales.

"'Penny Lane' is a bus roundabout in Liverpool," McCartney pointed out, "and there is a barbershop showing photographs of every head he's had the pleasure to know. No, that's not true, they're just photos of hairstyles, but all the people who come and go stop and say hullo. There's a banker on the corner so we made up the bit about the banker in his motor car. It's part fact, part nostalgia, for a place which is great, blue suburban skies as we remember it, and it's still there.

"And we put in a joke or two: 'Four of fish and finger pie. . . .' Most people wouldn't get it, but 'finger pie' is just a nice little joke for the Liverpool lads who like a bit of smut."

Of the parallel natures of the tunes, both are recollections of the duo's childhood days in Liverpool, but also represent something more. "We were always in competition," Paul remembers. I wrote 'Penny Lane' so he wrote 'Strawberry Fields.' That's how it was."

McCartney's tribute is bouncy, carefree, with trumpets heralding happy children at play, and bustling passersby, with a touch of humor that's just a bit bawdy. This slice-of-life chronicle exudes the flavor of a grandfather telling the kids about the good ol' days.

John's remembrance, on the other hand, is very much the flip side: heavy, plodding, and thickly layered. Whereas McCartney's view comes off in picture-postcard clarity, Lennon's choppy, often muddled brush strokes paint a more alienated surrealism. The lyrics are hazy, confused, and contradictory. Yet in his own distorted way, in the end, John's outlook is a positive one.

The late Nicholas Schaffner, in his stirring chronicle *The Beatles Forever,* offers this insight regarding the song: "The title was derived from a grim Liverpool orphanage called 'Strawberry Fields' and the song is no starry-eyed Utopian vision. The trip Lennon takes us on is a lonely, frightened, and confused one. Even after John publicly abdicated his role as 'the dreamweaver,' he called 'Strawberry Fields' one of his two or three best and [most] honest Beatle songs."

It is interesting that both composers at this point in their lives chose to look back at their youth, perhaps trying to recapture the security and innocence of simpler, saner times. Journalist John Jones calls it one identifying element of the Lennon-McCartney style: "Think of the echoes of melodrama. In 'Good Morning, Good Morning' we take a walk past the old school: 'Nothing has changed/It's still the same'; the complex compassion of 'She's Leaving Home' where the girl goes off, writes a note 'That she hoped would say more.' It is the specific past of good school days when the world was simpler and adults looked like fools.

"Their songs express the *good child's* hostility to grownups. This is why adults have been so keen to endorse the Beatles. This is safe play for children, mild naughtiness and much better than breaking up Margate or digging up Paris."

But for Lennon, these divergent journeys into the past, which began with *Help!* and would continue throughout his musical career, represented an often painful catharsis, one that would only show signs of resolving with his final contribution, *Double Fantasy.*

"Reality would be the missing element," he said of these retrospective ventures. "Because I was never really wanted. The only reason I am a star is because of my repression. Nothing else would have driven me through all that if I was 'normal.' Art is only a way of expressing pain."

When the double A-sided single was released in Britain on February 17, 1967, it peaked at number two in the charts, ending the string of Beatles' chart toppers at twelve. Martin, to this day, remains stumped. "For my money it was the best material we ever issued," he declared.

With the pressures of rushing out a hit single now out of the way, Lennon and McCartney turned their attention to the album. That same month McCartney brought in an old vaudeville ditty whose melody he'd penned at sixteen, "When I'm Sixty-four." At that early age Paul wasn't certain what direction his career might take and thought perhaps he might someday insert it in a musical. Later, he put words to it in honor of his father's sixty-fourth birthday.

McCartney claimed the song was never meant to be taken seriously. "So many of my things, like 'When I'm Sixty-four,' are tongue-in-cheek! But they get taken for real! 'Paul is saying, "Will you *love me* when I'm sixty-four."' But I say, 'Will you still *feed me* when I'm sixty-four?' That's the tongue-in-cheek bit."

The homespun patter was hardly John's bag, causing him to sarcastically quip, "I would never even dream of writing a song like that."

The whole "concept" idea of the album was born when McCartney brought the title track into the studio. George Martin remembers not being especially impressed with the song itself until Paul made a suggestion. "Why don't we make the album as though the Pepper band really existed, as though Sergeant Pepper was making the record? We'll dub in effects and things."

"You start to think," continued Paul, "there's this Sgt. Pepper who has taught the band to play and got them going so that at least they found one number. They're a bit of a brass band in a way, but also a rock band because they've got the San Francisco thing. And I had the idea that instead of Hell's Angels they put up pictures of Hitler and the latest Nazi signs and leather and that. We went into it just like that: Just us doing a good show."

It is often alleged that roadie Mal Evans dreamed up the Sgt. Pepper's Lonely Hearts Club Band moniker and perhaps even contributed to the song's construction. But McCartney heartily disagrees, insisting that the album, with its concept of role-playing as another band, was largely his influence. "I was trying to get everyone in the group to be sort of farther out and do this far-out album."

There seemed to exist a difference of opinion in the Beatles' camp. Neil Aspinall, for one, argues, "It wasn't a concept. They were just songs. . . . They were writing all the time. They didn't say, 'Let's do the *Pepper* album.' It's just a bunch of great songs."

Lennon agreed, pointing out that his contributions had no connection with the idea of Sgt. Pepper and his band. "But it works," he noted, "because we *said* it worked."

Even at this stage, the boys still enlisted the advice of their Medusa-coiffed mentor, Bob Dylan. "I played him some of *Sgt. Pepper,*" tells Paul, "and he said, 'Oh, I get it, you don't want to be cute anymore.' That summed it up, that was sort of what it was. The cute period had ended and it started to be art."

With that, the duo went to work on their groundbreaking technicolor dreamscape that bumped, floated, and soared upon innovative instrumentation and studio effects, all within a trendy drug-soaked framework. Asked about the life that was reflected in the album, McCartney responded, "Drugs basically. They got reflected in the music. When you mention drugs these days, heroin and cocaine and all of that, serious stuff comes to mind.

"Remember, drug taking in 1967 was much more in the musician's tradition. We'd heard of Ellington and Basie and jazz guys smoking a bit of pot and now it arrived on the music scene. It started to find its way into everything we did, really. It colored our perceptions. I think we started to realize there weren't as many frontiers as we'd thought there were. And we realized we could break barriers."

The innately conservative George Martin remembers how the Beatles would sneak off to the canteen to smoke their joints, away from his disapproving gaze. Had he taken part in their illicit behavior, he contends that the album would have turned out differently. "Perhaps," he speculated, rather tongue-in-cheek, "it was the combination of dope and no dope that worked, who knows?"

If any one song out of the thirteen cuts exemplified the complex and exquisite mastery of the work as a whole, it would be, hands down, the extraordinary "A Day in the Life."

The work's composition was pretty much a fifty-fifty effort from Lennon and McCartney. John revealed his impetus behind the lyrics. "I was reading the paper one day and noticed two stories. One was about the Guinness heir [Tara Browne] who killed himself in a car. On the next page was a story about four thousand potholes in the streets of Blackburn, Lancashire, that needed to be filled. Paul's contribution was the beautiful lick in the song, 'I'd love to turn you on,' that had been floating around in his head and couldn't use."

Even the orchestration was anything but conventional. "I suggested we write all but fifteen bars properly, so that the orchestra [forty-two members from the Royal Philharmonic and BBC Symphony] could read it," said Paul, "but where the fifteen bars began we would give the musicians a simple direction: 'Start on your lowest note.' How they got there was up to them, but it all resulted in a crazy crescendo. It was interesting because the trumpet players, always famous for their fondness for lubricating substances, didn't care, so they'd be there at the note ahead of everyone. The strings all watched each other like little sheep, 'Are you going up?' 'Yes.' 'So am I.' And they'd go up. 'A little more?' 'Yes.' And they'd go up a little more, all very delicate and cozy, all going up together. Listen to those trumpets. They're just freaking out."

Adds George Martin, "[John] explained what he wanted sufficiently for me to be able to write a score. For the 'I'd love to turn you onnnn' bit, I used cellos and violas. I had them playing those two notes that echo John's voice. However, instead of fingering their instruments, which would produce crisp notes, I got them to slide their fingers up and down the frets, building in intensity until the start of the orchestral climax."

The song was literally pieced together, which fit right into Lennon's disjointed method of writing. By this point, John was culling bits and pieces of material from newspapers, billboards, even television commercials, like the cornflakes ad that inspired "Good Morning, Good Morning."

According to Kenny Lynch, "he would always be writing," whenever Lennon was on the bus, in a hotel room, or a backstage dressing room he'd invariably jot down snatches of conversation on a cigarette pack. "Later I'd hear it crop up in a song."

"I couldn't sit down with Paul in some sort of working situation, like an office job," said John in a late-sixties interview. "If I was told the two of us had to sit at a table until we finished our next song, the job would never get done. I have to grab bits of inspiration when they fly by. I should carry a guitar. I never know when ideas will come. It's worse with individual words. I wait ages for the right rhyme and then it comes and goes before I am able to get it down. Once it's lost, the whole process has to begin again."

It is precisely this herky-jerky, cut-and-paste approach, or as John simply put it, "bits you join up," coupled with Paul's more fluid style that wove a brilliant magic. There is no better example than in "A Day in the Life," a merger of two totally different songs. Lennon took his segments and asked McCartney if he happened to have anything that might work for the middle section. Paul offered the now classic "Woke up, got out of bed . . ."

Following *Rubber Soul* and *Revolver,* on which Lennon and McCartney rarely collaborated, the *Sgt. Pepper* project found them pairing up on several tracks like in the old days. "A Day in the Life," "With a Little Help from My Friends," and "Getting Better" were true joint efforts.

The duo also teamed up for the moving and haunting "She's Leaving Home," dubbed in some circles as Paul McCartney's "soap opera." Paul's lyrical waltz of a teenage runaway was culled from the real-life pages of the *Daily Mirror.* Struggling to convey the realistic angst on the part of the parents, the composer called on Lennon to the rescue. Typically, John traded compassion for sharp-edged reality tinged with cynicism. His contribution of the parental lament: "Why should she treat us so thoughtlessly," came straight from his Aunt Mimi, who apparently voiced a similar sentiment when John moved into his first flat with Stu.

Neither Lennon, McCartney, nor the other Beatles played instruments on the track; that job went to session players who added strings and harp. This was a source of friction between McCartney and George Martin. Paul naturally wanted George to score the piece, but Martin had a session booked with Cilla Black. McCartney, instead of waiting, had Neil Aspinall run around and drum up someone else to do the job.

Said Paul callously, "Martin was busy and I was itching to get on with it; I was inspired. I think George had a lot of difficulty forgiving me for that."

"I was hurt," admits Martin. "I thought, 'Paul, you could have waited.' He obviously didn't think it was important I should do everything. To me, it was."

By the first of March the boys were laying down the Daliesque "Lucy in the Sky with Diamonds." Although definitely a Lennon creation, Paul's 20 percent contribution was evident in the line "Newspaper taxis appear on the shore," as well as in the last verse.

As to the rumors that the song's title spelled out the name of the dreaded heaven-hell drug LSD, Julian Lennon himself put me straight on a lovely spring day in Toronto back in 1983.

GEOFFREY: Did you, many years ago, bring home a drawing of a little girl named Lucy?

JULIAN: Yes. Well, I came up the drive from school, I'd just been dropped off and was waddling along up to the house with this big picture in my hand which was all watery and blurry. I mean, how well can you paint at five? It was just a school friend, "Lucy," I'd drawn. It had green grass at the bottom, a dark blue sky at the top with very rough looking stars and these long curly golden locks of hair on my school friend Lucy. Dad just said, "Well, what's that?" So I said, "That's Lucy in the sky with diamonds." I guess the song just got worked up from that.

GEOFFREY: Does the drawing exist anywhere or is it long gone?

JULIAN: I'm sure it's long gone by now.

GEOFFREY: They'd love it at Sotheby's now, wouldn't they?

JULIAN: You're not kidding!

Ironically, during one of this author's subsequent treks to Great Britain in the mid-eighties, I was staying with a friend of a friend just outside Bristol.

Upon being introduced to her lovely young daughter, I found, much to my amazement, that here was the original Lucy of Beatle lore. At the time, I believe, she was very happily engaged to a fellow who made his living by cooking pickles "inside the can" at a nearby factory. As to the sneaky left-handed fifteen minutes of fame afforded her by her immortalization in song, she smiled quietly and demurred, "We British are much too sensible to be caught up in anything like that."

McCartney noted sometime later:

> This one is really amazing. When you write a song and you mean it one way and then someone comes up and says something about it you didn't think of, you can't deny it. With "Lucy," people came up and said, very cunningly, "Right, I get it, 'L-S-D,'" and it was when all the papers were talking about LSD, but we never thought about it. . . .
>
> We did the whole thing like an *Alice in Wonderland* idea, being in a boat on the river, slowly drifting downstream and those great cellophane flowers towering over your head. Every so often it broke off and you saw "Lucy in the Sky with Diamonds" all over the sky. This Lucy was God, the Big Figure, the White Rabbit. You can just write a song with imagination on words and that's what we did.

Lennon, too, was perplexed at the tune's growing negative connotations. After all, it was not only a well-thought-out composition, but for Lennon, an important work. "The images were from *Alice in Wonderland,*" he said. "It was Alice in the boat. She is buying an egg and it turns into Humpty Dumpty. The woman serving in the shop turns into a sheep and I was visualizing that. That was also the image of the female who would someday come save me, a 'girl with kaleidoscope eyes,' who would come out of the sky. It turned out to be Yoko, though I hadn't met her yet." (Actually he had, as the song was written in March 1967.)

The entire *Pepper* project underscored to McCartney how much he still enjoyed working with Lennon and how much he needed him. "One of the best things about Lennon and McCartney," he said, "was the competitive element within the team. It was great. I could do stuff he might not be in the mood for. Egg him in a certain direction he might not want to go in. And he could do the same for me. If I'd go in a certain direction he didn't like he'd just stop it like that with a snap of his fingers."

"It was a peak," Lennon admitted.

Paul and I were definitely working together. . . . You'd write the good bit—the part that was easy—like "I read the news today," or whatever it was; then when you got stuck, or whenever it got hard, instead of carrying on, you'd just drop it. Then we would meet each other and I would sing half, and he would be inspired to write the next bit and vice versa. He was a bit shy about it because I think he thought it was already a good song.

"They hardly had anything in common," observed Peter Brown, "except their music and the fact that they both realized that if Paul wrote a song and they went into the studio John had a way of putting an edge on it while Paul had a way of softening a John song. It worked for both of them and they both got a lot out of it. It had become a family thing. They had been together since they were teenagers. If they had met later they would have had nothing in common."

That's not to say things were all rosy for Messrs. Lennon and McCartney. Professionally, yes, John was happier than he'd been in a long time. Certainly the project itself, with its creativity that fed into Lennon's inquisitive, active mind, had something to do with it.

Back home, however, John could not escape his problematic marriage and staid life in Weybridge. LSD became an escape that he sought with increasing frequency. "Acid went on for years," he related. "I must have had a thousand trips. Lots. I used to eat it all the time."

At one point Lennon even called a meeting at the Beatles' London office to announce that he had only recently discovered that he was, in fact, Jesus Christ come to earth yet again. "I got a message on acid that you should destroy your ego and I did," he said. "I was reading that stupid book of [Timothy] Leary's and all that shit."

Pete Shotton remembered the bizarre incident in his book, *Lennon: In My Life.*

The so-called inner circle—comprising the Beatles, Derek Taylor, Neil Aspinall, and myself—was summoned to a secret board meeting at Apple. All took their places in a state of keen suspense over the reason for this urgent conclave.

"Right," John began from behind his desk. "I've something very important to tell you all. I am Jesus Christ come back again. This is my thing."

Paul, George, Ringo, and their closest aides stared back, stunned. I found the scene utterly surreal, and was half-laughing inwardly, thinking to myself with real affection, "What the fucking hell is he going to get up to next?" That was really the magic of the man, you never knew.

Even after regaining their powers of speech, nobody presumed to cross-examine John Lennon, or to make light of his announcement. No specific plans were made for the new Messiah, as all agreed that they would need some time to ponder John's announcement, and to decide upon appropriate further steps. The meeting was quickly adjourned, as it was also unanimously agreed that we should all have a drink and a bite to eat.

At the restaurant, while we were waiting for a table, an affable older fellow recognized John and said, "Really nice to meet you. How are you?"

"Actually," John replied, as sincere as I'd ever seen him, "I'm Jesus Christ."

"Oh, really," said the man blandly. "Well, I loved your last record. Thought it was great."

Paul, for his part, was having his own difficulties. He found himself in the middle of a high-profile relationship where both parties were vying for public attention, where egos were bound to collide. "I want to be known as a Shakespearean actress, not as Paul McCartney's girlfriend," Jane quipped to an American reporter.

Asher, who had recently completed a five-month theatrical tour of the United States, returned to England to find a McCartney she didn't understand, much less appreciate. "Paul had changed so much. He was on LSD, which I knew nothing about. The house had changed and was full of stuff I didn't know about."

During the making of *Sgt. Pepper,* Paul uncharacteristically became the first Beatle to try cocaine.

I was the first one on coke at the time of *Sgt. Pepper,* actually, which horrified the whole group and I just thought, "No sweat." And the guys in the group were a bit, kind of, "Hey, wait a minute, that's a little heavier than we've been getting into." And I was doing the traditional coke thing, "No problem, man, it's just a little toot, no problem." But I remember one evening I went down to a club and somebody was passin' coke around and I was feelin' so great and I came back from the toilet and suddenly I just got the *plunge,* you know? The *drop.* And somebody said, "Have some more. Come on, get back up again." I said, "No, man, this isn't gonna work." I mean, anything with that big a downslide. . . . Anyway, I could never stand that feelin' at the back of the throat, it was like you were chokin', you know? So I knocked that on the head. I just thought, "This is not fun." The minute I stopped, the whole record industry got into it and has never stopped since.

Personal problems notwithstanding, nothing could remove from center stage the project that would forever stand as Lennon and McCartney's hall-mark achievement. Yet for all their renewed partnership, there could be no question that *Sgt. Pepper* was Paul's baby. John predictably aired his criticism regarding his colleague's dime-store fiction approach to songs, whose characters included meter maids, mailmen, and secretaries. "I'm not interested in writing third-party songs," he contended. "I like to write about me 'cause I know me."

"Fixing a Hole," however, was a McCartney composition with substance. Helped along with the tune by Mal Evans (who remained officially uncredited, but handsomely remunerated), the song elegantly encapsulates the compelling mindscape of McCartney as the wide-eyed, brooding visionary leading the way for future musical exploration.

Inspired, legend has it, by McCartney's having spent a drizzly afternoon repairing the roof on his farmhouse in Scotland, the actual recording was memorable in two regards: It was laid down at Regency Studio (Abbey Road was booked solid and even the Beatles couldn't get in) and a very special guest was in attendance.

Paul remembers,

The night we went to record that a guy turned up at my house and announced himself as Jesus. So I took him along to the session. You know, it couldn't harm, I thought. I introduced Jesus to the guys. Quite reasonable about it too. But that was it. The last we ever saw of Jesus.

This song is just about a hole in the road where the rain gets in, a good analogy, the hole in your makeup which lets the rain in and stops your mind from going where it will. It's you interfering with things; as when someone walks up and says, "I am the Son of God." And you say, "No you're not; I'll crucify you," and you crucify him. Well that's life, but it is not fixing a hole.

William Mann, writing in the London *Times,* remarked, "There is hope for all these pop genres and *Sgt. Pepper* provides it in abundance. 'Fixing a Hole' is cool, anti-romantic and harmonically a little like the earlier 'Michelle' and 'Yesterday.'"

A whimsical tale of a London civil servant who allows her heart to be "towed away" at the end of every romantic evening, "Lovely Rita" is based on a real-life encounter between McCartney and a St. John's Wood traffic warden who ticketed the Beatle's illegally parked Mini on Garden Street in 1967. "Lovely Rita" is, in reality, Meta Davis, today a retired nineteen-year veteran of the force.

"He saw that my name was Meta," remembers Constable Davis, "and he laughed and said, 'That would make a nice jingle, I could use that.' We chatted for a few minutes and then he drove off. I didn't think any more of it, but later the song came out and although I knew the record was about me I never bought a copy."

The final session, on April 1, saw the recording of the *Sgt. Pepper* reprise. "I think the reprise is more exciting than the first cut of *Sgt. Pepper,*" says engineer Geoff Emerick.

> There's a nice quality about it. We recorded in the huge Abbey Road number one studio which was quite hard because of the acoustics of the place. It's difficult to capture the tightness of the rhythm section in there.
>
> The way Ringo's bass and snare drums sort of thunder out on the *Sgt. Pepper* theme and reprise, no one had heard that in those days. The bass drum was just padded with woolen articles; later on we would take the front skin of the bass drum off. Before that, people recorded bass drums purely for the note and the beat value. So it became quite exciting to actually have it right up front and sort of slapped in your face. We wanted to get the snap of the hammer hitting the skin, and again we'd stuff the drums with cushions or rags to deaden it and make a solid note within there. That's now normal practice, but it wasn't then.

Despite the innovative technique, the normally affable Ringo was venting his feelings of alienation. The timekeeper in a pop band had suddenly become a session drummer in an orchestra, a role in which he felt hopelessly out of place. Despite the work's being universally touted as a Beatles "classic," Ringo pronounced it "Not my favorite album."

Once the album was finished, the next challenge was to create a jacket that would appropriately reflect and package the work's progressive musical content. The Beatles had commissioned the Fool, an aberrant trio of hippie designers from Holland, to do the job, but McCartney's friend, art expert Robert Fraser, convinced them their splashy swirling designs would date far too quickly, possibly having a detrimental impact on the record's longevity.

In order to expedite matters, EMI hired Fraser at £1,500 to oversee production of what would turn out to be the most ambitious and famous album sleeve, despite Brian Epstein's disapproval. He called the extravagance "foolish" and wanted the album released in a plain brown wrapper.

"Originally," relates Paul in the lavish giveaway program to his 1989–1990 world tour, "the idea was that this group was being given a presentation by a Lord Mayor on a kind of grassy knoll with a floral clock, which is very typical of Cleethorpes in Lancashire, all the parks, the floral clock. It was going to be that, and that might have said, 'Congratulations, Beatles' or something. And we were going to be standing, receiving a silver cup or something from this guy. I drew it all out, little sketches (being sold at Sotheby's regularly, these sketches, they got found). I took this to [designer and pop artist] Peter Blake and he started developing them. He said instead of the floral clock, couldn't we have all these heroes that we'd written these lists of."

Paul had been kicking around the novel idea of a cover that featured the Beatles' heroes. Each was asked to write down his twelve most popular historical figures. Not everybody made it. Lennon's suggestion of Adolf Hitler, for instance, was nixed for obvious reasons. It was also thought that Gandhi should be removed so as not to offend potential record buyers in India. Shirley Temple insisted on hearing the album before she finally gave her permission.

With the renowned cast of characters in place, Fraser brought on board Peter Blake to assemble the collage of famous faces to be used as a backdrop against which the Beatles would be photographed by Michael Cooper.

The trendy, elaborate uniforms commissioned for the *Pepper* band were the creation of the well-known London theatrical costumers Bermans, who had more than a little input from the Beatles themselves. At first the boys were going to dress in ordinary Salvation Army–style outfits, but when one of the tailors from the agency dropped by the studio with some fabric for them to examine, they immediately chose the brightest colors from a pile of satin samples. Four pairs of outrageous red and mustard yellow patent leather shoes were ordered, and arrangements were made for John, Paul, George, and Ringo to be measured and fitted for their costumes.

At Bermans, they sifted through mountains of frogs, braids, medals, hats, and trinkets to find just the right accents for their pseudo-military fantasy. Finally, the instruments the Beatles would hold on the cover were rented and collected by Mal Evans, who spent over four hours polishing them in preparation for the photo shoot.

After two weeks of almost continuous endeavor by Blake and his wife, sculptor Jann Haworth, the outrageous set was completed, and the photo session was held on March 30, 1967. It took Cooper only a little over three hours to get the shots he needed for both the front and back covers as well as the interior gatefold photo.

Following nearly four months and seven hundred hours of recording time at a cost of £40,000, *Sgt. Pepper's Lonely Hearts Club Band* was released on June 2, 1967, to near-unanimous acclaim and more than $1 million in advance sales. It remained high atop the *Billboard* charts for a staggering fifteen weeks.

London's leading underground newspaper, the *International Times,* commented, "Too many groups have been writing psychedelic music before they have achieved sufficient insight into its possibilities. The Beatles stayed cool until they had thoroughly explored the potential of freak-out sounds. . . . Tripping with this record is a mind-blowing experience. Musically it is highly sophisticated."

Allen Ginsberg, in a bit of poetic extravagance, added, "After the apocalypse of Hitler and the apocalypse of the Bomb it was here [in *Sgt. Pepper*] an exclamation of joy, the rediscovery of joy and what it is to be alive. They showed an awareness that we make up our own fate and they have decided to make it a cheerful one."

LSD prophet Timothy Leary offered this characteristically over-the-top assessment: "The Beatles are mutants, prototypes of evolutionary agents sent by God with a mysterious power to create a new species, a young race of laughing freemen. . . . They are the wisest, holiest, most effective avatars the human race has ever produced."

Perhaps the greatest acclaim came from Jimi Hendrix, just two days after the album's release, while playing Epstein's Saville Theatre. "It was the biggest compliment he ever paid me," grins Paul. "He opened with 'Sgt. Pepper's Lonely Hearts Club Band': *boom-boom-bahhm, boom-boom-bahhhm!* Oh man, that was so good. I mean, it had only been out for two days!"

In retrospect, what made this work such a standout? First and foremost, the album was lauded for its slice-of-life stories, which merged the short-fiction form with the pop song, a melding never before attempted on so grand a scale. Taking John's "Nowhere Man" and Paul's more complex "Eleanor Rigby" one step further, Lennon and McCartney drew engaging character studies: Lucy, Lovely Rita, Billy Shears, Mr. Kite. No longer were they penning innocuous love letters to their fans: "From Me to You," "I Want to Hold Your Hand," "Do You Want to Know a Secret"; now they had their sights pointed outward and employed a wider sociological perspective.

Lennon claimed it was all a simple matter of growth, saying the years had harvested a more intellectual, mature, and fertile approach to writing. "We were different," he pointed out. "We knew each other on all kinds of levels that we didn't when we were teenagers."

And then there was the album's numerous special effects: audience sounds dubbed in to make the record seem as if it were performed live; the pack of hounds and barnyard animals on "Good Morning"; the inclusion of a 20,000-hertz note only a dog could hear; the run-out groove that contained two seconds of gibberish that took eight hours to record.

"It's like a mantra in Yoga," suggested Paul, "and the meaning changes and it all becomes dissociated from what it is saying. You get a pure buzz after a while because it's so boring it ceases to mean anything."

Among the other "firsts" came the idea to sequel the entire album, making it a forty-one-minute single. "It makes the whole album sound more like a continuous show," John remarked at the time. "We've put everything in a sequence which is balanced just like a program of stuff for a concert. It should be listened to all the way through so there's no point in having a silence every few minutes."

From its opening sounds of the orchestra tuning up, to the reprise finale, this became the first rock LP, according to William Mann, "that was held together by a thematic device [that] gave it a sort of unity."

The success of the album promptly proved the axiom "imitation is the sincerest form of flattery." Before the year was out, artists were literally hopping on the *Sgt. Pepper* bandwagon in hopes of a big payoff. Pink Floyd was first to join the psychedelic foray with their *Piper at the Gates of Dawn* album. Bands such as Jefferson Airplane and Vanilla Fudge soon followed suit.

In retrospect, Mick Jagger probably wishes he'd never heard of *Sgt. Pepper.* Incensed over his rivals' enormous coup, he pushed the Stones to create their own *Sgt. Pepper* despite the prophetic claim by Brian Jones that it would flop. Sure enough, instead of topping the Beatles production, the

Stones offered *Their Satanic Majesties Request,* a dark and dour, poorly mixed psychedelic disaster, mercilessly trashed as a *Pepper* rip-off that quickly sent the band and a duly embarrassed Jagger scurrying back to their R&B roots.

The Lovin' Spoonful's John Sebastian admitted that trying to supersede the all-time blockbuster was but sheer folly. "It was like throwing down a hat in the center of the ring, it was a tremendous challenge. I remember having just finished an album that was fairly compact in its arrangement, and then hearing this incredible pile of tracks with stuff going backwards, entire orchestras playing very unconventionally, mechanical tricks which we'd never heard before and it seemed like an almost insurmountable task to come up with anything even in the same ballpark."

The most unique entry into the psychedelic musical sweepstakes was Frank Zappa's *Sgt. Pepper* put-on, *We're Only in It for the Money,* complete with an album sleeve in which Zappa appeared in drag surrounded by Liberace and characters from *Phantom of the Opera.* A miffed McCartney tried to block the project by holding up permission to parody the Beatles' masterwork, but only managed to delay it for a few months.

But McCartney and company needn't have worried about any challenge to the integrity of their tour de force. More than a quarter century later, *Sgt. Pepper* has weathered the test of time and is universally lauded by artists, critics, and fans alike as the most influential album of the rock era.

Sadly, however, Lennon and McCartney's rejuvenated partnership was to be short lived. Any further hopes of building on it were summarily dashed when an eccentric, strong-willed woman came storming unexpectedly into John Lennon's life.

Small Universe Running / Turning Inward

There is no small measure of irony to the fact that Paul McCartney had a hand in introducing Yoko Ono and John Lennon. The thirty-three-year-old Japanese artist had been on the London art scene for several months before meeting Paul at a charity function, requesting some original lyrics and manuscripts. McCartney, reluctant to pass over his material, suggested his partner might be willing to help out. "I kind of put her on to John and they hit it off, it was like wildfire."

Their initial encounter was at the Indica Gallery, where Yoko's so-called "Exhibition No. 2" was showing. John was particularly haggard after a three-day drug bender.

Lennon recalled those first fortuitous moments loitering near a sculpture in which people were requested to bang a nail. "The owner whispered to her, 'Let him hammer a nail in. You know, he's a millionaire. He might buy it.' And finally she said, 'Okay. You can hammer a nail in for five shillings.' So smart-ass says, 'Well, I'll give you an imaginary five shillings and hammer an imaginary nail.' And that's when we really met. That's when we locked eyes and she got it and I got it, and as they say in all the interviews we do, the rest is history."

Ono said of that memorable first meeting, "I decided that people should pay five shillings to hammer each nail. But when the gallery owner told John he had to pay he stopped a moment and asked if he could just hammer an imaginary nail! It was fantastic. It was my game. The two of us were playing the same game. I didn't know who he was. And when I found out I didn't care."

If timing in a relationship is everything, that perhaps explains why this pairing was one of such high combustion. Each was at an exceedingly despairing period in life when they met. "My life with the Beatles had become a trap," wrote John in 1978. "A tape loop. I made previous short excursions on my own, writing books and helping convert them into a play for the National Theater. I'd even made a movie [*How I Won the War*] without the others, a lousy one at that. . . . Although, even then my eye was already on freedom."

Yoko represented everything to John that wasn't the Beatles. She was Japanese, from a prominent Tokyo banking family, highly educated, and, most importantly, wasn't the least impressed with his celebrated stature. As Yoko herself once commented, "In the art world, a Beatle is, well, you know."

As for Ono, she was carrying the weight of six largely fruitless years trying to promote her highly conceptual avant-garde art. In addition, the financial strain placed enormous stress on her marriage to the equally penniless Tony Cox. "When I met John," she confesses, "I was at the point of disappearance, in the eyes of other people and myself. Where could I go after I'd done the Silent Music and they still didn't catch on? You see, the things I did then were in a field that no one has really touched on yet. I think I had something to offer, but people did all sorts of things to misunderstand me and I was very lonely.

"Because I can compose, I can paint, I can be in many fields, I was thinking, 'There's something wrong with me,' because everyone hated me for it. And then I met this man and for the first time I got the fright of my life because here was a man who was very genuine. And he can do anything I can do, which is very unusual. I really got surprised. And that happened at that first meeting. It was almost like fate that he came into the gallery."

Despite the immediate mutual attraction, the relationship would take more than a year to develop, smoldering on an intellectual level before finally erupting into romance. Yoko's eccentric art was initially very difficult to either absorb or accept, even for the free-thinking John. "I'd get very upset about it being all intellectual and fucking avant-garde, then I'd like it and then I wouldn't."

Meanwhile, with *Sgt. Pepper* barely in the can, Lennon and McCartney didn't stop to catch their breath before beginning work on their next project, *Magical Mystery Tour.*

Paul first got the idea for making an avant-garde film while he was in Denver, Colorado, with Mal Evans to help celebrate Jane Asher's twenty-first birthday on April 5.

"I had this idea," remembers Paul. "In England they have these things called Mystery Tours and you pay so much and you don't know where you're going. So the idea was to have this little thing advertised in the shop windows somewhere called *Magical Mystery Tours*. Someone goes in and buys a ticket and rather than just being the normal bus trip . . . the idea of the show was that it was actually a magical run . . . a real magical trip."

The concept was simple: The Beatles would invite a select group of close friends, fan-club secretaries, bizarre character actors, midgets, and circus freaks to travel around the English countryside with them in a rented bus and just see what happened.

Flying home on Tuesday, April 11, 1967, McCartney began working on the lyrics for the project's title track, mapping out further ideas for the proposed one-hour special with Evans. Borrowing some paper from one of the stewards, McCartney carefully drew a large circle and divided it up into several sections. He then penciled in various thoughts as to the film's content and structure, leaving several blanks for his colleagues back in London to work out.

A scant nine days later recording began on the title track, "Magical Mystery Tour." This one was literally written in the studio since only the title, the opening "Roll up, roll up!" line, plus a bit of the music had been developed. By all accounts this was one of the most off-the-cuff numbers the Beatles ever recorded, completing the backing track of piano, two guitars, and drums in only a couple of hours.

When session men arrived to play the song's dramatic trumpet flourishes they discovered firsthand that the Lennon and McCartney work ethic left much to be desired. Elgar Howarth, chairman of the Royal Philharmonic Orchestra, remembers showing up promptly for a one o'clock recording session and waiting four hours for John and Paul to show up.

"Where is the music for us to play?" asked an exasperated Howarth when the duo finally arrived.

"Oh, we haven't written it yet," they casually replied.

Sent over to the pub to wait while McCartney played one-fingered notes onto a tape that was to be the trumpet parts, Howarth and company returned and laid down their contributions. By this time it was after ten; as the haggard trio packed up their instruments Lennon cried out, "Where are you going? There's some more yet."

"Where is it?"

"We haven't written it yet," John replied.

They waited while Lennon sang the trumpet licks and Howarth wearily transposed them. Finally the parts were recorded. The scheduled three-hour session had turned into ten hours!

The lyrics, however, took on an even wilder free-form tone, as William Dowlding points out in *Beatlesongs:* "In an attempt to write more of the lyrics the Beatles shouted out ideas as Mal Evans took notes: 'Trip of a lifetime,' 'satisfaction guaranteed,' but they soon grew bored and decided to sing whatever words came to them later."

The Lennon-McCartney composition "Baby You're a Rich Man" was initially released as a single, the B-side to "All You Need Is Love." This one began in a most unusual fashion. Al Brodax was the producer for the Beatles' animated adventure, *Yellow Submarine,* a film that would be two years in the making. During the hectic production Brodax made some seventeen transatlantic trips.

On one of these occasions, he recalls,

> I was really testy because I hadn't slept the night and I had come across the Atlantic. I couldn't find my little overnight bag so I took a paper bag and put some underwear, aftershave, and so on in it. I went directly to EMI Studios and started screaming, "You are making all the money and all I am doing is going back and forth over the Atlantic." They started mumbling amongst themselves and Paul said, "You're a rich man, baby. Stop bitching." I said, "I'm not bitching. I'm just tired and I want to get some sleep." So a few weeks later they came up with the song: "Baby You're a Rich Man," meaning me. "He keeps all his money in a big brown bag." That's how "Baby You're a Rich Man" came about. They got the idea from that incident.

This was the second song to be composed in two separate parts, one by John, the other by Paul. Breaking it down, the title refrain was McCartney's while Lennon composed the "beautiful people" section. In fact, the two parts were recorded separately, but to this day have never been released.

Interestingly, the tape box for the original multitrack is inscribed: "The Beatles + Mick Jagger." The head Stone, it seems, was not only a visitor to Olympic Studios during its recording, but also joined in on the song's trippy extended backing vocals.

Rumor has it that John had originally entitled the number "Baby You're a

Rich Fag Jew" in honor of poor Brian Epstein. Some say at the very end of the song, buried way down in the mix, one can indeed hear the naughty lyric, interspersed with the more socially acceptable refrain.

But George Harrison claims there was a more noble purpose to the song. "For a while we thought we were having some influence and the idea was to show that we, by being rich and famous and having all these experiences, had realized there was a greater thing to be got out of life, and what's the point of having that on your own? You want all your friends and everybody else to do it, too."

Work on the *Magical Mystery Tour* project was interrupted by an invitation for the Beatles to join a worldwide satellite television linkup called *Our World.* With only two weeks' notice to come up with a song, Lennon penned the ultimate sixties' anthem, "All You Need Is Love."

"We had been told," said McCartney, "we'd be seen recording it by the whole world at the same time. So we had one message for the world, love. We need more love in the world."

With its dramatic entree to the flourish of the French national anthem in a very difficult 7/8 meter, the song flits unconventionally between waltz and march time. Notes George Harrison, "John has an amazing thing with his timing, he comes across with very different time signatures, you know. For example, on 'All You Need Is Love,' it just sort of skips a beat here and there and changes time. But when you question him as to what he's actually doing he really doesn't know. He just does what comes naturally."

According to Martin the song had to be kept top secret, "because the general idea was that the television viewers would actually see the Beatles at work recording their new single, although modern recording being what it is, we obviously couldn't do that for real; so we laid down a basic rhythm track first of all. I remember that one of the minor problems was that George had got a hold of a violin which he wanted to try to play even though he couldn't!"

Martin's score was an eclectic one indeed. Strains from the "Marseillaise" were joined with a bit of Bach, a snatch of "Greensleeves," and a spicy lick from "In the Mood." "I wove them all together," he said, "at slightly different tempos so that they all still worked as separate entities."

Said McCartney, "George is quite a sage. Sometimes he works with us, sometimes against us, but he's always looked after us. I don't think he does as much as some people think. He sometimes does all the arrangements and we just change them."

The song's debut, live on June 25, 1967, before more than half a million viewers, remains a nugget of classic television. The highlight was its all-star chorus of Eric Clapton, Keith Moon, Mick Jagger, Graham Nash, Keith Richards, Mike McCartney, and Marianne Faithfull, among others. As described by author Nicholas Schaffner, "The Beatles could still be irreverent as ever, in this case, about themselves, their earlier exhortations to 'say the word love' and the flower children who had so taken *the word* to heart. Decked out as the four letters of love, in beads and multicolored costumes, the Beatles previewed their new record for seven hundred thousand people, accompanied by a parade of signs translating the magic word into all kinds of languages."

Viewed as something of a parody, the song, complete with an offbeat refrain of "She loves you," made such an impact it was decided that it should bump "Magical Mystery Tour" as the next single and be rush-released at once. In fact, it was the fastest produced song in Fab history: written in late May, recorded on June 27, and released on July 7 throughout Britain.

Back to work on the album, the Beatles had just finished overdubbing the McCartney tune "Your Mother Should Know" at London's Chappell Recording Studios on August 23 when tragedy struck. Just four days later, they were informed of Brian Epstein's death from what was ruled an accidental overdose of sleeping pills. Rumors immediately swirled, citing Epstein's attempted suicide late in 1966, allegedly over a boyfriend who threatened to expose his sexual preference. Apparently Epstein had tried to take his life again several months later.

Epstein had been depressed throughout the Summer of Love, despondent over his father's unexpected death in July and apparently fearful that the Beatles would not renew his contract that fall. There was ample cause for his worry: Epstein had badly botched Beatles merchandising contracts to the tune of a spectacular $80 million loss.

Paul was particularly critical, which sparked many rows with the sensitive manager. "We got screwed for millions," he cried. "It was all Brian's fault. He was green. I always said that about Brian. Green."

Even Lennon, who was closer to Eppy than any of the Beatles, was outraged. "Brian definitely looked after himself and not us. He ripped us off on the Seltaeb thing [Beatles spelled backward, the licensee for Beatles products]. The myth is that he was a good guy. It's the same as the myth about Paul. Wonderful Paul and crazy John."

To add to Epstein's pressures, the Rolling Stones' cagey financial manager

Allen Klein was promising in the papers that he would "have the Beatles by Christmas."

Geoffrey Ellis, perhaps Epstein's closest confidant, contends a distraught Brian believed he was losing his hold over the Beatles. "In the last year of his life Brian may have been nervous about what the future held. They were independent cusses . . . would tease him and make Brian feel insecure, probably deliberately. There was an element of cruelty in them and a feeling that they had done a lot for him."

Speculation about Epstein's demise aside, there was little time to mourn their manager's death as McCartney quickly ushered them back into the studio. Peter Brown, who later dubbed McCartney "a control freak," maintained it was all part of Paul's reaction to Brian's death: to immediately start doing something.

"C'mon, let's not waste time," Paul would say, like a general mustering his troops. "Let's get on with the project. We can't be seen to be sitting around."

"I knew we were in trouble then," said Lennon. "I didn't have any misconceptions about our ability to do anything other than play music."

Epstein's passing, it seemed, had unleashed a torrent of bad luck. The *Magical Mystery Tour* LP, though another major seller, was a hit-and-miss venture, mostly the latter. McCartney's own "Your Mother Should Know" offered a regrettable slice of vaudeville fluff while Harrison's "Blue Jay Way," written around the street address of a rental house in Los Angeles, indicated George might be out of his element when away from Eastern mysticism. The redeeming factor about "Flying" was that it was the only track on which all four Beatles shared equal writing credit.

As for "Hello Goodbye," the single off the LP, which held the number-one slot for three weeks, its popularity was probably based more on its infectious repetitive quality than its musical craftsmanship.

Again, Al Brodax was indirectly involved in the song's origins. It seemed Ringo had been trying to call the producer overseas and kept getting Brodax's young daughter. "In those days you couldn't dial direct," related the producer. "You had to get the operator to get the number. And my daughter was only about five or six years old. So he called. And she'd say 'Hello.' And he'd say 'Hello.' And then she'd say 'Goodbye.' That happened several times. And from that came the idea for 'Hello Goodbye.'"

Lennon predictably didn't think much of this one. "That's another McCartney. It wasn't a great piece; the best bit was the end, which we all ad-libbed in the studio, where I played piano."

When the single was first issued in Britain on November 24, 1967, Pete Shotton related this story:

> Our old Liverpool friend, Bill Turner, happened to drop by 94 Baker Street on the afternoon Paul breezed into the offices to play us all the acetate. As soon as the song was over, all the employees gushed forth with superlatives like "wonderful," "lovely," and "Ooh, Paul, it's so fantastic!" Noticing that Bill had failed to join in this chorus, Paul demanded, "Well, what did *you* think, William?"
>
> "To be honest with you, Paul," replied Bill, "I thought it was a bit repetitious, really, and not one of your best records."
>
> Paul was visibly taken aback. Whatever the merits of "Hello Goodbye," it was clear that none of Paul's friends or associates had dared speak to him like that in years.

Two tracks on the album, however, do merit attention. The first, McCartney's drifting "Fool on the Hill," was written six months before in Paul's St. John's Wood home. While working on "With a Little Help from My Friends" McCartney came up with the insightful words.

"Better write them down so you don't forget them," John advised.

The song's Dostoyevsky-like theme depicts an apparent simpleton dismissed by society who, in fact, harbors a keen wisdom beyond them all. McCartney presents the underdog we all want to root for, the one we see in ourselves, and he pulls it off to perfection. Even Lennon was quick to praise the song as "Paul's major. Another good lyric. Shows he's capable of writing complete songs."

What really defines this one, though, is its constant and complex movement between major and minor keys, a frequent distinguishing characteristic of Lennon-McCartney tunes that harks back to the days of "I Want to Hold Your Hand." A total McCartney package, his elegant use of piano, flute, and, particularly, recorder lend the ballad a strikingly haunting mood.

Mystery Tour, however, will always be regarded for Lennon's chimerical shell-game play, "I Am the Walrus." Pete Shotton remembers the unlikely genesis of the piece.

> "Pete," John said to me one evening, "what's that 'Dead Dog's Eye' song we used to sing when we were at Quarry Bank?" I thought for a moment and it all came back to me.

Yellow matter custard, green slop pie
All mixed together with a dead dog's eye,
Slap it on a butty, ten foot thick
Then wash it all down with a cup of cold stick.

"That's it!" exclaimed John. "Fantastic!" He found a pen and commenced scribbling. . . . Such was the origin of "I Am the Walrus." . . .

Inspired by the picture of that Quarry Bank literature master pontificating on the symbolism of Lennon-McCartney, John threw in the most ludicrous images his imagination could conjure. He thought of "semolina" (an insipid pudding we'd been forced to eat as kids) and "pilchard" (a sardine we often fed to our cats). "Semolina Pilchard climbing up the Eiffel Tower . . ." John intoned, writing it down with considerable relish.

He turned to me smiling, "Let the fuckers work that one out, Pete!"

The heavy dirgelike opening is ushered in by Lennon on the Mellotron, a riff repeated six times on the British version, but curiously, only four times on the U.S. disc.

Lennon shared his thoughts on the remarkable tune.

The first line was written on an acid trip one weekend, the second on another trip the next weekend, and it was filled in after I met Yoko. . . .

I had just these two lines on the typewriter, then about two weeks later I wrote another two lines and then when I saw something, after these four lines I just knocked the rest off. Then I had a whole verse or verse and a half and then sang it.

I'd seen Allen Ginsberg and some other people who liked Dylan and Jesus, going on about Hare Krishna. It was Ginsberg in particular I was referring to. The words "elementary penguin" meant that it's naive to go around chanting Hare Krishna or putting all your faith in one idol.

The song's often jumbled imagery bore a striking resemblance to his earlier literary poems. Lennon explained, "Surrealism to me is reality. Psychedelic vision is reality to me and always was. When I looked at myself in the mirror at twelve, thirteen, I used to literally trance out into alpha. I would find myself seeing these hallucinatory images of my face changing, becoming cosmic and complete. I would start trancing out and the eyes would get bigger and the room would vanish; I read the same description years later by a famous person who took opium."

Released in America on November 27, *Magical Mystery Tour* (which contained the 1967 singles) remained at number one for eight weeks and generated some $8 million within three weeks.

The film itself, however, was another story. Setting off en route to Cornwall together on Monday, September 11, the Beatles and an entourage of thirty-nine began the arduous task of filming without benefit of any real script, competent technical advice, or even much of a clue as to where they were heading. Needless to say, right from day one, the *Magical Mystery Tour* was an unqualified disaster.

One of the most unfortunate setbacks occurred with the shooting of the dreamy "Fool on the Hill" sequence in Nice on October 30, 1967. Jetting off solo, McCartney soon realized he'd not only forgotten his passport, but his wallet as well, leaving him in grave difficulty with French customs officials. A series of frantic phone calls resulted in the document's being rush-delivered by air freight several agonizing hours later. To make matters worse, someone at NEMS had forgotten to include any money with the passport and McCartney's hotel refused to accept his signature for the room or advance him any credit whatsoever. Once again, the international phone lines were buzzing.

Lennon later observed:

> Paul made an attempt to carry on as if Brian hadn't died by saying, "Now, now, boys we're going to make a record." Being the kind of person I am, I thought, "Well, we're going to make a record, all right." . . .
>
> Paul had a tendency to come along and say well, he's written these ten songs, let's record now. And I said, "Well, give us a couple of days and I'll knock a few off." So Paul said "Well, here's the segment, you write a little piece for that," and I thought, "Bloody hell," so I ran off and wrote the dream sequence for the fat woman and whole thing with the spaghetti. George and I were sort of grumbling about the fuckin' movie, but we thought we'd better do it, as we had the feeling we owed it to the public to do these daft things.

Magical Mystery Tour first aired on Boxing Day 1967 over the BBC. The *Daily Mail* called it "blatant rubbish," while the *Los Angeles Times* reported, "Critics and Viewers Boo: Beatles Produce First Flop with Yule Film." Paul commented that if the film had been shown in color as originally intended rather than black and white it might have made more sense. Nevertheless,

American network officials ultimately canceled their option to broadcast the film in the United States.

A few years later the *Mystery Tour*'s critical failure still nagged McCartney, who said in 1974, "We didn't worry about the fact that we didn't know anything about making films and had never made one before. We realized years ago you don't really need knowledge to do anything. All you need is sense. It started out to be one of those things like *The Wild One* with Marlon Brando. At the time it couldn't be released. The real interest in it came later. *Magical Mystery Tour* was a bit like that. . . . You've got to be patient, I think it was a good show. It will have its day, you know."

In fact, the film did well on the American college circuit, with rentals grossing $2 million, ultimately making it a commercial success.

Magical Mystery Tour's artistic and commercial failure in Britain, however, uncorked a Pandora's box of conflict from which the Lennon and McCartney partnership would never really recover. And although the actual demise was still a couple of years away, this was a turning point—*the* turning point, according to Lennon. "After Brian died we collapsed," he said in the 1971 *Lennon Remembers*. "Paul took over and supposedly led us. But what is leading us, when we went round in circles? We broke up then. That was the disintegration."

Epstein's death pointed out how much the Beatles had needed and depended on him. As author Malcolm Doney pointed out, "Without Brian there was no one to temper the flights of imagination, no one to counsel caution or involve professional expertise."

Both Peter Brown and Neil Aspinall firmly contend that under Epstein's rein the film fiasco would never have occurred. "If Brian had been alive the film would never have gone out," asserted Aspinall. "Brian would have said, 'Okay, we blew £40,000, so what?' Brian would never have let it happen."

When a bitter, resentful Lennon blasted *Mystery Tour* as "the most expensive home movie ever made, a big ego trip for Paul," McCartney defensively fired back, "God, it was for *their* sake, to keep us together, keep us going, give us something new to do."

But John didn't see it that way, charging his partner with hoarding most of the songs, adding, "George just barely managed to get on."

It wasn't until two years later, in 1969, that Lennon was able to vent his frustrations of that period. "It was carte blanche because you'd come up with a *Magical Mystery Tour,*" he told Paul.

I didn't write any of that except "Walrus"; I'd accept it and you'd already have five or six songs, so I'd think, "Fuck it, I can't keep up with that." So I didn't bother, and I thought, I don't really care whether I was on or not, I convinced myself it didn't matter and so, for a period, if you didn't invite me to be on an album personally, if you three didn't say, "Write some more, 'cause we like your work," I wasn't going to fight!

I gave up fighting for an A-side or fighting for time. I thought, "Well, I'm content to put 'Walrus' on the B-side when I think it's much better than 'Strawberry Fields,' because I'm content to be on and get the cooperation of the group to produce a 'Walrus' and a 'Strawberry Fields' out of all of you." I didn't have the energy or the nervous type of thing to push it. So gradually I was submerging.

Even Paul couldn't fail to see that the relationship was badly floundering. But maybe there was "a way to get back home," as a future McCartney song would suggest. A way to arrest the bleeding, pick up the pieces, restore some element of harmony. And though it would ultimately prove only a stopgap measure, they looked all the way to the other side of the world. Deep in the mysterious Himalayan Mountains lay the next frontier, perhaps the ultimate frontier, and the lure of a vision well beyond even the realm of illicit mind-altering pharmaceuticals. Perhaps in India they would find the answers.

Just the summer before, at the urging of George Harrison, the boys attended a lecture at London's Hilton Hotel by the Maharishi Mahesh Yogi followed by a weekend conference in Bangor, Wales. John was particularly impressed with the Yogi's tenets of universal love and inner peace, and by his aura of contentment—a contentment that drugs and fame had not provided in Lennon's own life.

Thus it was with great enthusiasm all round that the Beatles, along with their wives, girlfriends, and a few close mates (including Donovan) flew to New Delhi on February 16, 1968, to begin serious study with the Maharishi at his extravagant Rishikesh retreat in Northern India. Joining them on their pilgrimage were Beach Boy Mike Love, Neil Aspinall, so-called electronics wizard and friend "Magic" Alex Mardas, as well as Mia Farrow, fresh from her doomed marriage to Frank Sinatra, and her younger sister, Prudence.

At the end of a rugged 250-mile drive to the ashram, the celebrated disciples, along with a throng of the world's press, were warmly welcomed by

George Harrison, Pete Best, John Lennon, and Paul McCartney in Liverpool, circa 1960.
PHOTO © GINA DELPONIO

BELOW: The Beatles on tour in America, 1964.
PHOTO © PHOTOGRAPHIC ARCHIVES INTERNATIONAL

LEFT: **John in top form, America, 1964.**
PHOTO © PHOTOGRAPHIC ARCHIVES
INTERNATIONAL

RIGHT: **Barnstorming America, 1964.**
PHOTO © BRAZEN IMAGES

LEFT: **The Beatles in Canada circa 1964.**
PHOTO © PHOTOGRAPHIC ARCHIVES
INTERNATIONAL

ABOVE: **With Labor leader Harold Wilson at an awards ceremony in London, March 19, 1964.**
PHOTO © GINA DELPONIO

LEFT: **On the set of** *A Hard Day's Night,* 1964.
PHOTO © BRAZEN IMAGES

Hamming it up out on the road, December 1965.

PHOTO © BRAZEN IMAGES

Impish behavior at a
press conference.
PHOTO © PHOTOGRAPHIC
ARCHIVES INTERNATIONAL

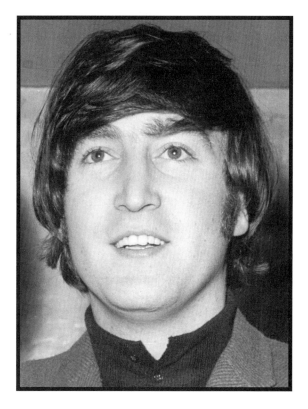

Big John at the pinnacle of his self-
proclaimed "Fat Beatle" period,
London, 1966.
PHOTO © BRAZEN IMAGES

The Maharishi Mahesh Yogi holds court with his most famous subjects, London,
August 24, 1967.
PHOTO © PHOTOGRAPHIC ARCHIVES INTERNATIONAL

"Padre" Lennon presides over a fancy
dress party in London, 1967.
PHOTO © PHOTOGRAPHIC ARCHIVES INTERNATIONAL

Celebrating the release of *Sgt. Pepper* at Brian Epstein's posh Belgravia town house, 1967.
PHOTO © GINA DELPONIO

A quiet moment during the shooting of *Magical Mystery Tour*, 1967.
PHOTO © BRAZEN IMAGES

Paul exiting Heathrow, London,
April 12, 1967.
PHOTO © PHOTOGRAPHIC ARCHIVES INTERNATIONAL

Macca with his charming former
fiancée, Jane Asher, on the way to
Greece for a holiday with the other
Fabs, 1967.
PHOTO © PHOTOGRAPHIC ARCHIVES
INTERNATIONAL

Lennon and McCartney leave London for New York to formally launch the Beatles' new umbrella company, Apple Corps Ltd., May 1968.
PHOTO © BRAZEN IMAGES

At the official Apple press conference in New York, 1968.

PHOTO © PHOTOGRAPHIC ARCHIVES INTERNATIONAL

Paul arrives at the premiere of *Yellow Submarine* at the London Pavilion Cinema in Picadilly, July 17, 1968.

PHOTO © PHOTOGRAPHIC ARCHIVES INTERNATIONAL

John and Yoko are hauled off to court in London for arraignment following their arrest for possession of marijuana at their Montague Square flat, London, 1968.
PHOTO © PHOTOGRAPHIC ARCHIVES INTERNATIONAL

McCartney walking his famous sheepdog Martha ("My Dear"), London, August 6, 1968.

Paul and Linda tie the knot Wednesday, March 12, 1969.

John and Yoko at the
height of their contro-
versial career together.

PHOTO © BRAZEN IMAGES

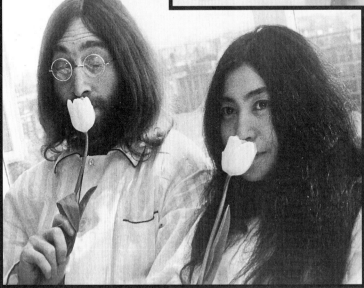

John and Yoko dazzle
the media during their
first Bed-In for Peace,
Amsterdam, March 25,
1969.

PHOTO © BRAZEN IMAGES

LEFT: At the Windsor Hotel in Toronto during the Lennons' brief North American peace campaign, 1969.

PHOTO © BRAZEN IMAGES

BELOW: At a press conference for an exhibition by Yoko Ono at the Everson Museum of Art, Syracuse, New York, 1971.

PHOTO © BRAZEN IMAGES

McCartney appears on Britain's *Top of the Pops* with the Wings original lineup.
PHOTO © PHOTOGRAPHIC ARCHIVES INTERNATIONAL

Denny Laine, Linda, and Paul attend a record-company function in London, late 1970s.
PHOTO © PHOTOGRAPHIC ARCHIVES INTERNATIONAL

the diminutive guru with a shower of encouraging words and endless cups of steaming almond drupe tea on the veranda of his comfortable stone bungalow.

Mal Evans gives us a hint of the amenities available to the meditators. "I suppose a total of about forty people were employed at the academy, including joiners, a full-scale printing works, numerous cooks, and cleaning staff. The room service was marvelous. On my first day I unpacked dozens of Beatles' shirts and other clothing and an hour later the lot disappeared. The same evening they were back, all freshly washed and pressed. And I hadn't even asked!"

As one day slipped casually into the next and the initial excitement of the trip subsided, the boys' pent-up tensions slowly began to unravel under the magic spell of the Maharishi's meditation. Most days, the normally sluggish Lennon was the first up, and following a half-hour's meditation he would take a leisurely stroll around the compound with Mal or George.

"The Maharishi was a wonderful teacher," recalls Cynthia. "His lectures were humorous, enlightening, and provided truly halcyon days. John and George, in particular, were in their element. They threw themselves totally into the Maharishi's teachings, were happy, relaxed and above all, found a peace of mind that had eluded them [for] so long."

McCartney, too, found himself very much absorbed in the philosophy. Starr, however, didn't particularly appreciate the simple Indian food or the numerous insects and complained that the stifling midday heat kept him from meditating properly. Only ten days into the program, he and Maureen fled back to London.

For those inside the Yogi's select inner circle of meditators, the key word was *endurance*. Students were encouraged to meditate for long periods, only to gradually taper off near the end of the course in an effort to "reconnect" with the material plane.

"To make sure we would meditate in peace," wrote Mal, "we had little printed cards saying, MEDITATING, PLEASE DO NOT DISTURB, which we stuck outside the doors of our rooms." Within the Beatles' clique, meditators John and George led the rest, each day clocking seven and nine hours respectively of sure-fire, tuned-in cosmic awareness.

While Lennon and Harrison steeped themselves in the Yogi's Vedic-inspired tenets, McCartney and Asher, accustomed to their swirling London life, began to grow weary of the tedious routine of silently muttering a Sanskrit syllable hour after hour. After sticking it out for six weeks, the couple jetted home.

That left John and George, the Maharishi's most ardent believers. So besotted were they with the holy man that even when Magic Alex introduced a rumor that the Maharishi had made a very definite bid for the earthly affections of Mia Farrow, they were loath to believe it. Within a week, however, Farrow had left on a tiger hunt in the south. It was suggested by the Maharishi's staff that she would be returning shortly thereafter. She never did.

Lennon, who had poured so much hope into the Maharishi's philosophical offerings, was left disillusioned by the entire affair, all the while enthusiastically counseled by his mate, Magic Alex, to drop the guru once and for all.

"An entire evening was spent trying desperately to sort everything out in their minds," revealed Cynthia. "That night of soul-searching by John and George produced a victory for Alex, but great unhappiness as far as I was concerned. Out of confusion and accusation came anger and aggression. Doubt and subterfuge replaced our joy and hard-won peace of mind."

Once the penny dropped, however, the two remaining Beatles were convinced there was no option but to confront the elderly master with the charges. The unseemly job fell to John Lennon, as he explained in a 1970 interview.

> There was a big hullabaloo about him trying to rape Mia Farrow and attempting to get off with a few other women. Anyway, we went to see him, after trying all night to figure out if it was possible. When George started thinking it might be true, I thought, "Well, it must be, because if George thinks it might be then there's got to be something to it." So I said to him, "We're leaving."
>
> "Why?" he asked and all that shit so I said, "Well, if you're so bloody cosmic, you'll know won't you?"
>
> "But I don't know. You must tell me."
>
> I kept saying, "You ought to know," and he gave me a look like, "I'll kill you, you bastard." I knew then.

The two Beatles stormed out of the bungalow and rang for a taxi from the ashram's dining hall before racing back to their quarters to pack. As they were filing out the main gate, a disciple was sent by the distraught master to make one last pitiful plea for them to calm down and talk things over. But it was too late. Like so many times in the past, Lennon had burned his bridges and was moving on.

Within thirty-six hours the Harrisons and the Lennons were safely back home on their lush estates in suburban London. The magical Maharishi Mahesh Yogi and Co. had become just another in a long series of bum trips.

Said John, "Maharishi was a father figure. There was nothing wrong with that until you give him the right to give you a recipe for your life. What happens is somebody comes along with a good piece of truth. Instead of the truth being looked at, the person who brought it is looked at. It's like when bad news comes, they shoot the messenger. When the good news comes they worship the messenger and don't bother listening to the message."

Echoed Paul, "We thought there was more to him than there was, but he's human. And for a while we thought he wasn't, we thought he was . . . uh . . . you know."

The incident, however, ultimately spawned Lennon's satirical "Sexy Sadie." "John, in particular, was furious at his new idol," reveals Beatles expert Bill Harry. "TM benefited him greatly. It had broken his drug addiction and opened his creative juices, resulting in a large number of songs being written in Rishikesh." Lennon channeled his fury into an angry exposé called "Maharishi," but later changed the title to "Sexy Sadie" to avoid possible lawsuits.

In retrospect, it has been suggested that in stumbling at the feet of the Maharishi, the Beatles were desperately trying to replace Brian Epstein. As time wore on, it became increasingly apparent that the boys were rudderless, setting sail on ill-advised journeys, in desperate need of real guidance.

Don Short, their reporter friend from the *Daily Mail,* termed their short-lived infatuation "a search for their next guru." Said Short, "There was some measure of compensation because all of them had found meditation and it did help them. There was no doubt about it."

The experience, too, spawned a wellspring of fine compositions, many of which would fill the ambitious *White Album.* The wistful, hypnotic "Dear Prudence," for instance, was Lennon's carefully crafted tale of Mia Farrow's kid sister.

Mal Evans explained: "Prudence was at the Maharishi's with us earlier this year. She used to spend much longer than most of us meditating in her room. This song of John's suggests that it's time Prudence came out into the sunshine to 'greet the brand new day.'"

"[She] seemed to go slightly balmy," Lennon remembered. "Meditating too long and couldn't come out of the little hut we were livin' in. They selected me and George to try and bring her out because she would trust us. If she'd been in the West they would have put her away."

Paul played piano and flügelhorn on the track while John and Mal added tambourine. The clapping and chorus comprised all four Beatles, Apple singer Jackie Lomax, and Paul's cousin, John. Several guitar overdubs lent the tune its rich, churning flavor.

Also culled directly from their Indian experience was Paul's "Wild Honey Pie," only fifty-three seconds in length, a fragment of an instrumental McCartney never intended to record. "But Pattie [Harrison] liked it very much," remembered Paul, "so we decided to leave it on the album."

"The Continuing Story of Bungalow Bill" was about a fellow meditator who took a break to go tiger hunting, which Lennon termed "a sort of teenage social comment and also a bit of a joke." Meanwhile, John's "I'm So Tired," about his insomnia while on retreat, was a dramatic turnabout from the lethargic "I'm Only Sleeping," off the earlier *Revolver*. Although Lennon considered this one of his favorite tracks, the tension depicted in the lyric was the result of the agitation he was going through over the state of his troubled marriage and preoccupation with Yoko Ono.

"Mother Nature's Son," inspired by a Maharishi lecture, is pure McCartney with its syrupy "Sit beside a mountain stream—see her waters rise." Not surprisingly, perennial lightweight John Denver soon added it to his repertoire.

Not all the material composed in Rishikesh bore the mark of peace and tranquility, however. Lennon's puncturing "Yer Blues," a parody of sixties British blues, was a piercing vocalization of the agony and confusion that had been there since the heady heyday of Beatlemania.

More immediate on Lennon's list of trials was his ever growing attraction to Yoko. Even as John had been communing in India with Cynthia he was slowly distancing himself, spurred on by his almost daily correspondence with Yoko, who would send him enigmatic postcards carrying messages: "Watch the light until dawn," and "I'm a cloud watch for me in the sky."

"It was beginning to happen," he said. "Our first attraction was a mental one, but I wasn't quite aware of what was happening to me."

By the time John returned to London something very potent was ready to ignite. One night in May, while Cynthia was out of town, Lennon sent for Yoko in his chauffeured Rolls. Following several awkward hours conversing in the downstairs lounge, the two decided to record some impromptu music in his third-floor studio.

"We improvised for many hours," Yoko later recalled. "He used two tape recorders, adding any sounds that came into his head. I sat down and did the voice. We were both involved and enjoying the uncertainty of how it would all turn out. And that was it. We called it *Unfinished Music.* The idea is that the listener can take from it or add to it in his or her mind."

Those tapes would ultimately become the controversial *Two Virgins* album, released later that year. But that night found the pair making another kind of music as well. Following the all-night session, Yoko and John succumbed to their long-pent-up desires and made love at dawn for the very first time.

Lennon later proclaimed,

> I've never known love like this before. It hit me so hard I had to immediately halt my marriage to Cyn. And don't think that was a reckless decision, because I thought very deeply about all the implications. My marriage to Cyn was not unhappy, but it was just a normal marital state where nothing happened, and which we continued to sustain. You sustain it until you meet someone who really sets you alight. With Yoko I really knew love for the first time.
>
> Some say my decision was selfish. Well, I don't think it is. Isn't it better to avoid rearing children in the atmosphere of a strained relationship? Initially our attraction was a mental one, but it happened physically too. Both are essential in a union, but I never dreamed I would marry again. Now the thought of it seems easy.

Three months later, on August 22, 1968, Cynthia Lennon would reluctantly file suit against her errant husband on the grounds of adultery with a decree nisi granted on November 8, ending their troubled six-year marriage. The long-suffering Cyn handled it with impeccable grace and dignity, along with a remarkably keen sense of perception.

"I didn't blame John or Yoko," she stated. "I understood their love. I knew there was no way I could ever fight the unity of mind and body they had with each other. Their all-consuming love had no time for pain or unhappiness. Yoko didn't take John away from me because he had never *really* been mine."

It seemed that no matter how chaotic their private lives, Lennon and McCartney continued to enjoy the abundant fruits of their success. "Lady Madonna" inaugurated McCartney's reign of dominance over the Beatles' singles; he would pen the remainder, except for Lennon's "Ballad of John and Yoko" and Harrison's torrid "Something."

Everything about "Lady Madonna," based on an arrangement of an old number called "Bad Penny Blues," oozed power and thrust. McCartney's Rickenbacker bass carries the song from one crescendo to the next, made stronger by the use of a cheap microphone and heavy compression. A stormy stroke of genius was the input of a saxophone quartet riff led by renowned London jazzman Ronnie Scott.

McCartney's vocals had never been stronger, dominating the piece with his Presley-like baritone. In fact, Ringo made a point of saying, "It sounds like Elvis, doesn't it? No, it doesn't sound like Elvis, it *is* Elvis, even those bits where he goes very high."

Who was Lady Madonna? A reference to the Virgin Mary? McCartney's own mother? As he finally replied in 1986, "Lady Madonna's all women. How do they do it—bless 'em—it's that one, you know. Baby at your breast, how do they get the time to feed them? Where do you get the money? How do you do this thing that women do?"

As the year progressed, another major episode in the Lennon-McCartney saga unfolded with the ill-fated creation of Apple Corps Ltd., headquartered at Number 3 Savile Row. The seeds were sown in late 1967 with the formation of the Apple Boutique, a business venture designed to assuage the Beatles' financial woes, resulting from their landing in a 96 percent tax bracket. Other divisions added late in 1968 included Apple Publishing, Apple Films, Apple Retailing, Apple Electronics, and the famed Apple Records.

McCartney, in typical fashion, took credit for the corporate undertaking, which John later hotly disputed. "One thing people never knew was that Apple was certainly not Paul's idea. . . . Apple was presented to us as a reality by the Epsteins in 1967, before Brian died, Brian and his furniture-salesman brother, Clive. And they hadn't the slightest fucking idea what they were doing."

Still, it began with lofty, idyllic visions, the altruistic, hip, corporate bene-factor out to lend a hand to promising young musicians. "It's ridiculous that people with talent like Dave Mason and Denny Laine have sometimes had to struggle to get their work accepted," Paul intoned at a 1968 New York press conference. "We want to help people, but without doing it like a charity. We're in the happy position of not needing any more money so for the first time the bosses aren't in it for profit. If you come to me and say, 'I've had such and such a dream' I'll say to you 'Here's so much money, go away and do it.'"

In reality, Apple was very quickly sinking under a deluge of tapes from hundreds of pop star wannabees. McCartney's commitment had suddenly rung hollow and the tapes were summarily tossed out.

The Apple record label, however, made an auspicious debut with the McCartney stalwart, "Hey Jude." "I happened to be driving out to see Cynthia," reveals Paul regarding the genesis of the now-classic tune. "I think it was just after John and she had broken up and I was quite mates with Julian. He's a nice kid. I was out in me car just vaguely singing this song and it was like, 'Hey Jules/Don't make it bad . . .' And then I just thought a better name was Jude. A bit more country and western for me.

"Once you get analyzing something and looking into it, things do begin to appear and do tie in. Because everything ties in and what you get depends on your approach. You look at everything with a black attitude and it's all black."

This marked quite a different attitude from his previous party line: "I never try to make any serious social point. Just words to go with the music, you can read anything into it you like."

McCartney credits Lennon for helping him decide to retain some of his initial phrases. "I was saying, 'These words won't be on the finished version,' . . . [but] John was saying, 'It's great!' I'm saying, 'It's crazy, it doesn't make any sense at all.' He's saying, 'Sure it does, it's great.' I'm always saying that, by the way. I'm always never sure if it's good enough. That's me, you know."

The first version of "Hey Jude," recorded at Abbey Road for a film feature about the music of Britain, was discarded and a second laid down at Trident Studios a day later, enlisting the services of a forty-piece orchestra. The musicians were used to hold single notes for long stretches as well as to clap and sing the "la la la" chorus.

"A special take," McCartney recalled of "Hey Jude." "In actual fact, Ringo was in the toilet. I started the song without drums, I thought he was in his drum booth. He heard me starting: 'Hey Jude, don't make it . . .' Hey, he does up his fly, leaps back into the studio and he's creeping past me. I'm doing this take realizing the drummer is trying to make his way back to the booth. He makes his way very quietly and just got there in time for his entry, so it was kind of a magic take."

But hardly magical in another sense, with McCartney resorting to his tired dictatorial ways. "I remember telling George not to play guitar. He wanted to echo riffs after the vocal phrases, which I didn't think was appropriate. He didn't see it like that and it was a bit of a number for me to have to *dare* to tell

George Harrison, who's one of the greats, not to play." An interesting comment—according to Harrison, his colleague never had problems vocalizing his wishes.

"It was like an insult," continued McCartney, "but that's how we did a lot of our stuff. The rule was, whosoever's song it was got to say how we did the arrangement for it. That pissed him off."

In 1980, Lennon suggested that the song's content was a personal message to him in the immediate aftermath of Yoko's appearance on the scene. Reading into the lyrics, John interpreted "Hey Jude" to mean "Hey John," and the line "Go out and get her" to mean, in effect, "Go ahead, leave me."

By this point, Yoko had successfully penetrated the Beatles' inner circle, having first been introduced at various Apple launch parties and the film premiere of *Yellow Submarine* on July 17. Eyebrows were raised among the three Fabs; the artsy Yoko just didn't seem to be a "Beatle woman," certainly not with her kooky art and outspoken views. Their allegiances had lain with the quiet and gracious stay-at-home, make-no-waves Cynthia.

But when Ono began showing up regularly at Abbey Road, breaking Lennon's longstanding unwritten rule of no women in the studio, she was pushing the avant-garde just a little too far. Lying stretched out atop the piano or perched on speakers, invading the control room, she even offered comments and suggestions about the recording.

To his credit, McCartney, realizing the couple's bond was such that verbalizing his feelings would only succeed in further driving a wedge between him and his old mate, suffered his lot in silence—except on one occasion. One EMI observer recalled how at one particular session Ono had begun to interfere with the development of several songs.

"I remember she turned to Paul and said, 'Why don't we try it this way?' He exploded and asked John: 'What the hell is going on? We never had anyone in the studio before. Why have we suddenly got somebody interfering in the way we work? Either she goes or I go.' John said, 'She's not going,' and Paul stormed out. It was about a week before they could get Paul back in the studio. That was the beginning of serious friction."

"Most galling of all," revealed Pete Shotton, "Yoko felt little hesitation about offering her own criticisms of their work [about which, of course, she knew next to nothing]. They also took vocal exception to the fact that John and Yoko expected Apple, i.e., the Beatles, to foot the bill for all the couple's artistic 'happenings.'

"At best, Yoko's presence tended to inhibit the other Fabs and stifle the extraordinary rapport the four musicians had heretofore enjoyed; at worst, Paul or George would let their resentment boil to the surface, thus putting John on the defensive and exacerbating tensions yet further."

It wasn't long before Ono's influence, complete with her caterwauling backing vocals, showed up on the blistering "Revolution," the B-side of the enormously popular "Hey Jude." McCartney was vocal about his dislike of the tune, charging that John's new paramour had given his music a distastefully hard and strident edge.

But to John, Yoko and her influences were a godsend.

> She inspired *all* this creation in me. It wasn't that she inspired the songs; she inspired *me*. The statement in "Revolution" is all mine. I wanted to put out what I felt about revolution; I thought it was time we fuckin' spoke out on it. The same as I thought it was about time we stopped not answering about the Vietnamese War when we were on tour with Brian and had to tell him, "We're going to talk about war this time and we're not going to waffle!" The lyrics stand today. They're still my feeling about politics: I want to see the *plan*.

John also accused his mates of trying to undermine the tune. "On the first take of 'Revolution' George and Paul were resentful and said it wasn't fast enough. But the Beatles could have afforded to put out the slow, understandable version whether it was a gold record or a fuckin' wooden one. But because they were so upset over the Yoko thing and the fact that I was again becoming as creative and dominating after lying fallow for a couple of years, it upset the apple cart."

As Pete Shotton viewed it, "Paul made little effort to mask his distaste for a few of John's more 'way out' compositions, specifically 'Revolution' and 'Revolution #9.' 'Revolution,' however, meant more to John at the time than any song he'd written in years and he was determined that it should appear as the A-side of the Beatles' next single. Apart from marking a return to the high-adrenalin no-frills rock 'n' roll that had always remained his first love, 'Revolution' was the first Beatles song to constitute an explicitly political statement. Which in turn is precisely why Paul felt so wary about it; nonpolitical to the core, he would have much preferred the Beatles to steer clear of such 'heavy' topics."

In fact, McCartney's views on the subject had been aired some three years previously, in October 1965, when he said, "We don't like protest songs, of course, because we're not the preaching sort and in any case we leave it to others to deliver messages of that kind."

When the single came out, many buyers believed they had purchased defective copies due to the muffled and distorted guitar sound. According to George Martin, that was done deliberately as John wanted a "dirty sound," and the only way to accomplish that was to overload one of the pre-amps.

Lennon, dissatisfied with his vocal, recorded it several times, but still didn't get it, mainly because he was so stoned. At last he resorted to lying down on his back on the studio floor while he sang the track.

In 1987 "Revolution" was utilized in a $7 million ad campaign for Nike Shoes over which Apple sued, claiming Nike used the Beatles "persona and goodwill" in its ads without permission. (Nike had licensed the rights to the song, but not the Beatles' version of it.) James Taylor, one of the first artists to sign with Apple, was dismayed. "For me and my generation, that song—I watched John Lennon creating at the Abbey Road Studios—was an honest statement about social change, really coming out and revealing how *he* felt. It was the truth, but now it refers to a *running shoe.*"

Creedence Clearwater Revival's John Fogerty chimed in, "I was one of the people who reacted violently the first time I saw the Nike commercial. I was really pissed off. I was mad, you know, because when Lennon wrote that song he wasn't doing it for the money. And to be using it for any corporate thing . . . it made me angry."

Meanwhile, in an abrupt turn, Paul and Jane were on the outs and a strawberry-blonde photographer from New York had breezed into McCartney's life faster than the click of her trusty Nikon. Linda Eastman first met McCartney at a press party marking the release of *Sgt. Pepper.* They were deep in conversation the entire evening and Paul later acknowledged, "Most people thought I was due to marry Jane Asher; I rather thought I was, too. But I just kept remembering Linda, this nice blonde American girl."

The development came as a shock to both insiders and outsiders; on Christmas Paul publicly announced his engagement to Jane, but Asher was adamant that all marriage plans were forever off. "Jane is obviously confused as to her priorities and is too selfishly caught up in her own career and doesn't see the obvious need to give it all up for me," McCartney said at the time. "That surprised me. True love should mean total devotion."

Apparently, though, that didn't quite cut both ways. "I was the biggest raver out," he confessed. "I didn't have one girl I could call a pal."

The blow-up with Asher finally erupted over one Francie Schwartz, a New York advertising copywriter who'd come to London in hopes of approaching McCartney to help produce a film she'd scripted. She soon settled into his St. John's Wood digs, apparently to replace Jane, away on yet another acting tour. Asher returned home unexpectedly and discovered the cozy scene at Cavendish Avenue, bringing an abrupt end to the five-year relationship.

For Francie, the incident served as a wake-up call. Shortly afterward, she, too, packed her bags and left. "Paul," she said later, "was an outrageous adolescent, a little Medici prince, powdered and laid on a satin pillow at an early age. But he was so pretty."

And Linda was there to pick up the pieces. One McCartney insider dubbed the opportunistic American a "yes-girl" whose clingy manner and blatant adoration seemed certain to turn off the independent bachelor.

But it was precisely this kind of all-out commitment McCartney was looking for. Family had always been very important to Paul, and he took an immediate liking to Linda's daughter, Heather. Moreover, Eastman was not out to hog the spotlight. "He was living with me, he knows I'm a good chick, he knows I don't have any bad motives," she pointed out. "I'm not a grabber, I'm not any of that."

In a situation mirroring John and Yoko's, Eastman soon found herself in considerable disfavor with the fans. After all, Jane was beautiful, innocent, waiflike; a serious actress from a fine family; a seemingly perfect match for the boyish, charming McCartney. Eastman, conversely, was depicted as an uppity New Yorker, the daughter of a big-time showbiz lawyer, a calculating divorcée out to sink her claws into their Paul.

"I was this ogre," recalled Linda. "I became a perfect foil. I was just a perfect person to knock in every way."

The Paul and Linda pairing symbolized the growing division between Lennon and McCartney. It was suddenly no longer Lennon-McCartney, but Lennon-Ono (or "JohnandYoko," as Lennon had taken to calling himself) and McCartney-Eastman.

A perceptive George Martin wisely noted, "I don't think Linda is a substitute for John Lennon any more than Yoko is a substitute for Paul McCartney."

This observation would sadly play out in a devastating final chapter. The tunesmiths each had begun to merge their personal and professional lives. It was the beginning of the end.

Burning Bush /
The Fall of Lennon and
McCartney

*P*ersonal upheavals aside, it was time to sift through material for the group's upcoming project. The public was clamoring for a new Beatles album, as it had been more than a year and a half since the release of *Sgt. Pepper.* The decision was made to release a double album, not only because of the backlog of tunes, but because Lennon and McCartney cleverly realized that they would owe EMI one less record under their current contract. It was a decision George Martin tried to overrule, arguing they didn't have enough first-rate material to fill four sides.

True enough, the work, comprised of a staggering ninety-four minutes of song, had its decided weak links, highlighted by Paul's insipid ditty "Rocky Raccoon." Nonetheless, the landmark album is packed with several stellar pieces over an eclectic mix of styles from country and western to blues, traditional Indian music and full tilt rock 'n' roll.

William Mann of the London *Times* called the work "inventive rather than creative.

"Even more than in *Sgt. Pepper,* the Lennon-McCartney numbers retraced already charted territory either to mock or further explore. There are overt references to their earlier songs, near-quotes from Indian and Greek poetry; while some tunes adopt the style of talking blues, shouting blues, rock 'n' roll, flamenco, and even the slushy ballad. There are too many private jokes and too much pastiche to convince me that Lennon and McCartney are still pressing forward with their race against other progressive composers. The genius is still there, though."

Artist Richard Hamilton suggested the white cover as distinctive in its simplicity and also as a contrast to the phantasmagoric technicolor splash of *Sgt.*

Pepper. In keeping with the understated artwork, the album—now known more commonly as the *White Album*—was officially called *The Beatles.*

Never was a title more ironic. Emblematic of the growing distance between Lennon and McCartney, this album, with only few exceptions, contains material each had written totally alone. "Every track is an individual track; there isn't any Beatles music on it," John pointed out. "It's like if you took each track off it and made it all mine and all George's. It was just me and a backing group, Paul and a backing group."

Although Lennon was critical about this fractured approach, he still chose this as his favorite Beatles album. "I thought the music was better," he stated simply. "The *Pepper* myth is bigger, but the music on the *White Album* is superior, I think. I wrote a lot of good shit on that."

More than ever, the album underscored that Lennon and McCartney were two individuals, poles apart in both composing styles and philosophy. Consider this trio of McCartney ditties: "Ob-La-Di, Ob-La-Da," "Martha My Dear," and "Honey Pie." All bear the familiar McCartney stamp of bouncy, toe-tapping, family entertainment. Infectious, but largely one-dimensional and ultimately lyrically inconsequential.

"Ob-La-Di, Ob-La-Da" includes an inadvertent gender-bender. The usually perfectionist Paul predictably recorded the vocal over and over again. Following one final take where he thought he'd given his best performance, Paul suddenly burst into laughter saying, "Oh shit! We'll have to do it all over again!"

"It sounded okay to me," John insisted.

"It was perfect," George nodded.

"But didn't you notice? I just sang, 'Desmond stays at home and does his pretty face' . . . I should've sung, 'Molly'!"

No one believed him until George Martin played back the tape. "Oh, it sounds great anyway," Paul finally concluded. "Let's just leave it in, create a bit of confusion there. Everyone will wonder whether Desmond's a bisexual or a transvestite."

Police drummer Stewart Copeland was quick to praise the song's construction. "Articulation of the words really should determine the overall riff of the whole thing. 'Ob-la-di' has an accent. 'Ob-la-da' has an accent, 'life goes on . . .' sort of leads you into that ska feel. There's a definite scansion to those lyrics, which is probably why they ended up playing a ska beat. In fact, that's one of the first examples of white reggae."

Lennon's own trilogy, in vivid contrast to McCartney's sunnyside-up perkiness, gave us the allusive "Glass Onion," the compelling "Happiness Is a Warm Gun," and the winsome "Julia."

"Glass Onion" finds John in a typically cynical mood, alluding in song to five previous Beatles songs. "Here's another clue for you all/The walrus is Paul," he sang.

Explained John, "I was having a laugh because there'd been so much gobbledegook written about *Pepper.* Even now I just saw Mel Tormé on TV the other day saying that 'Lucy' was written to promote drugs and so was 'A Little Help from My Friends,' and none of them were at all."

Highly unique lyrics earmarked the song, as Derek Taylor explains. "George told me John had been moved by a floral display peculiar to Parkes'—a haunt of the well-heeled in Beauchamp Place—whereby the designer bent tulip petals outwards and downwards to expose the stamen, pistil, etc. Hence . . . 'looking at the bent-back tulips/To see how the other half live,' i.e., the elusive rich and the secret parts of the flower."

Although Harrison deemed the song one of his favorites, Lennon dismissed it, and said that the reference to the walrus was simply a cover-up for his guilt over being with Yoko and leaving Paul. Said John, "It's a very perverse way of saying to Paul, 'Here have this crumb, this illusion, this stroke, because I'm leaving.'"

"Happiness Is a Warm Gun," hailed by McCartney as "my favorite on *The Beatles* album," was, once again, a product of Lennon's "stringing bits together." In fact, it was woven from some three pieces of different songs with complex imagery.

Incidentally, Ron Reagan, son of the former president, remembers borrowing the *White Album* from his sister, Patti, at the tender age of thirteen. "My mother got upset when she heard me listening to 'Happiness Is a Warm Gun.' It really bothered her a lot."

The delicately understated "Julia," according to Lennon, "was a combination of Yoko and my mother blended into one." John extended 20 percent credit to Yoko for the line "Julia oceanchild calls me" (*Yoko* literally means "ocean child") and 5 percent to poet Kahlil Gibran, "Julia seashell eyes," from *Sand and Foam.* This was the only piece performed totally on his own right down to the solo vocal and backing of two acoustic guitars.

McCartney, likewise, also managed to come up with a couple of genuine winners. This time it was the poignant "Blackbird." Although the song is said to have been inspired by a newspaper account of the 1968 race riots, the delicate tapestry does not appear to suggest such an intense metaphor. More likely is the suggestion that it was conceived in the tranquil setting of India.

When Eastman arrived from New York to shack up with McCartney, Paul was spotted perched on the windowsill with an acoustic guitar, serenading the lovely Linda with his new song. He'd also done the same for several lucky Apple scruffs who braved the often harsh London nights hanging around his front gate in hopes of catching a glimpse of the famous bachelor Beatle.

According to Alistair Taylor, who, along with Linda, was one of the first to hear the song, it changed dramatically from its inception to the finished piece. He explains,

> High up on a wall at the corner of Cavendish Avenue is an old gaslight. Paul stopped here, the dim rays of the lamp showing his ankle-length brown tweed coat and his acoustic guitar, which was suspended from his neck by a piece of frayed string. "I've just written a new song. Would you like to hear it?" Paul asked.
>
> And he gently took his guitar and, standing in the pale cone of light, sang very quietly, a haunting song about a blackbird with a broken wing. Paul's plaintive, boyish voice was the only sound in London, it seemed. Several yards away two fans stood, silent, happy that their long vigil had brought them this reward. Paul sang the song once, beautifully in the chilly street and then he slung the guitar across his shoulder and casually broke the spell.
>
> Later, Paul played me the demo of "Blackbird." I was terribly disappointed he had used all sorts of production effects which smothered the delicacy of what I'd been privileged to hear. A second demo even had bird noises added! Paul never could stand leaving a hole in a song unplugged.

The bird noises were, in fact, genuine blackbird calls recorded at his father's home in Liverpool. Taylor, by the way, wasn't the only one to question the inclusion of the sound effects. The overdubbing of the chirping was hotly debated in the studio. Nevertheless, the innate, stark beauty of the song manages to shine through the addition of percussion and double tracked vocals.

"Birthday," written in the studio, was Paul's answer to the fifties hit "Happy Birthday." Lennon rebuffed the catchy tune as "a piece of garbage."

Engineer Chris Thomas remembers, "Paul was the first one in and he was playing the 'Birthday' riff. Eventually the others arrived by which time Paul had literally written the song right there in the studio."

The melody featured a rollicking bass line by George, but what really percolated the tune was Paul's piano work at an old upright that was adjusted to affect a harpsichord sound. The background singers incidentally were none other than Yoko and Pattie Harrison.

If nothing else, the *White Album*, with its varied individual statements, was a preview of Lennon and McCartney's future solo ventures. For all its strengths, however, there were also many clearly delineated weaknesses. For one thing, John was not around to corral Paul's tendency toward triteness, especially by lending some bite to those tricky middle eights.

Conversely, John's "Revolution 9," voted by fans in the *Village Voice* as the "worst Beatles song ever," sharply demonstrated how Yoko had now overwhelmingly usurped Paul's position. McCartney despised the cut and wanted it pared down, and even George Harrison claimed he never listened to the whole thing. Although McCartney probably would have fought to keep it off the album altogether, his light touch might have made it more palatable, shaped it more rhythmically perhaps, even added a bit of melody. Yoko was the mastermind in this strident collage of tape loops and pieces of dialogue that build to a numbing crescendo of gunfire and over-the-top screaming.

Explained John, " 'Revolution 9' was an unconscious picture of what I actually think will happen when it happens. It was just like a drawing of revolution. I had about thirty loops going and fed them onto one basic track. I was getting classical tapes, going upstairs and chopping them up, making it backwards and things like that to get the sound effects. One thing was an engineer's testing tape and it would come on with a voice saying, 'This is EMI Test Series number nine.' I just cut up whatever he said and I'd number nine it."

After the track was finally laid down Lennon exuded, "*This* is the music of the future. You can forget all the rest of the shit we've done, this is it! *Everybody* will be making this stuff one day, you don't even have to know how to play a musical instrument to do it."

Oddly enough, "Revolution 9," coupled with the dreamy "Good Night," made the juxtaposition one of the most abrupt on record. Lennon's lazy lullaby, written for Julian, was appropriately given to Ringo to sing. The tune was winsome, but even Lennon, who told Martin to "arrange it like Hollywood—corny," admitted it was horrendously overdone. With a thirty-piece orchestra, plus harp, backed by an eight-member children's chorus, he was probably right.

During the five-month ordeal of putting together the thirty tracks, the Beatles juggernaut was beginning to seriously unravel. This was evidenced in the unexpected abdication by Ringo during the recording of "Back in the USSR." The discord had continued throughout the *White Album* recording, exacerbated once more by Paul's desire to do things his own way.

As Peter Brown recalls, "Most of the time [Ringo] spent in the studio he sat in a corner playing cards with Neil and Mal. It was a poorly kept secret among Beatle intimates that after Ringo left the studio Paul would often dub in the drum tracks himself. When Ringo returned to the studio the next day he would pretend not to notice that it was not his playing."

Tensions finally came to a head on August 22, the recording date of Paul's ballsy "Back in the USSR." McCartney openly chastised Starr for not getting his drum part right, thus causing an indignant Ringo to storm from the studio. "I'm sure it pissed Ringo off when he couldn't quite get the drums to 'Back in the USSR' and I sat in. It's very weird to know that you can do a thing someone else is having trouble with. If you get down and do it, just bluff right through it, you think, 'What the hell, at least I'm helping.' Then the paranoia comes in: 'But I'm going to show him up!' I was very sensitive to that."

Funny how Paul's so-called sensitivity emerged only after the damage was done and he'd once again gotten his way.

Commented Starr later on, "I felt I was playing like shit. And those three were really getting on. I had this feeling that nobody loved me; I felt horrible. So I said to myself, 'What am I doing here? Those three are getting along so well and I'm not even playing well.' That was madness, so I went away on holiday to sort things out. I don't know, maybe I was just paranoid. To play in a band you have to trust each other."

Ever the diplomat, however, the wily McCartney smoothed things over with Starr by luring him back with bouquets of flowers strewn over his drum kit. "When I came back everything was all right again," Ringo recounted. "Paul is the greatest bass player in the world. But he is also very determined; he goes on and on to see if he can get his own way. While that may be a virtue it did mean that musical disagreements inevitably arose from time to time."

Incidentally, Paul would cite Ringo's temporary defection as the first step in the Beatles' demise. "The real breakup of the Beatles was months ago," he'd say in 1970. "Ringo left while we were doing the *White Album* because he said he didn't think it was any fun playing with us anymore."

Starr, though, wasn't the only victim. McCartney had not only continued to tell George Harrison how to play his solos, but according to Harrison, turned a cold shoulder to his compositions. It has been suggested that Paul was growing resentful of Harrison's increasing writing ability; George managed to garner three tracks on the *White Album,* notably "While My Guitar Gently Weeps." It was one reason, said John, that Paul never liked the *White Album.* "He was always upset over it because on that one I did my music, he did his, and George did his. And first, he didn't like George having so many tracks, and second, he wanted it to be more of a group thing, which really means more Paul."

"Paul would always help out when you'd done *his* ten songs, then when we got 'round to doing one of my songs he would help. It was silly. It was very selfish, actually," Harrison said in 1977.

"George was writing more," tells Ringo. "He wanted things to go his way, where, when we first started, they basically went John and Paul's way. George was finding his independence and wouldn't be dominated as much by Paul."

"I was pissed off at Lennon and McCartney for the grief I was catching," says George. "I said I wasn't guilty of getting in the way of their careers. I said I wasn't guilty of leading them astray in our going to Rishikesh to see the Maharishi." The guitarist's frustrations would later appear in song on "Not Guilty," off the 1979 *George Harrison* album.

Justin DeVilleneuve, manager of sixties super model Twiggy and close McCartney friend, recalls the climate at Abbey Road during those days. "The strange thing was that when they were all together they went peculiar, as if an invisible barrier had fallen. Paul, my pal, blanked me completely; Ringo looked elsewhere; George gave me a long stare; John was the one I didn't know well—we were only nodding acquaintances—so I couldn't speak to him. After ten minutes talking to myself, I turned round, calling them 'fucking Scouse gits,' or words of that effect, and stormed out of the studio. Footsteps behind me. It was John. He put his arms round my shoulders. 'Sorry, Justin, we're a bunch of eyes fronts,' but he didn't say 'eyes fronts' if you get my gist. . . . The mad thing is, when I met Paul next he behaved as if nothing had happened. Weird. Together they were weird."

Also a strain on the band was the ongoing and increasingly disturbing presence of Yoko; by now an appendage to John, she followed him even into the bathroom. During pregnancies and other periods of delicate health she had a bed brought into the studio, complete with a microphone dangling overhead, ready to capture for posterity any moment of creative inspiration.

Defending herself, Yoko said in 1972, "Paul began complaining I was sitting too close to them when they were recording and that I should be in the background. He said to John, 'Do you have to spend so much time with her?' And we stood up to it. We just said, 'No. It's simply that we have to be together.'"

Added John, "Paul was always coming up to Yoko and saying, 'Why don't you keep in the background a bit more?' It was going on behind my back."

The bespectacled Beatle vented his feelings in a 1971 interview.

> They despised her. They insulted her and they still do. . . . They don't even know I can see it and even when it's written down it will look like I'm just paranoid or she's paranoid. . . . George insulted her right to her face in the Apple office at the beginning; just being "straightforward" you know, that game of, "Well, I'm going to be upfront because this is what we've heard. Dylan and a few people said she'd got a lousy name in New York and you gave off bad vibes." That's what George said to her and we both sat through it and I didn't hit him. I don't know why, but I was always hoping they would come around. . . . They all sat there with their wives like a fucking jury and judged us. . . . Ringo was all right, so was Maureen, but the other two really gave it to us. I'll never forgive them . . . although I can't help still loving them either.

George Martin confirmed the growing rift. "The disruption really came with the women. When you have very close personal relationships between two men and one of them goes off and gets a girl there's a divergence. I don't think Paul minded Yoko, Yoko's fine, nothing wrong with Yoko, except that she was *always* there. When she wasn't, well, she had a bed in the studio and the other boys got fed up with that. I think that was the beginning of it. And almost in self-defense Paul got Linda."

McCartney's opinion was typically tactful. "Maybe we should have taken to Yoko a little more. I often feel not too clever about not talking to her because we didn't get on too well. She was very different from anything we'd encountered. I figured, well, he loved her and I tried to respect her through him. But we were being so set against each other that his unreasonable bitterness was almost inevitable, I think. It's such a pity he felt that way."

Apparently the public saw the fray as fair game too, and in a particularly cruel move, posters began cropping up around London depicting a caricatured Ono as some hideous slanted-eyed beast perched on John's back with talons driving into his rounded shoulders. Lennon, in a more tolerant mood, penned his response in the rock 'n' roll nugget "Everybody's Got Something to Hide Except for Me and My Monkey." Letting it all slide off his back, he said, "We've got nothing to hide. Yoko inspires me, she doesn't destroy my ability to write good songs."

Another factor contributing to the ongoing turmoil was the absence of George Martin for the final two weeks of the project. With the Beatles' producer off on vacation, the production reins went to engineer Chris Thomas. Without Martin's presence, the project soon fell into disarray, according to technical engineer Brian Gibson. The original version of Paul's "Helter Skelter," recorded under Martin's guiding hand, was not the one to appear on the album. The second recording, done two months later, was the result of an absurd notion on Paul's part to imitate the Who.

"[Pete Townshend] said the Who made some track that was the loudest, most raucous rock 'n' roll, the dirtiest thing they'd ever done. It made me think, 'Right. Got to do it.' I like that kind of geeking up. And we decided to do the loudest, nastiest, sweatiest rock number we could do. That was 'Helter Skelter.'"

For the Beatles to try to outdo the Who was foolhardy. As Gibson confirmed, "The version on the album was way out of control. They were completely out of their heads that night. But a blind eye was turned to what the Beatles did in the studio. . . . They were really a law unto themselves."

The double album, released in America on November 25, 1968, was viewed as a triumph. Jann Wenner of *Rolling Stone* commented, "*The Beatles* is a history and synthesis of Western music," while authors Roy Carr and Tony Tyler cited the effort "Easily as good as anything they'd done. McCartney's material reveals the eclecticism which had always dodged him, he hardly ever falters [while] Lennon's unhappiness and resurgent iconoclasm came through powerfully."

Steven Spielberg remembers the impact the album had on him: "I resented [the Beatles] at first because it wasn't a fad I'd discovered for myself. I wasn't a Beatles fan until I listened to the *White Album,* but then I became an instant convert."

But even as the album piled up plaudits, the Beatles' day was on the wane. "The album," wrote Malcolm Doney, "was a collection of bits and pieces and stands as a memorial to the death of the Beatles. John Lennon and Paul

McCartney needed each other. It has become a truism now, but the Beatles myth was so strong in 1968 that no one saw past it into the story the music was telling."

Suddenly into the mix entered cult leader Charles Manson. In a bizarre set of interpretations, Manson took the meaning of the song "Helter Skelter" (*helter skelter* being the British term for an amusement-park slide) to indicate the apocalypse between the races he felt was forthcoming. The Beatles, he believed, represented the four angels of the Apocalypse and left personal messages throughout the album to prophesy a mass war about to erupt throughout the world. "Revolution 9," in Manson's mind, represented Revelation: Chapter Nine, which set the stage for Armaggedon, while "Blackbird" signified black revolutionaries, and Harrison's "Piggies," their white, establishment victims.

Manson and his "family" of troubled young people inferred from the *White Album* that it was their mission to trigger the apocalypse by carrying out the August 1969 Bel Air murders of actress Sharon Tate and the Leo LaBianca family. In the aftermath of the horrendous slayings, Mansonites scrawled slogans in blood at the crime scenes: "Helter Skelter" and "Political Piggy." Publicly it did the Beatles no good at all.

By the fall of 1968 Apple was slowly rotting away, losing a reported £20,000 a week from gross mismanagement and employee pilfering. First to go was the Apple Boutique, with other divisions soon to topple. Only Apple Records was left standing, with promising artists like James Taylor, Billy Preston, and Mary Hopkin, whose top-selling "Those Were the Days" managed to pay a few bills.

Bad news, however, just kept coming. On October 18, John and Yoko were busted for possession of one and a half ounces of cannabis. Lennon took the entire rap and was fined a mere £150, but the ramifications would erupt several years later when he would be refused a U.S. visa.

That November saw the release of John and Yoko's experimental *Two Virgins,* complete with its explicit cover exposing the pair "stark bullock naked." McCartney was reportedly outraged, not so much by the impropriety—after all, he had written on the sleeve, "When two great Saints meet, it is a humbling experience"—but rather how the fallout would affect sales of the *White Album,* where John also appeared nude, on the free poster included inside.

As John said in 1972, "Paul and Derek [Taylor] and all of them were in collusion to kill *Two Virgins.* They had meetings where Paul said, 'Let's kill it.' I sent a telegram to Neil because I'd heard that he'd been doing things behind my back and I said, 'Don't bite the hand that feeds you.' I was the one who protected him many times from Paul. Paul had no love for Neil and vice versa. And all of a sudden now he's a Paul man. They clung to Paul because they all thought he was the one who was going to hold it all together. You see, they were under the delusion that they are the Beatles. That they are the source of power."

As it turned out, *Two Virgins* was an unqualified disaster, limping to the 124 position on the charts and convincing absolutely no one that this was "the music of the future."

The work was certainly no threat to the *White Album,* which made more than $4 million in one month. Ironically, on the same day the record was released in Britain, November 21, Yoko suffered a miscarriage with life-threatening complications.

By now, McCartney knew he was on a sinking ship and was desperately searching for a lifeboat. "I said, why don't we make a film, it'd be great," remembers Paul. "So I slightly badgered them into it. At one point we were going to take a boat, an ocean liner, and make up a story about that, play in the ballroom or something. But the final idea was to go down to Twickenham to a big studio, rehearse, shoot the rehearsals and have this beautifully filmed concert at the end."

John, George, and Ringo were less than enthusiastic. "In a nutshell," John unveiled, "it was getting time for another Beatles movie or something so Paul thought up the idea of us playing live somewhere and then filming it raw, as it happened with no icing. But where? Someone mentioned the Coliseum in Rome and I think originally Paul might have even suggested a bloody boat in the middle of the ocean. As for me, I was rapidly warming to the idea of an asylum!"

Despite McCartney's bullheaded enthusiasm, no one really cared and it shows on film. "It was hell making *Let It Be,*" revealed Lennon. "When it came out, a lot of people complained about Yoko looking miserable. But even the world's biggest Beatle fan couldn't have sat through those six weeks of misery. It was the most miserable session on earth."

At least a partial explanation for the couple's bad experience with the film was that they were secretly using heroin. Rumor had it that Yoko first introduced John to the deadly drug back in July 1968, a claim which Ono hotly denies.

[We took it] as a celebration of ourselves as artists. George says it was me who got John on heroin, but that wasn't true. John wouldn't take anything he didn't want to.

John was just very curious. He asked if I'd ever tried it. I told him that while he was in India with the Maharishi I had a sniff in a party situation. I didn't know what it was. They just gave me something and I said, "What was that?" It was a beautiful feeling. John was talking about heroin one day and he said, "Did you ever take it?" and I told him about Paris. I said it wasn't bad, because the amount was small and I didn't get sick. It was just a nice feeling. So I told him that. When you take it, "properly" isn't the right word, but when you do a little more, you get sick right away if you're not used to it. So I think maybe because I said it wasn't a bad experience, that had something to do with John taking it.

Taking his first line at his and Yoko's temporary digs in Montague Square, Lennon discovered that he loved the comfy rush of the drug and snorted up gleefully at nearly every opportunity. "I felt," he later explained, "like a baby wrapped in cotton wool floating in water." The "baby," unfortunately, almost drowned.

Still, they managed to keep their habit under wraps from their cohorts as the Beatles' latest project pushed ahead. Originally entitled *Get Back,* a pointed reference to the more streamlined music of their glory days, the album's concept was one of a live performance with no fancy overdubs or overblown production. George Martin would be there to assist, but not to produce. All the Beatles had to do was turn up and play, just like they did in the old days in Liverpool and Hamburg when they were just a scruffy basement band.

But the old Thomas Wolfe adage, "You can't go home again," never rang truer. As work in the studio began on January 2, 1969, George Martin noted, "Right from the beginning, everything about *Let It Be* seemed to be out of sync with what we had done before. It was not at all a happy experience. It was a time when relations between the Beatles were at their lowest ebb."

The month-long project was filled with endless creative differences and even a defection, this time by George Harrison. On January 10, Harrison stormed off, mortally pissed off by the entire *Let It Be* plan. Just prior to the sessions, George had returned from America where he had enjoyed playing with a variety of musicians. The cooperation and atmosphere there contrasted dramatically with the deteriorating Beatles situation.

When I came back from the States I was in a very happy frame of mind, but I quickly discovered that I was up against the same old Paul. . . . In front of the cameras, as we were actually being filmed, Paul started to "get at" me about the way I was playing.

There's a scene where Paul and I are having an argument . . . and we're trying to cover it up. Then in the next scene I'm not there. Yoko's just screaming, doing her screeching number. Well, that's when I went home and wrote "Wah Wah" [later to appear on Harrison's 1970 *All Things Must Pass*]. I had such a headache with that whole argument.

Martin, witnessing the acrimony, added, "In order to get things together Paul would try to get everybody organized and would be rather over-bossy, which the other boys would dislike. But it was the only way of getting together. John would go wafting away with Yoko. George would say he wouldn't be coming in the following day. It was just a general disintegration."

Even the proposed raw, spontaneous feel went out the window with endless takes; on one song alone there were some sixty-seven versions.

The material was almost equally divided into hit-and-miss songs. McCartney's "Two of Us," a pleasant but bland ditty about his early relationship with Lennon, and John's "Dig a Pony," which he later declared "yet another piece of garbage," got the record off to an inauspicious beginning. "Dig It," the second and final track to credit all four Beatles, was merely a listing of famous persons and places, while "Maggie Mae," a traditional melody, was noted only for its historical significance in being a song performed by the Quarry Men at that now famous Woolton fête. "I've Got a Feeling" was the final song on which Lennon and McCartney shared equal writing duties, taking turns at the verses.

The album's noteworthy pieces are Lennon's two sterling contributions. The first, "Across the Universe," was another song to survive McCartney's alleged tampering. John called it, "One of my best songs, one of my favorites." Lennon penned the tune in 1967 after the words "pools of sorrow, waves of joy" leaped into his head. According to its author, the song simply came to him and demanded to be written. "It *drove* me out of bed. I didn't want to write it, I was just slightly irritable and I went downstairs and I couldn't get to sleep until I put it on paper."

Lennon categorized the tune's unusual meter as one he was never able to reproduce and, as for the extraordinary lyric "Words are flowing out like endless rain into a paper cup," he hadn't the slightest notion where they came from. Lloyd Rose of the *Boston Phoenix* wrote, "It's as if they had washed up on the beach of his mind, beautiful many-whorled shells complete in themselves."

Another vintage Lennon number is the infectious "One After 909," written nearly a decade before at Paul's house while cutting school. One of John's favorites, its references to the number nine in the title were part of a well-known Lennon obsession. He was born on the ninth, as was his son Sean; Brian Epstein spotted the Beatles at the Cavern on November 9, 1961, and secured a record deal on May 9, 1962. He also met Yoko on November 9, 1966. "It's just a number that's followed me around," he later commented.

Once again, the big three on this record belong to Paul McCartney, starting with the stirring "Get Back" (initially released as a single on April 11, 1969, in Britain and on May 5 in the States) to worldwide sales of over $4.5 million.

This universal number-one smash was created in the studio on the set of *Let It Be.* "A song to roller coaster by," Paul called it, distinguished by its stellar, thumping guitar work by Lennon, McCartney, and Harrison. Billy Preston took credit for the opening electric piano lick and was the first "guest artist" ever to be credited on a Beatles single.

One widely bootlegged version of the tune caused a bit of controversy over whether or not Beatle McCartney was, in fact, a racist, because it contained the lyrics "Don't dig no Pakistanis taking all the people's jobs."

McCartney, however, defended the work as staunchly antiracist. "There were a lot of stories in the newspapers then about Pakistanis crowding out flats, living sixteen to a room or whatever. So in one of the verses to 'Get Back,' which we were making up on the set of *Let It Be,* one of the outtakes has something about, 'Too many Pakistanis living in a council flat,' that's the line. Which to me, was talking *against* overcrowding for Pakistanis. . . . If there was any group that was not racist it was the Beatles. I mean, our favorite people were always black. We were kind of the first people to open international eyes, in a way, to Motown."

Lennon, who hailed the song as "a better version of 'Lady Madonna,'" also charged that it was a subtle put-down of Yoko, particularly the line, "Get back to where you once belonged." John submitted: "Every time he sang the line in the studio, he'd look at Yoko."

According to Lennon, the title track, "Let It Be," was Paul's reaction to "the shock of Yoko and what was happening," as John put it. McCartney's response to the chaotic state of the world was depicted in a child's clinging to his mother for security.

"Mother Mary," for a long time believed to be the Virgin Mary, was later revealed to be his own late mum. "I had a lot of bad times in the sixties," he confessed. "We used to lie in bed and wonder what was going on and feel quite paranoid. Probably all the drugs. I had a dream one night about my mother. She died when I was seventeen so I hadn't really heard from her in quite a while and it was very good. It gave me strength."

Known as the Beatles' swan song, Paul's wistful "The Long and Winding Road," complete with its "yeah yeah yeah" ending, took the group full circle. By the time it was released in May 1970, it was not at all the same tune Paul had initially recorded nearly a year and a half earlier. Considering the demoralized state the boys were in, they were not particularly enthusiastic over the results and, in fact, the entire *Let It Be* project was indefinitely shelved. But when Apple was sorely in need of the money their one remaining cash cow could desperately provide, Lennon and Harrison decided to give the tapes to famed producer Phil Spector to remix.

Lennon loved the results, saying shortly after its completion, "Phil listened to about one thousand million miles of tape, none of which had ever been marked or catalogued. Which is why the Beatles couldn't face the album, because there was too much shit and nobody was interested enough to pull it all together. And Phil pulled it together, remixed it, added a string or two here and there. I couldn't be bothered because it was such a tough one making it. We were really miserable then. Spector has redone the whole thing and it's beautiful."

McCartney, meanwhile, passionately disdained the final product. Nowhere was the often heavy hand of Spector more apparent than on "Winding Road." Extensive overdubbing of choir, strings, and harp had turned McCartney's unadorned ballad, backed by acoustic guitar and piano, into Spector's famous wall of sound. McCartney was so angered he tried, unsuccessfully, to get all the production extras removed.

"I couldn't believe it," he said of the final version. "I would *never* have female voices on a Beatles record."

Spector also added a heavenly choir plus an orchestra, perhaps more effectively, to "Across the Universe," Harrison's "I Me Mine," and "Let It Be." Gone, however, was the stripped-to-the-bone, down-home philosophy that had spawned the album originally.

Paul said, "The best version was before anyone got hold of it. Glyn Johns's early mixes were great, but they were very spartan; it would be one of the hippest records going if they brought it out. But before it had all its raw edges cut off, that was one of the best Beatles albums because it was a bit avant-garde. I loved it."

Even George Martin was critical of his longtime colleague. "I thought the orchestral work on it was totally uncharacteristic. We had established a particular style over the years . . . and I felt that what Phil Spector had done was not only uncharacteristic, but wrong. . . . I was totally disappointed with what happened to *Let It Be*."

The *Let It Be* reviews almost unanimously reflected these assertions. *Rolling Stone* stated, "The Beatles cast the fate of [their] get-back statement to the most notorious of over-producers."

Alan Smith of the *New Musical Express* callously ventured, "If *Let It Be* is to be their last then it will stand as a cheapskate epitaph, a cardboard tombstone, a sad and tatty end to a musical fusion which wiped clean and drew again the face of pop music."

As for the resulting *Let It Be* documentary, it gave a woefully accurate and closeup look at a band losing its wheels. The highlights lay mainly in the live performance sessions atop the Apple roof, notably of "One After 909" and "Get Back." But the bigger picture is seen in the listless response from his cohorts as Paul tries desperately to cajole, exhort, and even harass them to enthusiasm. Although it is somewhat tedious to watch, the film did well at the box office and earned an Academy Award for best original score.

Meanwhile, the sense of competition was still alive between Lennon and McCartney, this time in their personal lives: Within eight days of each other they each exchanged marriage vows. McCartney tied the knot with a pregnant Linda Eastman on March 12, 1969, at London's Marylebone Registry Office; Lennon and Ono married in Gibraltar on March 20 before conducting their very public Bed-In for Peace honeymoon in Amsterdam and Montreal that, more than anything, signaled Lennon's cutting ties with the Beatles.

"I think we spurred each other into marriage," said McCartney. "They were very strong together, which left me out of the picture, so then I got together with Linda and we got our own kind of strength. I think they were a little peeved that we got married first."

If fans disapproved of Linda replacing Jane Asher in Paul's affections, they were downright outraged by this sudden and permanent move. McCartney has commented on some of the stresses put upon him and his new bride. "To the world, of course, she was a divorcée, which didn't seem right. People preferred Jane Asher. Jane Asher fitted. . . . People tend to disapprove of me marrying a divorcée and an American. That wasn't too clever. None of that made a blind bit of difference though; I actually like her, I still do, and that's all it's to do with."

The media circus fallout from the Lennons' honeymoon cum antiwar campaign spawned the modest hit "The Ballad of John and Yoko." As usual, Lennon found himself embroiled in more controversy by retaining lines involving Christ and referring to crucifixion, which resulted in the song's being banned by both the BBC and numerous American radio stations. Where it received heavy play, however, the song hit number one, suggesting that if not for the ban it could have been a mega-success for Lennon and Apple.

McCartney attended the recording session on April 14, and together, with John on guitar and Paul on bass, drums, and piano, the two laid down the track. Flashes of the old camaraderie made for a spirited session with the two playing back and forth: "Go a bit faster, Ringo!" John kidded Paul while McCartney grinned, "Okay, George!" In fact, things went so well John later reciprocated by giving Paul coauthorship credit for "Give Peace a Chance," even though his partner had nothing whatsoever to do with it.

But the warm feelings didn't last. As spring unfolded, an event of enormous consequence took place: the official signing of Allen Klein as the Beatles' business manager. The New York mogul wasted no time in pruning the overrun Apple orchard, with wholesale firings right down to Peter Asher (Jane's brother) and even Ron Kass, head of Apple Records, the one division to show a profit. It was no secret that McCartney detested the brash, streetwise Klein, calling him "nothing but a New York–trained crook," and campaigned instead for Linda's father, the more refined and elegant Lee Eastman, to run their multimillion-dollar empire. John, meanwhile, trusted the self-made orphan who'd climbed his way to the top, feeling Klein's rough edges were more like his. "He's one of the lads, whereas Eastman and all them other people are automatons," quipped Lennon.

McCartney's refusal to recognize Klein as the Beatles' manager left Paul pitted against the other three. The house had become divided against itself and was now surely destined to fall. Still, Paul clung even more desperately to the group, wanting to wash the bitter taste of *Let It Be* from his memory. He approached George Martin with the proposition, "Let's get back and record like we used to. Would you produce an album like you used to?"

Martin cautiously agreed and the sessions commenced. "And that's how we made *Abbey Road,*" he explained. "It wasn't quite like the old days because they were still working on their own songs. And they would bring in other people to work as kind of musicians for them rather than being a team." In fact, when the project was completed, the first Beatles LP to be recorded on eight-track equipment, Martin hailed it as his favorite Beatles album.

Malcolm Doney observed, "The mutual challenge brought together some of the finest songs of Paul, John, and George. Musically it contained some of the best playing ever by all four of them. George's guitar lines have a fluidity he must have learned from his great friend Eric Clapton. Ringo's drumming was simple but eloquent. And John and Paul let their instruments speak as well as they ever did. *Abbey Road* shared the inner unity, the sense of singleness of purpose that *Sgt. Pepper* had. Each track flowed into the next."

Still, there was no getting around the fact that from a composing standpoint this was a package, fine as it was, of staunchly individual contributions. Even sides one and two were a creative split, with Lennon commandeering the former and McCartney the latter. "By the time we made *Abbey Road*," comments Paul, "John and I were openly critical of each other's music. I felt he wasn't much interested in performing anything he hadn't written himself."

If you'd have asked Lennon, it's fairly certain he would have said the exact same thing about Paul, which was just as well with both of them. But it wasn't very good for the Beatles. "We were never really close," Lennon said of McCartney. "But we were working so hard and so long, that's all we were ever doing. I thought very highly of him, of course, but ours was the sort of relationship I imagine soldiers develop during wartime. The situation forces them together and they make the most of it."

Work had actually begun in April 1969, with the labyrinthine "I Want You (She's So Heavy)." "This one's about Yoko," confirmed John. "She is very heavy and there was nothing else I could say about her other than, 'I want you, she's so heavy.'" One reviewer actually submitted, "He seems to have lost his talent for lyrics, it's so simple and boring."

But, in fact, Lennon asserted he was simply moving away from the layered Dylanesque manner of expression to streamline his images. "Like Yoko said, when you're drowning you don't say, 'I would be incredibly pleased if someone would have the foresight to notice me drowning and come and help me,' you just scream! And in 'She's So Heavy' I just sang, 'I want you, I want you so bad, she's so heavy, I want you,' like that. I started simplifying my lyrics then."

A pop torch song reminiscent of the late fifties was McCartney's "Oh! Darling." Paul prepared for the raspy-voiced rendition by coming into the studio early every morning and singing it by himself to achieve the gravelly effect. Noted second engineer Alan Parsons, "He'd come in and sing it and say, 'No that's not it, I'll try it again tomorrow.' He only tried it once per day. I suppose he wanted to capture a certain rawness which could only be done once before the voice changed. I remember him saying, 'Five years ago I could have done this in a flash,' referring, I suppose, to the days of 'Long Tall Sally' and 'Kansas City.'"

Praising the tune as one of Paul's greatest, Lennon was quick to add, "I always thought I could've done it better; it was more my style than his."

A McCartney tune that Lennon didn't dig at all was the whimsical "Maxwell's Silver Hammer." Its tinkling four-to-the-bar jauntiness conflicts with the bizarre subject matter of the quirky Maxwell thumping off everyone with his trusty tool.

"It's quite like 'Honey Pie,'" commented Harrison, "a fun song, but it's pretty sick because Maxwell keeps on killing everyone." But according to McCartney, serial murder was the last thing on his mind. "This epitomizes the downfalls in life. Just when everything is going smoothly, 'bang bang' down comes Maxwell's silver hammer and ruins everything."

His strange play on words (even Paul dubbed this "the corny one") is evidenced in the line ". . . studied pataphysical science in the home." McCartney drew this from a Parisian club called the Pataphysical Society, in reality a drinking club. "But to be a professor of pataphysics sounds great," he grinned.

Lennon said of the tune, "The Beatles can go on appealing to a wide audience as long as they make . . . nice little folk songs like 'Maxwell's Silver Hammer' for the grannies to dig."

Paul defended these so-called lightweight tunes by saying, "We are family grocers. You want yogurt, we give it to you. You want corn flakes, we have that too. Mums and Dads can't take some of our album stuff so we make it simple for them on the singles."

John's rumbling, funky "Come Together" drew its inception from an unusual source. Timothy Leary, who was pondering, of all things, a race for the California governorship against Ronald Reagan, asked Lennon to write a campaign song. Although he tried to produce one, all John could come up with was "Come Together," which was hardly ideal.

From that peculiar beginning Lennon found himself in hot water when he was sued for plagiarism for having allegedly pinched the opening melody and the first two lines from Chuck Berry's "You Can't Catch Me." Lennon insisted, "'Come Together' is *me,* writing obscurely around an old Chuck Berry thing."

The settlement, unlike the more serious George Harrison case of "subconscious plagiarism" from the Chiffons' "He's So Fine" for "My Sweet Lord," was simply that Lennon agreed to record three songs published by Big Seven Music: Berry's "Sweet Little Sixteen," the aforementioned "You Can't Catch Me," both on his 1975 *Rock 'n' Roll* LP, plus "Ya Ya" by Lee Dorsey and Morris Levy, which appeared on the 1974 *Walls and Bridges.*

While McCartney's slinky bass line defines the tune, in an eerie sidebar Lennon whispers the words, "Shoot me!" followed by a handclap. In view of John's tragic murder in December 1980, it is today very unnerving.

"On the finished record," clarifies Geoff Emerick, "you can really only hear the word 'shoot!' The bass guitar note falls where the 'me' is."

For McCartney, the session stands out for a rare bit of plaudits from his partner. "Whenever John did praise any of us it was great praise because he didn't dish it out much. If ever you got a speck of it, a crumb of it, you were quite grateful. With 'Come Together' for instance, he wanted a piano lick to be very swampy and smoky and I played it that way and he liked that a lot. I was quite pleased with that."

Just as Jane Asher opened the world of classical music to McCartney, so Lennon absorbed the genre via Yoko. Classical influences showed up on the floating "Because," which Nicholas Schaffner described as "a Beethoven sonata in a Hawaiian setting."

As Lennon remembered it, "I was lying on the sofa in our house listening to Yoko play Beethoven's 'Moonlight Sonata' on the piano. Suddenly I said, 'Can you play those chords backward?' She did and I wrote 'Because' around them."

McCartney and Harrison voted this track their favorite on the album, largely due to the exquisite three-part harmonies made into nine-part harmonies by recording the voices three times. Said Harrison, "It's so damn simple. The lyrics are uncomplicated, but the harmony was actually pretty difficult to sing. We had to really learn it, but I think it's one of the tunes that will definitely impress people."

In the midst of a heavy summer recording schedule to finish up the project, a wrench was thrown into the proceedings. On July 1, en route to Scotland, John and Yoko were involved in a serious automobile accident that sent them both to the hospital. The resulting intense pain, according to Yoko, got them back on heroin. Just when they'd managed to get a grip on their habit, they were seduced once more into addiction. Locking themselves away in Tittenhurst Park, their newly purchased 74-acre Ascot estate, they were content to submerge themselves deeper in their narcotic-induced lifestyle. Ironically, it was Paul, motivated by the urgent need to finish up the album, who hauled John from his bedroom to Abbey Road, where Yoko once again demanded that a bed be set up in the studio with a microphone.

At first, they tried unsuccessfully to withdraw in the swank London Clinic before deciding to kick the habit on their own. Explains Yoko, "We just went straight cold turkey. The thing is, because we never injected, I don't think we were sort of, well, we were hooked, but I don't think it was a great amount. Still, it was hard. Cold turkey is always hard."

Finally, by the morning of August 24, they had won the battle; to celebrate, John penned the harrowing "Cold Turkey" and tried to get it released as a Beatles single. Paul, however, would have none of it, and the song was instead released by John and Yoko's newly formed Plastic Ono Band. Banned by both the BBC and American radio stations for its explicit content, it did, however, manage to crawl into the British top twenty.

Lennon later defined his tussle with junk as a reaction to the previous two years of business, personal, and creative conflicts. "I never injected it or anything," he stated. "We sniffed a little when we were in real pain. I mean, people were giving us such a hard time. . . . I've had so much shit thrown at me and at Yoko, especially at Yoko. People like Peter Brown, after we came home from six months he comes down, shakes my hand and doesn't even say hello to her. We were getting so much pain we had to do something. . . . We took 'H' because of what the Beatles and their pals were doing to us. But we got out of it."

Several years after the fact McCartney reflected on his former partner's addiction: "I really didn't like that. Unfortunately, he was drifting away from us at that point, so none of us actually knew. He never told us; we heard rumors and we were very sad. But he'd embarked on a new course, which really involved anything and everything. Because John was that kind of guy he wanted to live life to the full as he saw it. John'd always wanted to jump off the cliff. He once said that to me, 'Have you ever thought of jumping?' I said, 'Fuck off. You jump and tell me how it is.' That's basically the difference in our personalities."

At this stage McCartney was finally coming to grips with his often overbearing tactics. "I was beginning to get too producery for everyone. George Martin was the actual producer, and I was beginning to be too definite.

Harrison and Ringo turned around and said, 'Look, piss off! We're grown-ups and we can do it without you!' For people like me who don't realize when they're being very overbearing it comes as a great surprise to be told. So I completely clammed up and backed off, 'Right, okay, they're right, I'm a turd.'"

But it was a lesson learned too late, as even the never-say-die McCartney finally accepted the Beatles' imminent demise. The clues are found on side two of *Abbey Road,* which launches McCartney's "pop opera," as Lennon dubbed it. The telltale "You Never Give Me Your Money," for instance, is a clear snipe at the ongoing Apple entanglements: "You never give me your money/You only give me your funny paper." The sixteen-minute medley includes three Lennon interludes: "Sun King," "Mean Mr. Mustard" (actually recorded as one song), and "Polythene Pam," sliding into McCartney's memorable "She Came in Through the Bathroom Window," again recorded as one song.

The latter had Paul recounting an incident whereby a fan broke into his home, making off with some items including a treasured photo of his father, the return of which he was forced to negotiate. Initially McCartney reserved the song for Joe Cocker, who eventually recorded it shortly after the Beatles' version.

"Golden Slumbers" owes its original inspiration to a four-hundred-year-old poem by Thomas Dekker. McCartney had run across the composition during a visit to his father's house in Cheshire in a songbook belonging to his stepsister, Ruth. "I thought it would be nice to write my own 'Golden Slumbers.' I can't read music and I couldn't remember the old tune so I started playing my tune to it and I liked the words so I just kept that."

The album concludes with the deliberate "Carry That Weight," an inference to the heavy burden that being Beatles had now become, leading naturally to "The End." But was Paul leaving the door open? John pointed out it was simply another case of his partner writing an unfinished song. He did, however, praise the line "The love you take is equal to the love you make" as "very cosmic, philosophical."

Almost as if by design, each Beatle had a turn on lead guitar one bar at a time, while Ringo performed a drum solo despite his natural aversion to such displays of showmanship. "We could never persuade Ringo to do a solo," says McCartney. "The only thing we ever persuaded him to do was that rumble on 'The End.' He said, 'I hate solos.'" The actual finale, the twenty-three-second tribute to the Queen of England, "Her Majesty," was never intended to wrap up Abbey Road. In fact, it was slated to be dropped in between "Mean Mr.

Mustard" and "Polythene Pam." John Kurlander, the second engineer, tagged it on the end by mistake. "This is why 'Her Majesty' doesn't have a final guitar chord—it lays, unheard, at the beginning of 'Polythene Pam.' And the jarring electric guitar chord that begins 'Her Majesty' is actually from the end of the original 'Mean Mr. Mustard,'" said Kurlander.

Although the collapse of the Apple business empire would legally spark the group's split, it was, at heart, a case of four individuals ready to move on, as evidenced by the solo albums soon released by all four: Harrison's *Wonderwall*, Starr's *Sentimental Journey*, McCartney's *McCartney*, and, of course, Lennon's freaky quartet: *Unfinished Music I & II, The Wedding Album*, plus *Plastic Ono Live Peace in Toronto.* The Beatles box could no longer hold them; it was a simple case of the sum of the parts now exceeding the whole.

Submitted Lennon, "In the old days Paul and I would knock off an LP together, but nowadays there's three of us writing equally good songs and needing that much more space. The problem is, do you make a double album every time, which takes six months of your life, or do you make only one? We spend a good three or four months making an album and maybe we get only two or three tracks on each LP. That's the main problem."

Creatively, John was also feeling stifled. "What was there to sing about? On *Abbey Road* I sing about Mean Mr. Mustard and Polythene Pam, but those are only bits of crap I wrote in India. When I get down to it I'm only interested in Yoko and peace. I don't write for the Beatles, I write for myself."

"There were just too many limitations based on our being together for so long, everybody was sort of pigeonholed," added Harrison.

Yet even with his magical empire collapsing around him, Paul refused to give up. One late September day in 1969 in an Apple meeting, he even suggested the Fab Four recharge their batteries by doing a tour of the club circuit.

Lennon launched a bombshell. "I think you're daft. In fact, I wasn't going to tell you, but I'm leaving the group. I've had enough. I want a divorce, like my divorce from Cynthia."

"Our jaws dropped," remembers Paul. "And then he went on to explain that it was a rather a good feelin' to get it off his chest, a bit like when he told his wife about a divorce, that he'd had a sort of feeling of relief. Which was very nice for him, but we didn't get much of a good feeling."

While the four agreed to keep quiet about the pending split, a nasty situation unfolded, swirling around Paul's first solo effort *McCartney.* Just as John had penned *Two Virgins* at Weybridge with Yoko, the situation was strikingly similar with Paul composing the tunes at High Park on a four-track machine, playing all the instruments with Linda on backup vocals: his own personal Declaration of Independence.

McCartney wanted the release date for April, but Klein moved to block him as April 17 was the scheduled release for *Let It Be.* Tempers were flaring and Ringo was sent in to mediate. At Paul's Cavendish Avenue home, Starr claims his bandmate finally went over the top. "He went completely out of control prodding his fingers towards my face saying, 'I'll finish you all now! You'll pay!' He told me to put on my coat and get out. Whether he was right or wrong I felt that since he was our friend and that the date was of such immense significance to him, we should let him have his own way."

The victory for McCartney, with the release of *Let It Be* pushed back to May, was a Pyrrhic one. With the official press release for *McCartney* was a self-penned interview, the proclamation, for all the world to see, that the Beatles were breaking up. Part of the extended transcript read:

Q: Are all these songs by Paul McCartney alone?
A: Yes, sir.
Q: Did you enjoy working as a solo?
A: Very much. I only had to ask me for a decision and I agreed with me. Remember, Linda's on it too, so it's really a double act.
Q: Will Paul and Linda become a John and Yoko?
A: No, they will become Paul and Linda.
Q: Are you planning a new album or single with the Beatles?
A: No.
Q: Do you foresee a time when Lennon-McCartney becomes an active songwriting team again?
A: No.

Lennon, as expected, was livid, accusing Paul of staging the announcement to coincide with his album release, to cash in at the expense of the other three.

"The Beatles were my fucking band," he later said. "I put the band together and I took it apart!"

Apparently Lennon had once before threatened to disband the group as far back as 1964 when Lew Grade offered Brian Epstein £100,000 for the Beatles.

"I told [Brian] if you sell we'll never play again. We'll disband. The funny thing was, when it was all over, Paul wanted credit for breaking up the band. 'I'm leaving,' he kept saying. But he couldn't because I had already left."

In retrospect, McCartney called his action "a dumb move." He said in 1986, "When I look back on it it looks very hard and cold. John got quite mad about that, apparently. This was one of the things he said really hurt him and cut him to the quick. Personally, I don't think it was such a bad thing to announce to the world after four months that we'd broken up. It had to come out sometime. I think maybe the manner of doing it I regret now, I wish it had been a little kinder or with the others' approval. But I felt it was time."

Ironically, the final single to be mixed by the Beatles, released on March 11, 1970, was the comic sizzler "You Know My Name, Look Up the Number," later voted the all-time favorite track by both John and Paul. Originally recorded over several sessions in 1967, Rolling Stones bad boy Brian Jones was recruited to play saxophone on the track.

"It was a real killer," Jones commented shortly afterward. "When Paul asked me along to play I'm sure he thought I would be playing guitar or something. For some reason, though, my driver, Tom Keylock, only packed the alto sax that morning so that's what I played. I remember the track was originally about twenty minutes long or something. There were all sorts of silly sound effects too that were tagged on, but later edited out. If memory serves, they were calling it 'Instrumental-Unidentified' or some such nonsense. Anyway, in the end it was a pretty good track even though there weren't any vocals on it. It was a good time, man."

"That was a piece of unfinished music I turned into a comedy record with Paul," Lennon recalled of the composition. "I was waiting for him in his house and I saw the phone book on the piano with the words, 'You know the name, look up the number.' That was like a logo and I just changed it."

McCartney, too, remembers the tune with great affection. "Probably my favorite Beatles track. Just because it's so insane. All the memories. I mean, what would you do if a guy like John Lennon turned up at the studio and said, 'I've got a new song.' I said, 'What's the words?' and he replied, 'You know my name, look up the number.' I asked, 'What's the rest of it?' 'No other words, those are the words. And I wanna do it like a mantra!'

"We had these endless, crazy sessions. It was just hilarious putting that record together. It's not a great melody or anything, it's just unique."

Sadly, those happy days were only fading echoes by December 1970. In an effort to dissolve the partnership, McCartney sought to file a lawsuit against manager Allen Klein, only to discover the sole way to free himself from the

Beatles was to also sue Apple Corps Ltd.—and that meant suing the Beatles. The divorce Lennon had alluded to was, in fact, cold, messy, and very public—the worst kind of celebrity litigation in which Paul was painted the heavy.

"I didn't leave the Beatles," he bitterly submitted. "The Beatles have left the Beatles, but no one wants to be the one to say the party's over."

Officially it would take nearly five years for the split to be finalized, initially hastened by the other three launching their own lawsuits against Klein, which undoubtedly gave McCartney some small measure of satisfaction.

George Martin said shortly after the split, "People talk about the breakup of the group as though it was a tragedy, which is nonsense. They don't say it's amazing how long they lasted together. What other group has lasted as successfully as they? And as amicably? For nearly a decade—it really is pretty remarkable. It's amazing to me, human nature being what it is, that they didn't break up earlier under the strain of superstardom. They were living in a golden prison all the time and not growing into individual lives. Now they're living individual lives and enjoying it. Good luck to them."

In the face of the public shock and outcry, Lennon downplayed the whole Fab phenomenon. "Whatever wind was blowing at the time moved the Beatles too. I'm not saying we weren't flags on the top of the ship; but the whole boat was moving. Maybe the Beatles were in the crow's nest shouting, 'Land ho,' or something like that, but we were all in the same boat."

Most significantly, the breakup of the Beatles marked the end of the Lennon-McCartney partnership. The blow of their professional demise notwithstanding, it was perhaps even more tragic on a personal level, this acrimonious and bitter rupture of two still very young men who'd once bonded through the loss of their mothers and found solace, and each other, in their music. Tony Bramwell, a keen Beatles watcher for many years as well as a close friend and former employee of the group, sums up the nuts and bolts of the incomparable Lennon-McCartney relationship:

> Although John and Paul very seldom tackled a songwriting project as a team of two equal contributors, each needed the other as a catalyst. Neither would admit dependence upon his partner in terms of creative abilities, but it's quite clear now with the benefit of hindsight that the duo's best work was done within the context of the Beatles.
>
> Of the two, Paul McCartney always appeared more confident to the

extent that he did occasionally believe that he had yet another new hit when it wasn't good enough, something common to most songwriters. That's where the basic benefit of working in collaboration with a pal who was also a rival talent took on a great value. Paul might get carried away over the strength of a tune he'd just penned. John might be full of satisfaction about a set of intricate lyrics he'd just worked out. In each case, the second opinion balanced truth against emotion and sensible compromises were struck.

By the time Lennon and McCartney finally called it quits, their legacy was staggering. They'd sold over $200 million in records worldwide. They'd earned Grammys, Oscars, numerous Novellos, they'd been film stars and filmmakers. They'd gone from teen heartthrobs to Members of the British Empire, and their music had been hailed as the best since Beethoven. They'd reached the toppermost of the poppermost. It was no surprise that they were eager to get on with their separate lives: What more could they accomplish? And yet, considering their extraordinary talents, it was a realization laced with both sadness and wonderment that they were leaving their best work behind before they'd even reached the age of thirty. And although they had found other partners, partners for life, and each would work with new collaborators, neither would come close to re-creating the indelible magic that was Lennon and McCartney. This, after all, was a partnership for the ages.

Chocolate Wings / Lennon and McCartney Alone

John Lennon once said, "You could say that [Paul] provided a lightness, an optimism, while I would always go for the sadness, the discord, the bluesy edge."

As the pair retreated back to their respective musical corners, these divergent philosophies would essentially define their solo careers. As McCartney put down roots in the bucolic Scottish highlands, gathering material from the warm, safe hub of family, Lennon laid anchor in New York City, whipping up the world's social conscience. Their respective song titles say it all: McCartney's "Hi Hi Hi," "Little Lamb Dragonfly," and "Silly Love Songs" contrasted with Lennon's "Power to the People," "Woman Is the Nigger of the World," and "Mind Games."

By the time the *McCartney* LP was issued in April 1970, John was an old hand at the solo game, already scoring the first gold record of any former Beatle for "Instant Karma." Although *McCartney* sold some 2 million copies, it was clear to critics and listeners alike that this was a feeble offering, one Paul himself called "nothing much."

One real diamond, though, was the passionate "Maybe I'm Amazed." "That was very much a song of the period," he said. "When you're in love with someone—I mean, God, this sounds soppy—but when you are in love and it's a *new* love like that, as it was for me and Linda with the Beatles breaking up, that was my feeling. Maybe I'm amazed at what's going on— maybe I'm not—but *maybe* I am! These were things happening at the time and these phrases were my symbol for them."

Denouncing Paul's album as "rubbish," Lennon said, "I think he'll make a better one when he's frightened into it. But I thought that first one was just a lot of crap. I think it [the Plastic Ono Band] would probably scare Paul into doing something decent. . . . I think he's capable of great work. He will do it. I can't see him doing *McCartney* twice."

Despite his more polished follow-up, whose title, according to McCartney, inspired him to "ram forward, press on, be positive," *Ram* was pounded by critics as vacuous puff littered with off-key harmonies by wife Linda. Still, to many, this author among them, *Ram* resonates with a childlike air that puts it right there with the composer's most original work.

It did, however, spawn McCartney's first number-one single as a solo artist with "Uncle Albert/Admiral Halsey." Cast in the title role was his real-life Uncle Albert, "a good bloke who used to get drunk and stand on the table and read passages from the Bible," revealed Paul. "I can never explain why I think of a particular person when I write. 'We're so sorry, Auntie Edna,' you know, it could have been her. I use these things like a painter uses colors."

Meanwhile, fresh from his "primal scream" therapy with Hollywood psychotherapist Arthur Janov, Lennon was releasing twenty-nine years of demons with his first Plastic Ono Band LP, anchored by the riveting anti-establishment anthem "Working Class Hero." This powerfully raw and elemental purging featured pungent lyrics framed within stark arrangements driven by Ringo's drumming and bassist Klaus Voormann's thumping lines. John called the LP his "Sgt. Lennon," the ultimate "concept album of life."

Critiqued John, "In one way it's terribly uncommercial, it's so miserable in a way and heavy, but it's reality and I'm not going to veer away from it for anything."

Sometime later Lennon also had this to say: "Songwriting is about getting the demon out of me. It's like being possessed. You try to go to sleep, but the song won't let you. So you have to get up and make it into something, and then you're allowed to sleep. . . . So letting go is what the whole game is. Every time you try to put your finger on it, it slips away."

Even as Lennon and McCartney forged ahead on their own, the Beatles still loomed as a painful memory. Freed from the group, the former partners volleyed rockets of acrimony at one another in the form of song. It began with McCartney's none too subtle remarks off *Ram,* right from the back cover depicting two beetles copulating, or as Lennon put it, "One beetle fucking another."

His musical shots aimed directly at Lennon included "Too Many People"— "Too many people preaching practices"—and the more overt "Dear Boy"— "Dear boy, I hope you never know how much you missed."

"Okay," admitted McCartney, "there was a little bit of it from my point of view, certain little lines, I'd be thinking, 'Well, this will get him.' You do, you know. Christ, you can't avoid it. 'Too Many People' I wrote a little bit in that. . . . He'd been doing a lot of preaching and it got up my nose a bit. That was a little dig at John and Yoko."

The response from Lennon was far more vitriolic. In his 1971 album, *Imagine,* John fired a fierce diatribe via "How Do You Sleep?" in which he said the only thing notable Paul had written was "Yesterday" and that "Those freaks was right when they said you was dead."

John likened it to the Dylan approach of character assassination. "It's using somebody as an object to create something. I wasn't really feeling that vicious at the time, but I *was* using my resentment towards Paul to create a song. . . . There were a few little digs on *his* albums, which he kept so obscure that other people didn't notice 'em."

This began a feud that would continue in public, Paul calling John a "maneuvering swine" while Lennon derided his former partner with taunts of "Englebert Humperdink." The following bitter exchange took place in the *Melody Maker:*

PAUL: I just want the four of us to get together somewhere and sign a piece of paper saying it's all over and we want to divide the money four ways. . . . But John won't do it. Everybody thinks I'm the aggressor, but I'm not. I just want out.

JOHN: For the millionth time. . . . I repeat, what about the *tax*? It's all very well playing "simple honest ole human Paul" in the *Melody Maker,* but you know damn well we can't just sign a bit of paper. You say, "John won't do it." I will if you *indemnify* us against the tax man! . . . If *you're* not the aggressor (as you claim) who the hell took us to court and shit all over us in public?

PAUL: John and Yoko are not cool in what they're doing.

JOHN: If *we're* not cool, *what does that make you?*

PAUL: I like . . . *Imagine,* but there was too much political stuff on the other albums.

JOHN: So you think *Imagine* ain't political, it's "Working Class Hero" with sugar on it for conservatives like yourself!

Paul admitted he was deeply hurt by all the slagging off, a product of jealousies inherent in their life-long love/hate relationship. "I hated it. You can imagine, I sat down and pored over every little paragraph, every little sentence. 'Does he really think that of me?' Gradually I started to think, 'Great, that's not true. I'm not really like Engelbert; I don't just write ballads.' And that kept me kind of hangin' on; but at the time, I tell you, it hurt me."

For the record, though, McCartney did offer an olive branch via the song "Dear Friend," off his Wings' *Wild Life* LP.

"It was written for John, to John. It was like a letter. With the business pressures of the Beatles breaking up it's like a marriage. One minute you're in love, the next minute you hate each other's guts. It's a pity, because it's very difficult to cut through all that. So you do what we all seemed to do, which was write it in songs. I wrote 'Dear Friend' as a kind of peace gesture."

Although John never publicly acknowledged this attempt at fence-mending, McCartney said in 1987 that it was a gesture that "got through. . . . Thank the Lord, because otherwise it would have just been terrible. I would have brooded on the fact that we were always bitching with each other forever."

In 1971, Lennon beat his old partner to the LP hit parade with the million-seller *Imagine.* Far from the starkness of *Plastic Ono* and the general weirdness of *Unfinished Music,* this LP, under the guiding hand of Phil Spector, was more musically layered, with guest appearances by Badfinger's Tom Evans and Joey Molland; pianist extraordinaire Nicky Hopkins; saxophone legend King Curtis; and even John's old mate George Harrison. From the touching love ballad to Yoko, "Oh My Love," to the hypocrite-bashing "Gimme Me Some Truth," to the vulnerable, apologetic "Jealous Guy," Lennon's refreshing genius, coupled with the record's Beatlelike sound, struck a positive chord with record buyers.

But it was the title track that quickly became the Lennon standard-bearer. "Imagine," with its simple piano backing, affectingly fragile vocal, and utopian message, was ripe for the quixotic times yet remains a classic to this day. It was written in typical Lennon style, while on an airplane on the back of a hotel bill.

Comedian turned activist Dick Gregory gave John and Yoko a booklet dealing with the concept of positive prayer, whose precepts closely mirrored Lennon's own antiwar philosophy. "All you have to do is imagine it; if you can *imagine* a world at peace, then it can be."

Once again, it was Lennon's work that dominated the charts just as it did in the early days of the Beatles. His singles, "Give Peace a Chance," "Happy

Xmas," and "Instant Karma," all sailed into the top five, proving, at least in the initial stages, that John was a formidable force as a solo artist.

While Lennon was out pursuing this stellar success, McCartney was busy getting his own new band together. Wings, named in a moment of McCartney familial bliss, introduced a lineup that included Denny Seiwell on drums, guitarist and founder of the Moody Blues Denny Laine, and Linda, who would pick her way along on the keyboard. The decision to include Linda in the band causes great controversy to this day.

Paul, shedding the excessive trappings of the Beatles, led what was essentially a band of gypsy troubadours traveling the club and university circuit in caravans. Even Lennon was envious of his old mate's new venture.

"I kind of admire the way Paul started from scratch, forming a new band and playing small dance halls because that's what he wanted to do with the Beatles, he wanted us to go back to the dance halls and experience that again."

The group's fledgling effort, *Wild Life,* recorded in over just two weeks, was a critical and commercial disaster, tainted by such mindless pap as the innocuous "Bip Bop" and "Mary Had a Little Lamb." At his most terminally insufferable, McCartney gave critics like Tony Palmer full rein to lower the boom: "McCartney is a lyricist of dubious sentimentality [who] still whistles tinkly little tunes which please the Mums and Hayley Mills."

Historically adept at taking these slings and arrows, Paul finally shot back in 1980, saying, "Nearly everything I've ever done or been involved in has received some negative critical reaction. You'd think the response to something like 'She Loves You' with the Beatles would have been pretty positive. It wasn't. The very first week that came out it was supposed to be the worst song the Beatles had ever thought of."

Even the scrutinizing Lennon hailed the next Wings effort: "*Band on the Run* is a great album. Wings is almost as conceptual a group as Plastic Ono Band. I mean, they're back-up men for Paul. It doesn't matter who's playing. You can call them Wings, but it's Paul McCartney music. And it's good stuff. It's good Paul music."

Meanwhile, rampant rumors of a Beatles reunion left fans on a roller coaster of raised and dashed hopes. The interest refused to die down, largely due to promoters offering incredible incentives, each more lucrative than the last. Two of the biggest came in 1976. Bill Sargent, a West Coast entrepreneur, offered the Fabs $50 million for a July 5 concert in Montreal.

New York promotor Sid Bernstein shamelessly fed on the sympathy factor by penning an open letter in *The New York Times* saying the Beatles must reunite for the sake of world harmony. "In a world that seems so hopelessly divided, engaged in civil war, scarred by earthquakes and too often in fear of tomorrow's encores of tragic headlines, more than ever, we need a symbol of hope for the future. . . . Let the world smile for one day. Let us change the headlines from gloom and hopelessness to music and life and a worldwide message of peace. You are among the very few who are in a position to make the dream of a better world come together in the hearts of millions in just one day."

As George Harrison told this author in 1983, "All this stuff about the Beatles being able to save the world was rubbish. The thing about the Beatles is that they saved the world from boredom."

Chimed Ringo, "The silliness goes on even without us."

John, though, delivered the most passionate rendering. "Don't you think the Beatles gave every sodding thing they had? That took our whole lives . . . a whole section of our youth. When everybody else was just goofing off we were working twenty-four hours a day."

Even George Martin concurred. "I think it would be a terrible mistake for them ever to go into the studio together. . . . Whenever you try to recapture something that existed before you're walking on dangerous ground, like when you go back to a place that you loved as a child and you find that it's been rebuilt. It destroys your illusions."

It was Paul, predictably, who kept his options open, carefully treading the waters of possibility. "For me, the only way the Beatles could come back together again would be if we wanted to do something musically, not lukewarm, just for the money. . . . But I know my feeling and I think the others' feeling in a way is we don't want to close the door to anything in the future. We might like it someday."

Meanwhile, as McCartney and Wings were touring the world, piling up hit after hit, Lennon was undergoing yet another crisis. His split from Yoko in the fall of 1973 spiraled into his famed eighteen-month "lost weekend" and caught everyone, including close friends, off guard. His famous offhand explanation, "I went out one day and didn't come back," belied the far more precarious state he was in.

Being with Yoko literally twenty-four hours a day had turned Lennon into a nervous chain smoker who'd drifted into some very serious drinking. John had become far too dependent on her, Ono claimed, and she shuffled him off to Los Angeles to work with Phil Spector on an album of rock classics simply entitled *John Lennon Rock 'n' Roll.*

There Lennon became a public spectacle, engaging in one drunken display after another. "It was one big hangover," as he described it. Yoko, however, was never very far out of the picture, conducting a tailor-made therapy for John that included a carefully manipulated fling with their young personal secretary, May Pang.

Yoko's orchestrated maneuvers finally reaped rewards on several fronts. Out of the experience came Lennon's cathartic *Walls and Bridges,* a forthright musical diary of his painful bloodletting. "I got the title," he unveiled, "from one of those public service announcements I'm always watching on TV. . . . I heard the phrase 'walls and bridges,' and filed it in my head because I liked it."

"Scared," for example, portrays John's fears about growing older and being alone while "Nobody Loves You When You're Down and Out" depicted the combination of profound depression and alcoholic haze John was suffering from; he was so dysfunctional he couldn't even record the song until he returned to New York. The purposely vague "Steel and Glass" was thought by many to again be about Paul with lines like, "Your teeth are clean, but your mind is capped." The fact is, it was about the unhappy composer himself.

His bottoming out led him, oddly enough, to a friendship with Elton John. During the sessions for *Walls and Bridges,* Elton showed up, playing piano on the rocking "Whatever Gets You Through the Night." The cagey Elton then proposed that if the song made it to number one Lennon would have to appear with him on stage. John called it "a shot in the arm."

As the tune catapulted to the top slot, Lennon made good on his promise, joining Elton during a Thanksgiving 1974 concert at Madison Square Garden before a surprised and nearly hysterical crowd. "I was very moved by it. . . . It was a great high night, a really high night," he admitted.

The occasion capped off Lennon's full comeback as well as his reunion with Yoko, who'd been in the audience and made her way backstage. "The separation didn't work out," John announced. "We got back together because we *love* each other. I've been on Sinbad's voyage, you know. I've battled all those monsters and I've got back."

Paul almost enviously commented, "John was lucky. He got all his hurt out. I'm a different sort of personality. There's still a lot inside me that's trying to work its way out."

For the emotionally tight-lipped McCartney, these few lines spoke volumes about his inability to express his deepest feelings and finally provided a clue to his often superficial approach to songwriting.

Just when Lennon had honed himself into the best physical and mental state of his life, to the shock of friends and fans alike, he retreated into a five-year hiatus to play house-husband and raise his second son, Sean. His hibernation, however, began a slow mending of fences with McCartney. Initially, John resented Paul's intrusions, telling his former partner when he impulsively showed up at the Dakota, "We're not in Liverpool anymore, do you mind calling before you come round next time?"

McCartney recalled his follow-up attempts to contact his old pal. "I happened to be on my way to the Caribbean, so passing through New York I rang John up. But there was so much suspicion even though I came bearing the olive branch. I said, 'Hey, I'd like to see you.' He said, 'What for? What do you *really* want?' It was very difficult. Finally he had a great line for me: He said 'You're all pizza and fairy tales.' He'd become sort of Americanized by then so the best insult I could think of was to say 'Oh, fuck off, Kojak' and slam the phone down. . . . That was about the strength of our relationship back then, very, very bitter and we didn't get over that for a long, long time.

"At the very end," said McCartney, "we suddenly realized that all we had to do was not mention Apple if we phoned one another. We could talk about the kids, talk about his cats, talk about writing songs; the one paramount thing was not to mention Apple. . . . I remember he once said to me, 'Do they play me against you like they play you against me?' Because there were always people in the background pitting us against each other. And I said, 'Yeah they do. They sure do!'"

To John, Paul represented the past and its pain, wounds that were still far too fresh. To McCartney's credit, though, he refused to back off and finally won over his old friend. "He visits me every time he's in New York like all the other rock 'n' roll creeps," said John good-naturedly. "He comes over and we just sit around and get mildly drunk and reminisce!"

The year 1980 proved fateful. January marked McCartney's notorious Japanese drug bust, in which he was jailed for possession of marijuana and summarily kicked out of the country. According to John's personal assistant, Fred Seaman, Lennon followed the story with gleeful relish, asking Seaman's father to buy all the British papers so he and Yoko could share a good laugh over Paul's predicament. "I can just picture Paul sitting in a bare jail cell,"

John said. "They've taken away his shoelaces and his belt so he won't hang himself if he becomes despondent singing: 'Yesterday, all my troubles seemed so far away.'"

It was Lennon's theory that Paul subconsciously wanted to get busted "to show the world he's still a bad boy."

Nineteen-eighty signaled the end of Wings as well, fueled by Denny Laine's bitter defection. The band's guitarist charged that Paul had cheated him out of millions in royalties and left him uncredited in several key compositions he claimed to have coauthored.

The grounding of Wings ended an astounding chapter in music history. Over the group's decade-long tenure they sold more records than even the Beatles!

In the cruelest of ironies, December marked a new beginning for Lennon with his first release in five years, the melodic, challenging, and eminently listenable *Double Fantasy*. This was John Lennon hitting forty, fully mature and finally at peace, taking on McCartney-like themes of home and family and displaying a tender, settled, even sentimental side. The titles were an eloquent testimony to his newfound serenity: "Beautiful Boy," written for Sean; "Woman," a tribute to not only Yoko, but women everywhere; and the anthemic "Hard Times Are Over."

Of the first hit single from the LP, "Starting Over," Lennon remarked, "That's just what I'm doing. It took me forty years to grow up. I'm saying 'Here I am, now how are you? How's your relationship going? Did you get through it all? Wasn't the seventies a drag? Well, here we are, let's make the eighties great."

But this, his final work, had far deeper roots. Even ten years removed from his partnership with McCartney, Lennon was still taking up the gauntlet, according to Fred Seaman. "I realized that after years of lying dormant, John's competitive nature had been aroused again. As long as Paul kept turning out mediocre 'product,' John felt justified in keeping his own muse on a shelf. But if Paul were writing decent music, then John felt compelled to take up Paul's challenge. It was a conditioned reflex, nurtured during years of friendly (and later fierce) rivalry in the Beatles. John told me that Paul was the only musician who could scare him into writing great songs, and vice versa. That was the nature of John and Paul's relationship: creative sibling rivalry."

McCartney biographer Chet Flippo put it this way: "John and Paul badly needed each other in the musical process. Not in writing, actually, because they had quit truly writing together years earlier. It was the bullshit detector that each brought to the other's work. . . . John and Paul always brought out the best in each other and discouraged the worst."

The most shocking blow of all came on December 8, 1980, at 10:49 P.M., when Lennon was brutally cut down outside his Dakota apartment home by a faceless punk with a cheap Charter Arms revolver. The artist's obsession with number nine stood even to the end, as John's passing came within one hour of December 9. Back in Liverpool it was already the ninth.

When informed of the tragic news, McCartney's public response, "It's a drag," was grossly misunderstood. Explains Paul, "When John was killed somebody stuck a microphone [in my face] and said 'What do you think about it?' I said 'It's a dra-a-ag' and meant it with every inch of melancholy I could muster. When you put that in print it says, 'McCartney in London today when asked for a comment on his dead friend said, "It's a drag."'' It seemed a very flippant comment to make."

In reality, affirms McCartney, he was overcome with grief, gathering his family close and crying for days. "We just couldn't handle it, really," he confessed.

"I talked to Yoko the day after he was killed and the first thing she said was, 'John was really fond of you.' The last telephone conversation I had with him we were still the best of mates. He was always a very warm guy, John. His bluff was all on the surface. He used to take his glasses down—those granny glasses—and say, 'It's only me.' They were like a wall, you know? A shield. Those are the moments I treasure."

Only much later, nearly a decade after Lennon's death, was McCartney able to assess the depth of the acrimony centered around Yoko. At a Sotheby's auction he came across an Apple booklet with John's comments in the margins. One, for example, showed a photo of Paul and Linda's wedding where John had crossed out "wedding" and scribbled in "funeral." Under another photo depicting the set of *Let It Be,* the caption reads "Paul goes to Hollywood." John added "to cut Yoko and John out of the film." Said Paul in 1986, "A lot of the accusations John made in public were slightly wild. Maybe we should've taken to Yoko a little better. I often *do* feel not too clever about not talking to her because we didn't get on too well. She was very different from anything we'd encountered. A lot of people still find her a little difficult to take. I felt I tried to . . . respect her through him. But we were being so set against each other that his unreasonable bitterness was almost inevitable. It's such a pity he felt that way. But the bottom line is we loved each other."

Double Fantasy swept into mass popularity, in part due to the tragic circumstances, and sold seven million copies in seven months. Meanwhile, McCartney found himself once again on his own, launching himself for the second time as a solo artist. The albums he put out over the next decade, unfortunately, signaled a steady creative and commercial decline.

Interestingly, he wrote poignantly of his relationship with Lennon in "Here Today," off *Tug of War*. Behind a subtle string quartet Paul sang, "I am holding back the tears no more/I love you."

"We actually did know each other, we were very close," he acknowledged.

Still, it seemed McCartney needed Lennon more than ever. He was unable to sustain that high level with three straight commercial and critical bombs: The well-intentioned but largely ignored *Pipes of Peace,* the limp film flop *Give My Regards to Broad Street* (pulled from theaters after just three days), and the only occasionally engrossing *Press to Play* represented the worst showing of his career.

It appeared he'd lost his touch.

Proving his seemingly endless resilience, Paul rebounded with the universally acclaimed *Flowers in the Dirt.* The album's success was largely due to Paul's four-song collaboration with Elvis Costello, whose personality curiously resembles that of John Lennon.

"Elvis is a very good foil for me," Paul said in 1989. "With Elvis, it's you're opinionated, narrow-minded, and full of yourself, but I like that in a guy!"

On one joint effort, "You Want Her Too," McCartney reveals in the liner notes, "My God, that's me and John's whole style. I'd write some romantic line and John does some sort of acid acerbic put down."

The album reached number one in Britain, if only for one week.

As for John and Paul's permanent partners, Yoko and Linda, their impact was often overstated by their prejudicial husbands. Linda, for one, never claimed to be a real creative force with Paul, despite his naming her cowriter on several tunes and her self-penned reggae composition "Seaside Woman." Yoko possessed more artistic flair perhaps, but despite John's dubbing her the power behind the throne, her input was essentially in driving John to cross boundaries that he probably would not have explored on his own.

As John Rockwell wrote in *The New York Times,* "His touted avant gardism never quite rings true. John was, at heart, a rock & roller until the moment he died."

The question of talent notwithstanding, Linda and Yoko were too similar to their husbands to make effective collaborators. As Pete Shotton put it,

"Linda reinforced Paul's bourgeois aspirations as surely as Yoko brought out the subversive artist in John." On his post-Beatle efforts, John clearly could have benefitted from Paul's subtlety. His solo work was often overbearing, with the too-frequent overt full frontal relentless attack that characterized 1973's appalling *Sometime in New York City*. Radical, clichéd images of the Attica prison uprising, women's lib, and Irish politics, all no doubt spurred on by Yoko, became a major turn-off even for the most ardent Lennon followers. Moreover, John's persona of the working-class hero often unintentionally crossed the line to the role of martyr, which he despised.

By the same token, Paul desperately needed John's drop kick out of the complacency in which he too often wallowed. "The greed is gone," he admitted in the early 1990s. "If you get a bit content then you might not write savage lyrics and stuff."

It is particularly revealing to note that Paul's greatest success came when he teamed up with others: Denny Laine, Stevie Wonder, Michael Jackson, and Elvis Costello. It's not so much a case of needing their creativity, but more as a vital sounding board.

As George Harrison observed in a 1988 interview, "Paul should work with various other people and hopefully he'll find somebody who will actually tell him something because most people who work with Paul are afraid to say anything to him. And I think that's no good. You need to have somebody you can work with who'll tell you you're no good when you're no good. Otherwise, it's no help at all."

As Lennon once said, "It's easier to say what my contribution was to him than what he gave to me." Which is probably true. *Double Fantasy* was proof that, on his own, Lennon could please the mass, middle-of-the-road audience as well as the more culturally aware without compromising his artistic integrity.

Still, when the public at large list their favorite Beatles songs, it's generally Paul's titles they'll cite: "Yesterday," "Hey Jude," "Michelle," or "All My Loving." According to George Martin, sentiment generally wins over substance. "It's quite likely," he observed back in the early eighties, "that, in terms of success, Paul's songs will last longer than John's because they get more to the average man, to the heartstrings, than John's did. That's being really commercial about it. But personally, I couldn't put a cigarette paper between them."

In the end, the genius that was Lennon and McCartney was in the combination, their wholly unique chemical reaction. "It only really worked with the two of them," noted Malcolm Doney. "When they wrote together, sparks flew. Each with their individual genius was able to counterpoint the other, excess held in check, a creative clash of opposites. What they produced is evidence of a pairing of minds that transcended the mechanics of the making." Author Ross Benson has his own take on the indelible magic of this incomparable partnership. "One of the best things about Lennon-McCartney arose, not out of their similarities, but out of their differences: McCartney, smiling, pert, ever the matinee man, Lennon drawing off the vein of a dark appeal; Lennon a continuous improvisation, McCartney hanging on tight to conventional values; contradictory yet complementary."

Both understood and appreciated this all too rare gift and, in addressing it, revealed the pride in their teamwork. Stated Paul in 1990, "I've collaborated with Lennon, and anybody else will not be as good, which I still do feel; if you've written with the best who else is going to be as good?"

Echoed John, "I had two great partners, Paul and Yoko. And I discovered both of them. That isn't bad going, is it?"

Meanwhile, the Paul McCartney of the nineties has stepped into the comfortable shoes of pop's elder statesman, still putting out records and music videos, if far off the chart-busting path he once so routinely traveled. He also uses his celebrity in other ways these days, to promote kinder and gentler, politically correct issues such as the preservation of the rain forests and animal rights.

Musically, though, he's still willing to take chances. His 1991 ninety-minute choral undertaking, *Paul McCartney's Liverpool Oratorio,* two years in the making, was a monumental stretch. Yet, even in this classical arena the shadows of Lennon still haunt. *The Guardian*'s Paul Fisher wrote, "McCartney's literary self is more uncertain than his musical self and the sugary libretto needed an editor with even a fraction of Lennon's cynicism."

He is still a commanding, energetic presence on stage, performing to sold-out venues on worldwide tours, serving up Beatles chestnuts, coming to terms with his inherited role of keeper of the flame.

By 1995, the long-awaited Beatles reunion seemed to be finally coming to pass. *The Beatles Anthology,* a documentary and CD project in the works for many years, took Paul, George, and Ringo back into the studio to record some new material. Through the latest achievements in technology, even John's voice, extracted from unreleased masters supplied by Yoko, was laid down in the mix, rendering a veritable Beatles reunion from the grave.

But try as they might, the past can never be recaptured, as Paul himself fondly recounted: "What I cherish is that I know I sat there and we wrote 'Love

Me Do.' And I sat there and we wrote 'I Want to Hold Your Hand' and we screwed around with the lyrics. I know he brought in 'In My Life' and he had the first verse and the rest of it wasn't written. And I know he brought in 'Norwegian Wood' and we developed the idea of setting the place on fire. I remember sitting there doing 'Help!' and then I'd come in with, 'When I was younger, so much younger than today,' and he'd have the main melody and I'd do the counter melody. I can remember where we were, how it was, and just magic moments where I'd be writing, 'It's getting better all the time' and John would be sitting there, 'It can't get much worse.' Those moments. That's what I cherish. No one can take it away from me."

John Lennon and Paul McCartney were the single greatest force in popular music. That time has worn away much from those heady bygone days is both inevitable and somehow strangely reassuring. Skyrocketing headlong into the next century, we carry with us a singular gift of music and hope wrought by two motherless boys from the very back of beyond. Their image forever etched within the spiraling imprint of our generation, perhaps the only thing left to say is "thank you."

Or as someone once said, "There's nothing you can do that can't be done."

It's a timeless, treasured legacy, and as for me, I still choose to believe it.

All You Need Is Cash /
Marketing a Myth

*W*atching Paul McCartney watching his young designer daughter Stella ease down the runway with an arm full of flowers following her first big fashion show for Chloé in Paris in spring 1998, one is struck by how far the fifty-something multimillionaire seems from the lighthearted hippie prince who turned the world on all those years ago with his psychedelic pal, John Lennon. Of course, no one can blame Macca for the passage of time, but it is unfortunate that so few dynamics of the young, adventurous Paul are apparent in the old, puffy one. As seemingly self-satisfied as he is smug, Sir Paul has gotten just about everything he ever wanted out of life with the exception of John Lennon's reputation as the tortured, creative inspiration behind the Beatles. In Barry Miles's recent marshmallow biography, *Paul McCartney: Many Years from Now,* Paul goes out of his way to tell the world that it was he, and not John, who was there in London burning the midnight oil with the likes of William Burroughs, Allen Ginsberg, and wild Stone Brian Jones. It was he, and not his bespectacled buddy, sitting on his stoned ass in Weybridge who brought to life *Sgt. Pepper, Magical Mystery Tour,* and even the raw splendor of the *White Album.*

If McCartney could make a last-minute deal with the devil, I wonder how much he'd pay for John Lennon's avant-garde reputation? No matter how many times he sits down with the media to discuss the perils of global warming, the obvious dangers of nuclear power, the legalization of pot, or even ethical vegetarianism, Paul is still a natural-born square. It was his jealousy of John Lennon that motivated much of his great work. Now that his best years are long behind him, one wonders what he actually thinks about late at night lying in bed. Just about everyone who cares realizes that John was *the man* in the Beatles and that despite Paul's colossal talent, energy, organizational skills, and drive, that's the way it will always be, no matter how much revisionist history Mr. McCartney indulges in.

Not surprisingly, along with the creative battle, the financial battles live on today. Beatle fans knew for years that the *Anthology* was pretty much inevitable; others, perhaps more sensible types otherwise busy with their lives, lost track and thus became vulnerable to Derek Taylor's almost biblical PR campaign that swept the earth in the months preceding its release. Even the late, great Taylor, however, couldn't hide the fact that here was the world's first official bootleg, right down to the usual outtakes and random bits of dialogue. With three double CD releases on tap, Apple obviously was going for quantity. The *Anthology* is a commodity that certainly has its place, especially with greedy Beatle fans in love with every dangling eighth note or rolling drum beat wrought by the group. I must confess that, when routing through my CDs in preparation for an extended trip through rural India, I scooped up parts two and three for my listening pleasure on the subcontinent. Now, I'd be lying if I told you that the instrumental version of "Within You Without You" was what I was really looking forward to hearing in the land of the sacred cow, but when I got there I was amazed at just how good Messrs. Lennon and McCartney sounded some thirty-plus years after the fact.

Perhaps more interesting than the mammoth six-CD offering from Apple was the nicely packaged six-video (or, better yet, laserdisc) *Anthology* documentary with the classy box aptly illustrated by longtime Beatles cohort Klaus Voorman. Here was something both fans and couch potatoes everywhere could really sink their teeth into. Clocking in at over ten hours of high-quality video (a relative rarity in the shaky realm of vintage Beatle visuals), the exhaustive effort did a good job in sanitizing the group's excruciating myth. Heavy on sweet-sixteen Beatlemania and suspiciously light on the Fabs' fairly sensual home life, it all seems rather like the New York City police investigating themselves, or, worse, the kind of wishful whitewash in which Maestro McCartney excels. Being fairly close to the Beatles phenomenon via their various family members and friends over the years (coupled with well over two decades of concentrated study), I can say that, despite a few insightful comments from George Harrison, the truth level inherent in this package is pitifully substandard. Of course, without the direct input of John Lennon, how could it be otherwise? But who knows? Had Lennon lived, he would've been well into middle age by the time the *Anthology* finally hit the streets, and perhaps by then he might have let the truth slide in favor of a more cohesive, immediately palatable product. And would anyone care? At a price tag of well over $200 for the deluxe laserdisc version, the epic box set would not find an audience among many rock 'n' roll dissidents.

As time goes by, the Beatles have become bitter about the untold millions that have been generated in their name by unauthorized entrepreneurs around the globe and therefore decided to cash in while there was still interest among the rapidly aging boomers. These days one can find dozens of items bearing the heralded Apple logo—from hemp tote bags to baseball hats, sweatshirts, watches, and a mountain of other pricey goodies available to the faithful. It's certainly true that the group's management was sound asleep for many years in regard to the illicit marketing of the Fabs by hip profiteers. It's equally true that now that their managers have successfully stemmed the tide of these often questionable product lines, they are gleefully diving in headlong, ready to market the Beatles' beloved image to the hilt.

Perhaps the most blatant offender in the realm of Beatles marketing in 1999 is Beatlefest founder Mark Lapidos. Since way back in the mid-seventies Mr. Lapidos has made a career of giving fans what they want: more and more John, Paul, George, and Ringo. That's not to say he is popular with either the faithful or even the group themselves, but he does certainly fill a niche. These days anyone who calls his Beatles hotline is bound to receive a fancy four-color catalog offering more cheesy Beatles memorabilia than was ever made during the sixties. Posing immodestly with his wife and grinning kids wearing this and that silly T-shirt, the dour Lapidos epitomizes all that is suspect about obsessive-compulsive hero worship as he rakes in the big bucks by identifying himself with the tidal wave of goodwill the Beatles have generated over the years. Although he's never directly had a Beatle in attendance at one of his dos, he does apparently have some sort of relationship with Yoko Ono that insulates him somewhat from the Beatles' natural distaste for this kind of money-hungry dog-and-pony show. As for Yoko, I'm sure she's grateful for the attention.

To be fair, Lapidos swears that John Lennon gave his blessing to the event when the former record store manager approached him back in 1974 in a New York hotel. What the former Beatle would think about it *now*, however, is another thing entirely. Both John and Paul have always shared an affinity for vintage Beatles memorabilia, but these days most of the good stuff has all been snatched up by serious collectors and squired away to some musty closet somewhere. But that is not what Beatlefest is really about. Take a walk into the dealers' room, past the Beatles look-alike booth, the "have your picture taken with a life-size cardboard cutout of the group," and the "give some money to the Lennon's Spirit Foundation table," and you enter a world of endless rock 'n' roll garbage all designed to line the pockets of those still banging the Beatles drum. Still, anyone looking for purity in the cult of popular music these days is unlikely to find much of anything that reminds them of the eye-to-eye honesty of John Lennon singing "Revolution" on *The David Frost Show* back in the turbulent final days of the Beatles. In short, these days it's only, and always, about money.

During the production of both the Beatles audio and video comeback of the nineties there was a hell of a lot of speculation by the PR circus surrounding the event that had John lived he would have been front and center for this latest joint venture. My best guess, however, is that he would not have. Lennon had long ago made a deep covenant with the fact that the Beatles were well and truly over. As complex and convoluted a person as he was, John had a very strong sense of detachment from things past and it is doubtful that anything as jolly as this opportunistic reunion would have drawn him out of hiding. Back in the seventies, John wouldn't even get involved with George's Concert for Bangladesh after Harrison pretty much begged him to do so. Nor would he lend his name to either the aborted UN-sponsored Boat People Concert, or promoter Bill Sargent's $50-million offer for the Fabs to reunite to save the whales, or the world, or something. And that was during a period when John really needed the money. It seems unlikely that, especially given the formidable Ono factor, Lennon would have stuck his neck out to buddy up with his old cohorts just for a few million lousy bucks.

Looking over the small mountain of clippings relevant to the Beatles' eleventh-hour reunion for the *Anthology,* it becomes immediately clear that the Fabs' actual physical participation was basically limited to a few days in the recording studio and a number of ad hoc video editing sessions in suburban London. Perhaps more telling were the things left unsaid by the aging trio. Nowhere was the import of the Beatles' various wives and children addressed, nor was much said about their long-standing business hassles, or even the death of John Lennon! McCartney, however, quite predictably waxed sentimental as often as he could, perhaps hoping people would be so high about the Beatles' being finally "back together" that they wouldn't notice the glaring Grand Canyon–size holes in the storyboard. In a press conference about the *Anthology* project, McCartney said,

It was actually a very joyous experience. It was a lot of fun seeing the guys and working with them. There were nice little things, like sitting down trying to work out the piano part and Ringo would just come on the drums so we'd have a little jam. And I'd think, "My God, it's twenty years since we did that." And, of course, you just fell in, it was like it was yesterday. We just read each other so easily, it was a lot of fun. . . . It was also good fun for me to have John in the headphones when I was working, it was like the old days and it was a privilege. . . . Of course, getting back in the band and working on this *Anthology,* you're in the band again. It was good being with them again for a little while. We work well together, that's the truth of it, we just work well together. And that's a very special thing. When you find someone you can talk to, it's special. But if you find someone you can play music with, it's really something. . . . It was a cool thing, the Beatles. Looking back on the Beatles, I'm glad about the content of what we said. Our songs were, you know, "Let It Be," peaceful, and "All You Need Is Love." They weren't anthems of rebelliousness and "come on, kids, kill your parents," the whole thing. So I think if there is any sort of love for the Beatles, it was because we were on a very loving vibe, that was genuine. I really don't think there is much else between families and people, I think a lot of the problems are because there isn't really enough of it. It's really good that our message still remains a very positive, loving one. I'm very pleased with that. We could have just gone off on the psychedelic thing and really majored in that and forgot the love thing, but it was important to us. . . . There was a period where John and I were just writing together, "I Want to Hold Your Hand," "She Loves You," that kind of thing. Where we were just very equal, and the two of us were putting equal effort into the songs. As you go through the story you find things like me doing "Yesterday," "Let It Be," or "Hey Jude," which was very me. John doing 'Strawberry Fields,' 'Walrus,' which are very him. We were able to discover our own identities within this chemistry as well, which is a good thing. So that became the growth factor and you could actually see us growing. Part of that was because we just complemented each other. So the chemistry of the combination of these four people was obviously something very special. We felt it. . . . We were a very good little band. I always used to feel that if we ever sat down and had a little jam, it always used to work.

Of course, John Lennon's participation in the video version of the *Anthology* had to be limited to whatever tape they could find of him holding forth on the rigors and rewards of Beatlemania. For the uninitiated, perhaps, this worked well, but the fact is, a lot of the interviews the producers chose were actually quite well known, thus dampening things a bit for the confirmed Lennonite. Then there is the whole question of Yoko and the Beatles' utilizing two of John's unreleased demos as the basis for the new tracks. Again, I'm not sure Lennon would have been pleased. First of all, these were songs that John did not release for whatever reason. Now that he's dead, Yoko hands them over to the other Fabs, the tapes are obsessed over in the studio for a few days, and suddenly the Beatles are back together with two "new" tunes! As curiosities I suppose they're interesting, but what Paul, George, and Ringo really should have done if they wanted to make some new music was to roll up their sleeves, dig in, and record an album's worth of original tunes. That would have really accounted for something. Unfortunately, the lure of doing things the easy way was just too great. After all, they're not exactly hungry anymore, are they? Strangely, almost all of the best artists from the sixties seemed to have peaked very early creatively and then, by and large, simply parodied their earlier hits with a succession of vaguely copycat works. Not even the Beatles were very good at reinventing themselves once the fire of their collective brilliance burned out. They were reasonably successful, each having several solo hits since the breakup of the group in April 1970. But it was never really the same. Lennon and McCartney, especially, should have had more artistically meaningful careers than they did. Undoubtedly, "Imagine" was inspirational, and Wings wasn't too bad, but without each other to lean on, a good part of their magic was forever extinguished.

Certainly John Lennon paid a big price for hooking up with the ever difficult Yoko Ono. The stress level of their lives together was overwhelming, as were John's various emotional maladies near the end of his life. Writing and recording very little from 1975 to his death in 1980, Lennon was secretly jealous of his old partner's commercial success and was almost persuaded by various friends to at least think about working with Paul again. Had he lived, who knows? For his part, Paul certainly would have jumped at the chance to have written with Lennon again, knowing full well just what the world would pay for more well-crafted Lennon-McCartney songs. Unfortunately, all of this falls into the realm of speculation, as a series of big-money business deals and ego problems kept them at arms' length until the end.

As the world spins, the baby boomers and their lush Beatle dreams have faded slowly into history. John Lennon is now the icon he never wanted to be and Paul McCartney, sadly, isn't. Still, frozen in time is the icy image of two young guys from suburban Liverpool who changed the world forever by their hip presence, stirring poetics, and astonishing music. It is an ideal that is ours forever. At least as long as time allows.

Chronology

1933–1970

18 February 1933 Yoko Ono is born in Tokyo, Japan, into a prominent banking family.

10 September 1939 John's first wife, Cynthia Powell, is born in Blackpool.

23 June 1940 Stuart Sutcliffe is born in Edinburgh.

7 July 1940 Richard ("Ringo") Starkey is born to Richard and Elsie at 24 Admiral Grove, the Dingle, Liverpool.

9 October 1940 John Winston Lennon enters this world during a German air raid over Liverpool at seven o'clock in the morning. Shortly after his birth he is placed under his mother's sturdy iron bed at the Liverpool Maternity Hospital. He is named John after his grandfather and Winston in honor of the cigar-chewing prime minister. His father, Alfred, is away at sea.

15 April 1941 Paul McCartney's parents are married at St. Swithin's Roman Catholic Chapel, Liverpool.

24 September 1941 Linda Louise Eastman is born in Scarsdale, New York, to parents Lee and Louise.

24 November 1941 Randolph Peter Best, the Beatles' first professional drummer, is born in Madras, India.

18 June 1942 James Paul McCartney is born to Mary Patricia Mohin and James McCartney in Liverpool.

1942 Finally giving in to family pressure, Julia Lennon reluctantly agrees to temporarily turn over care of her infant son to her sister Mimi and her husband, gentleman dairy farmer George Smith.

Despairing of her globetrotting husband's ever settling down, Julia finally ends their on-again off-again relationship. She soon meets and falls in love with congenial barman John Albert Dykins. Together they take a small flat in the tatty Gateacre district of Liverpool.

25 February 1943 George Harold Harrison, the youngest child of Harry and Louise Harrison, is born at 12 Arnold Grove, Wavertree, Liverpool.

September 1945 Young John begins attending school at Dovedale Primary just around the corner from his aunt Mimi's home at 251 Menlove Avenue in Woolton.

July 1946 Alf Lennon returns from sea unexpectedly and convinces Mimi to allow John to accompany him on an impromptu holiday trek to Blackpool, secretly intending to spirit the boy away to a new life together in New Zealand. At the last moment Julia locates the two and takes John back home to Liverpool.

1950 George Martin accepts a position as assistant A&R man for EMI's Parlophone label.

September 1950 Young John is awarded a beginner's swimming certificate by the Liverpool Association of Schoolmasters.

July 1952 John leaves Dovedale Primary.

September 1952 John enters the Quarry Bank High School for Boys.

September 1953 Paul enters the Liverpool Institute.

1954–1955 Paul McCartney and schoolmate George Harrison get together for the first time and begin bashing out Lonnie Donegan material in the front room of the Harrisons' home at 25 Upton Green, Speke.

31 October 1956 Mary McCartney dies unexpectedly of breast cancer.

11 November 1956 Paul sees Lonnie Donegan in concert at Liverpool Empire for the first time.

16 January 1957 A former wine cellar on Matthew Street in Liverpool is opened as a showcase for local jazz and skiffle groups and called the Cavern Club. Rock 'n' roll is strictly forbidden by order of the management.

March 1957 John Lennon receives a £17 guitar and forms a group with Pete Shotton.

9 June 1957 The Quarry Men unsuccessfully audition for Carrol Levis's *TV Star Search*.

6 July 1957 Paul McCartney meets John Lennon for the first time at a Saturday afternoon performance by Lennon's schoolboy skiffle group, the Quarry Men, at St. Peter's Parish Fête in Woolton. Shortly afterward, he is invited to join the group by Pete Shotton (the Quarry Men's erstwhile washtub player).

7 August 1957 John Lennon's Quarry Men play the Cavern Club for the first time.

September 1957 Cynthia Powell, aged eighteen, enrolls as a lettering student at the Liverpool Junior Art School. She soon transfers to Liverpool Art College where she meets her future husband, John Lennon.

18 October 1957 At the New Clubmoor Hall in Liverpool, Paul McCartney does his first gig with the Quarry Men, playing lead.

7 November 1957 The Quarry Men play Wilson Hall, Speke Road, Garston, Liverpool, for the first time.

6 February 1958 Fourteen-year-old George Harrison is accepted into the band.

1958 Percy Phillips, owner of a bare-bones recording studio in his Liverpool basement, records the Quarry Men performing two high-powered skiffle numbers. It is Lennon and McCartney's first bona fide recording. Paul buys the only existing copy on disc in July 1981.

15 July 1958 Julia Lennon, John's mother, is killed when she's hit by a car being driven by an off-duty police officer suspected of drinking; this happens outside Mimi's home on Menlove Avenue while John and his sisters are at home with John Dykins. Julia's final words to Mimi just before the accident were, "Don't worry."

December 1958 Lennon and McCartney briefly perform together as the Nurk Twins.

20 December 1958 The Quarry Men play at George's brother Harry's wedding to Irene McCann.

1 January 1959 While on school holiday, the Quarry Men play for the Speke Bus Depot Social Club at Wilson Hall.

3 February 1959 Early rock legends Buddy Holly, Ritchie Valens, and J. P. "The Big Bopper" Richardson are killed in the crash of a private plane near Clear Lake, Iowa. Twenty years later, the cuff links worn by Holly on the fatal flight will be presented to Paul McCartney by Holly's widow, Maria.

29 August 1959 The Quarry Men are invited to play at the opening-night party of the Casbah Club at 8 Haymen's Green, Liverpool. They become regulars at this teenage coffee club run by Mona Best, drummer Pete Best's fun-loving mother.

18 October 1959 Renamed Johnny and the Moondogs, the band auditions for British television personality Carrol Levis at Liverpool's Empire Theatre, and qualifies for the finals.

26–31 October 1959 Again, Johnny and the Moondogs audition for *TV Star Search* at the Empire. They go on to finals held at the Hippodrome Theatre in Manchester.

15 November 1959 Johnny and the Moondogs fail their audition for Carrol Levis because they didn't have funds to stay overnight, meaning they couldn't stay late for the final judging.

January 1960 Stuart Sutcliffe joins the group after buying a Hofner bass with the proceeds he earned from an art show.

23 April 1960 While on school holiday, John and Paul visit Lennon's relatives in Caversham, Berkshire. They perform as the Nurk Twins in the Fox and Hounds pub.

24 April 1960 John and Paul perform as the Nurk Twins for the last time before returning to Liverpool.

May 1960 Allan Williams becomes booking agent and manager until April 1961.

14 May 1960 The Silver Beetles play a gig for promoter Brian Kelly under the name of Silver Beats.

18–28 May 1960 Now called the Silver Beetles, John, Paul, George, and Stuart begin a tour of Scotland, backing British balladeer Johnny Gentle.

30 July 1969 The group plays the Grosvenor Ballroom in Wallasey as the Silver Beatles.

12 August 1960 Paul McCartney invites Pete Best to join the Beatles as their regular drummer on their first trip to Germany.

17 August 1960 The Beatles begin their Hamburg gig, which takes them through 30 November. They perform a series of engagements at Bruno Koschmeider's seedy Indra Club in Hamburg's red-light district.

Autumn 1960 The Beatles make their first professional recording with members of Rory Storm and the Hurricanes, at Akustik Studios in Hamburg.

21 November 1960 The Beatles' trek to Germany is interrupted after George is found to be under age by German immigration officials and is unceremoniously deported. The other Beatles soon follow and end up back in Liverpool, feeling beaten and dejected.

December 1960 The Beatles play Liverpool's Cavern Club on Matthew Street after a long absence.

21 February 1961 In a lunchtime session, the band appears as the Beatles at the Cavern for the first time. Over the next two years they will play some 292 gigs at the celebrated Liverpool cellar.

15 March 1961 Stuart Sutcliffe leaves the Beatles in order to marry German photographer and early Beatles supporter Astrid Kirchherr. Paul takes over duties on bass guitar.

24 March 1961 The Beatles depart Liverpool for their second trip to Hamburg.

May 1961 The Beatles play a three-month engagement at Hamburg's Top-Ten Club.

June 1961 While in Hamburg the Beatles participate in a Polydor-sponsored session with British singer Tony Sheridan, performing as the Beat Brothers. They record a Lennon-fronted version of "My Bonnie" backed by "The Saints."

9 October 1961 John and Paul take off on a two-week hitchhiking trip to Paris.

28 October 1961 A patron named Raymond Jones walks into NEMS Record Store in Liverpool's Whitechapel shopping district and asks proprietor Brian Epstein for a copy of "My Bonnie."

9 November 1961 Wealthy Liverpool record retailer Brian Epstein unexpectedly drops in to the Cavern to hear the Beatles after being deluged with requests for their first official release, "My Bonnie" (a German Polydor import).

3 December 1961 Epstein invites the group to his office to discuss the possibility of his taking over as their manager. They readily agree.

21 December 1961 The Beatles record "Sweet Georgia Brown," backing Tony Sheridan.

21 December 1961 The Beatles record "Sweet Georgia Brown," backing Tony Sheridan.

December 1961 The Beatles top the *Mersey Beat* popularity poll in Liverpool.

1 January 1962 The Beatles travel down to London to audition for Mike Smith at Decca Records. Despite a rousing performance by the Fabs, they were ultimately turned down by Decca executive Dick Rowe, who told Brian that groups with guitars were on the way out.

24 January 1962 Brian Epstein officially becomes the Beatles' manager.

5 February 1962 Pete Best is ill so Ringo Starr, drummer for Rory Storm and the Hurricanes, fills in on his day off.

12 February 1962 The Beatles audition for Peter Pilbeam of the BBC. They pass the audition.

13 February 1962 Brian Epstein meets George Martin, EMI's A&R man, for the first time and plays him the group's demo.

March 1962 In London, Decca Records turn down the Beatles.

10 April 1962 Stuart Sutcliffe tragically dies of a brain hemorrhage in Hamburg. He was just twenty-one years old.

11 April 1962 John, Paul, and Pete leave for Hamburg to begin a seven-week engagement at the Star Club, where they are met by Astrid Kirchherr.

9 May 1962 Brian Epstein wires the Beatles in Germany that EMI Records has agreed to audition the group at their recording facility at 3 Abbey Road, St. John's Wood, London.

4 June 1962 The Beatles are offered a recording contract with Parlophone Records, a tiny offshoot of the vast EMI entertainment empire. Their recording manager is the brilliant George Martin.

6 June 1962 The Beatles perform six songs for EMI/Parlophone staff producer Martin in London.

16 August 1962 For reasons that remain a mystery to this day, drummer Pete Best is unceremoniously sacked by Brian Epstein. Ringo Starr is quickly brought in to fill the gap.

18 August 1962 Starr plays his first session with the Beatles at the Cavern.

23 August 1962 John Lennon marries Cynthia Powell in a civil ceremony at the Mount Pleasant Registry Office in Liverpool. Fellow Beatles Harrison and McCartney attend.

4 September 1962 The Beatles arrive in London to begin recording with George Martin at EMI Studios in St. John's Wood, London. The group's first single, "Love Me Do" backed by "P.S. I Love You," is culled from these sessions.

5 October 1962 "Love Me Do" is released throughout Britain.

29 October 1962 The Beatles once again travel to Hamburg to begin a two-week engagement at the Star Club.

18 December 1962 The Beatles begin their final engagement at the Star Club. Alleged McCartney love child Bettina Heubers is born.

31 December 1962 The Beatles make their final club appearance in Hamburg.

22 February 1963 "Please Please Me" becomes the number-one single on the *New Musical Express* charts. Twenty-four hours later it will do the same on the *Disc* charts.

2 March 1963 "Please Please Me" hits the coveted number-one position on the *Melody Maker* chart.

8 April 1963 John Charles Julian Lennon is born to John and Cynthia at 6:50 A.M. at Sefton General Hospital, Liverpool.

18 April 1963 Following the Beatles' first performance at London's Royal Albert Hall, which was broadcast as the BBC radio special "Swinging Sounds '63," Paul McCartney meets actress Jane Asher.

26 April 1963 "From Me to You" reaches number one on the British pop charts.

18 June 1963 McCartney celebrates his twenty-first birthday at his Auntie Gin's home on Dinas Lane, Huyton.

7 September 1963 "She Loves You" becomes the number-one song on the *Melody Maker* singles chart, remaining there for the next five weeks.

September 1963 The Beatles perform at London's Royal Albert Hall.

13 October 1963 The Beatles appear on Britain's top television show, *Sunday Night at the London Palladium.*

17 October 1963 London's normally conservative Bond Street is overrun with teenyboppers when Paul McCartney arrives to dine with the winner of the "Why I Like the Beatles" magazine contest.

4 November 1963 The Beatles play a Royal Command Performance.

31 December 1963 Heather See is born to Linda Eastman and her first husband, American college professor Melvin See.

30 January 1964 *Mersey Beat* magazine prints an interview with Brian Epstein in which he assures McCartney fans that the Beatle has no plans to be either engaged or married to Jane Asher or anyone else.

1 February 1964 "I Want to Hold Your Hand" becomes the number-one record in America.

7 February 1964 The Beatles and their entourage land at Idlewild Airport in New York, where they experience their first taste of the intensity of American Beatlemania.

9 February 1964 The Beatles appear on *The Ed Sullivan Show.* During their performance an estimated 73 million television viewers experience John, Paul,

George, and Ringo for the first time. Across America not a single crime is committed by a teenager during the performance.

March 1964 The Beatles hold a staggering twelve slots on *Billboard*'s top one hundred (singles) charts.

20 March 1964 While taping an appearance on the popular British television series *Ready, Steady, Go!* McCartney denies the persistent rumor that he will soon marry Jane Asher.

23 March 1964 John Lennon's first book, *In His Own Write,* is published. Almost overnight it becomes an international bestseller.

4 April 1964 The Beatles hold the top five positions on the American pop charts.

10 July 1964 A civic reception is held in Liverpool to honor its most famous sons; over 100,000 people attend. Among them are John's sisters Julia and Jacqui as well as most of Lennon's family.

18 August 1964 The Beatles make their second trek to the United States to begin a rigorous twenty-five city tour.

October 1964 The Beatles commence an autumn tour of Great Britain.

24 November 1964 Paul McCartney gains a stepmother and stepsister when his father, Jim, marries thirty-four-year-old widow Angela Williams, whose little girl is named Ruth.

8 December 1964 McCartney hints to the media that he may indeed marry Jane Asher although he hastens to add that no specific date has been set.

4 February 1965 Paul and Jane vacation together in Hammamet, Tunisia.

15 February 1965 John Lennon finally passes his driving test (after driving illegally for years).

February 1965 The Beatles are in the Bahamas for the shooting of their second feature, *Help!*

13 April 1965 It is reported that Paul McCartney has purchased a home at 7 Cavendish Avenue in St. John's Wood for £40,000.

12 June 1965 Buckingham Palace announces that the Beatles will be awarded MBEs later that year.

24 June 1965 John's second book, *A Spaniard in the Works,* is published.

3 August 1965 John buys his aunt Mimi a lovely seaside bungalow in Poole, Dorset.

15 August 1965 Jane Asher hints to the media that her marriage to Paul is imminent. While the Beatles are in the United States, Bob Dylan visits them in their suite at the Delmonico Hotel.

22 August 1965 The Minneapolis vice squad raids McCartney's room at the Lexington Motor Inn, where he is in the company of a young woman who is under age. The incident receives sporadic media coverage but is effectively suppressed by Brian Epstein.

27 August 1965 The Beatles visit Elvis Presley at his Bel Air mansion, where they spend the evening drinking Cokes, jamming, and playing billiards with the King.

26 October 1965 The Beatles receive MBEs from Her Majesty Queen Elizabeth II in the Great Throne Room at Buckingham Palace. Afterward, the group holds a press conference at the Saville Theatre, a new pet project of Brian Epstein's.

November 1965 Paul and John travel to Manchester to film a television special, "The Music of Lennon and McCartney."

8 December 1965 The Moody Blues, who have been touring with the Beatles, dine with the group after a concert at Sheffield City Hall.

31 December 1965 Alfred Lennon suddenly reappears, this time to release his one and only record, "That's My Life (My Love and My Home)." Although initially it receives quite a lot of airplay, it is critically panned and sells poorly. Today it is a much-sought-after collector's item.

16 January 1966 Martha, Paul McCartney's celebrated Old English sheepdog, is born in High Wycombe.

17 January 1966 McCartney purchases High Park Farm near Campbeltown, Scotland.

26 January 1966 While the Beatles are in Hamburg, Paul and a former girlfriend visit the Star Club and the Indra.

March 1966 The Beatles pose for the famous "butcher" photograph for the American compilation LP, *Yesterday and Today.*

March 1966 McCartney spends the evening at Dolly's, a swank London nightclub, with Bob Dylan.

4 March 1966 John makes his infamous remark about the Beatles being more popular than Jesus Christ during an interview with British journalist Maureen Cleave.

31 July 1966 Radio stations across America join together in an ad hoc ban on Beatles music as a direct result of John's controversial remarks. Over the next few weeks there are reports of record burnings and other protests by groups ranging from the Ku Klux Klan to the Daughters of the American Revolution. In the midst of this furor, John is persuaded by Brian Epstein to recant his remarks in an effort to calm Middle America's shattered faith in the group.

26 August 1966 McCartney denies rumors that he will wed Jane Asher during the Beatles' brief stay in Los Angeles.

29 August 1966 The Beatles give their final American concert at Candlestick Park in San Francisco.

9 November 1966 John meets Yoko Ono for the first time at a special preview showing of her one-woman conceptual art show, "Unfinished Paintings and Objects," at the Indica Gallery in London.

November 1966 John Lennon completes filming on *How I Won the War.*

6 December 1966 Recording sessions for *Sgt. Pepper's Lonely Hearts Club Band* begin.

18 December 1966 *The Family Way,* starring Hayley Mills, premieres in London. McCartney wrote the incidental music for the film. Paul and Jane attend.

12 January 1967 Jane Asher leaves for America to tour with the Bristol Old Vic Repertory Theatre. Meanwhile, Paul and Ringo attend a high-powered performance by Jimi Hendrix at the Bag O' Nails in London.

7 February 1967 Paul McCartney spends the evening at home with Mickey Dolenz of the Monkees.

March 1967 The Beatles earn three Grammy Awards, including Song of the Year for "Michelle."

30 March 1967 Photographic sessions for the cover of *Sgt. Pepper's Lonely Hearts Club Band* are held in the Flood Street Studios of Michael Cooper.

5 April 1967 McCartney catches up with Jane Asher in Denver to celebrate her twenty-first birthday.

15 May 1967 While attending a Georgie Fame performance at the Bag O' Nails, McCartney meets his future wife, photographer Linda Eastman, for the first time.

26 May 1967 *Sgt. Pepper's Lonely Hearts Club Band* is released just in time to kick off the infamous "Summer of Love."

May 1967 Linda Eastman attends a press party at Brian Epstein's Chapel Street flat to celebrate the release of *Sgt. Pepper.*

4 June 1967 Paul and Jane attend a concert by the Jimi Hendrix Experience, Procol Harum, Denny Laine and His Electric String Band, and the Chiffons at the Saville Theatre.

19 June 1967 McCartney confirms that he has taken the controversial drug LSD.

24 August 1967 The Beatles and an entourage of girlfriends, wives, and hangers-on attend an introductory lecture on Transcendental Meditation given by the Maharishi Mahesh Yogi at the Hilton Hotel, London.

27 August 1967 While attending a special weekend meditation seminar held in Bangor, Wales, the Beatles receive word that Brian Epstein has been found dead in his London town house, the cause of death being an unexplained overdose of drugs. The Maharishi attempts to comfort them by reminding them to try and "be happy" and "don't worry."

October 1967 *How I Won the War* premieres in London.

25 December 1967 Paul McCartney and Jane Asher announce their engagement, ending four years of speculation by the media.

5 January 1968 Alfred Lennon and his nineteen-year-old fiancée, Pauline Jones, meet John to seek his blessing for their forthcoming marriage. Lennon is not too happy about this unexpected romance, but reluctantly gives the two of them his support.

16 February 1968 John, Cynthia, George, and his wife, Pattie, join the Maharishi in Rishikesh, India, for an intensive two-month instructor's course in Transcendental Meditation.

19 February 1968 Paul and Jane, accompanied by Ringo and Maureen Starr, join John and George at the Maharishi's exclusive country ashram.

26 March 1968 Paul and Jane return to England, somewhat disillusioned with the Maharishi and his otherworldly philosophy.

April 1968 Apple announces its plans to promote unknown musical artists.

12 April 1968 John, George, and wives leave the peaceful mountain ashram two weeks ahead of schedule after a nasty rumor circulates that the giggly Indian fakir attempted to compromise the virtue of fellow meditator Mia Farrow.

15 May 1968 Linda Eastman slips Paul her phone number at a New York press party held to mark the launch of the Beatles' Apple Corps Ltd. They spend the night together at business associate Nat Weiss's Manhattan apartment.

21 May 1968 Paul and Jane dine with singer Andy Williams and later attend his concert at the Royal Albert Hall.

7 June 1968 Paul and Jane attend Paul's brother Mike's marriage to first wife Angela Fishwick. Paul is best man.

22–24 June 1968 McCartney is ensconced in a bungalow at the Beverly Hills Hotel with Linda Eastman.

20 July 1968 Jane Asher announces on British television that her seven-month engagement to McCartney is over.

August 1968 McCartney hanger-on Francie Schwartz moves into his St. John's Wood home and stays for three weeks.

22 August 1968 Cynthia Lennon sues John for divorce, citing his adultery with Yoko Ono as the cause.

12 October 1968 Jane Asher publicly discusses her on-again, off-again romance with McCartney for the first time.

18 October 1968 John and Yoko are arrested for possessing 219 grains of hashish at their flat at 34 Montague Square, London. A charge of obstructing justice is also brought against the couple, who, according to old chum Pete Shotton, had been forewarned of the impending bust.

25 October 1968 Word leaks to the press that Yoko is pregnant. John Lennon is reportedly the father.

31 October 1968 McCartney calls Linda Eastman from London and invites Linda and her seven-year-old daughter, Heather, to move in with him. Days later Linda arrives, alone, in St. John's Wood.

8 November 1968 Cynthia Lennon is granted a divorce from John in an uncontested suit brought before magistrates in London.

21 November 1968 Yoko suffers her first miscarriage. John remains constantly at her bedside at Queen Charlotte's Hospital where he beds down next to her in a sleeping bag for several days.

28 November 1968 John pleads guilty to unauthorized possession of cannabis at Marylebone Magistrates Court. A fine of £150 is imposed as well as court costs of 20 guineas. The obstruction of justice charges against both him and Yoko are dropped.

29 November 1968 John and Yoko's infamous *Unfinished Music Number One: Two Virgins* is released. The scandalous album cover depicts the free-spirited couple nude.

December 1968 The first universal "Beatle Day" is celebrated.

30 January 1969 The Beatles play their last live public performance ever on the rooftop of Apple headquarters. The impromptu gig is filmed for inclusion in the Beatles' eclectic cinematic swan song, *Let It Be.*

2 February 1969 Yoko Ono is granted a divorce from her husband, Anthony Cox.

12 February 1969 Paul McCartney's personal corporation, Adagrose Ltd., is formed in London. He will later change the name to McCartney Productions Ltd (MPL).

March 1969 Construction begins in Beverly Hills on the posh headquarters for Apple USA.

11 March 1969 The Apple press office announces Paul McCartney's intention to wed Linda Eastman the following afternoon.

12 March 1969 Paul and Linda are married at the Marylebone Registry Office, London amidst great publicity.

17 March 1969 The McCartneys, along with Linda's daughter, Heather, fly to New York for a visit with the Eastmans.

20 March 1969 John and Yoko are married in a quiet civil ceremony on the island of Gibraltar.

24 March 1969 Reporters from *Life* magazine track down McCartney at his farm in Scotland to try to quash rumors that the reclusive Beatle is actually dead.

8 May 1969 Allen Klein becomes the Beatles' new business manager. Paul, however, is adamantly opposed to the appointment. It is the beginning of a bitter feud between John and Paul that would never be fully resolved.

15 May 1969 The McCartneys vacation on the island of Corfu. Publicists announce that Paul and Linda are expecting a child.

26 May 1969 The Lennons fly to Montreal to hold an eight-day "Bed-In for Peace" at the Queen Elizabeth Hotel. While there they record the now-famous counterculture anthem, "Give Peace a Chance."

14 June 1969 Peter Asher resigns his position as A&R director of Apple.

July 1969 Recording sessions for *Abbey Road* begin.

1 July 1969 While visiting John's Aunt Mater in Durness, Sutherland, Scotland, the Lennons and their children, Julian and Kyoko, are involved in a car accident in Golspie. Although no one is seriously injured, John requires seventeen stitches on his face and head. Julian is treated for shock.

28 August 1969 Paul and Linda's first child together, Mary Louise McCartney, is born at Avenue Clinic in London.

September 1969 Jim McCartney is hospitalized in Cheshire. Both Mike and Paul visit him frequently.

12 October 1969 Yoko miscarries again. This time, however, the pregnancy is sufficiently long for the child, a little boy, to be given the name John Ono Lennon; he is buried in a tiny white coffin somewhere outside London. Only John and Yoko attend the service.

November 1969 Rumors that "Paul is dead" fuel one of the biggest hoaxes in media history.

14 January 1970 McCartney purchases Low Ranadran Farm, adjacent to his property in Scotland.

March 1970 The Beatles appear via film on *The Ed Sullivan Show.*

2 April 1970 In an interview with the *Evening Standard,* McCartney hints that the Beatles may soon go their separate ways due to the rapid disintegration of their multimillion-pound Apple empire.

9 April 1970 McCartney appears on a *London Weekend Television* segment performing "Maybe I'm Amazed."

10 April 1970 Paul McCartney publicly quits the Beatles.

11 April 1970 The *Daily Mirror* reports that Paul McCartney has officially left the Beatles.

17 April 1970 Paul's solo *McCartney* album is released in Great Britain.

31 December 1970 Paul McCartney brings suit against the other Beatles in an effort to legally dissolve the group.

—Compiled by Vrnda Devi and Sesa Giuliano

The Beatles Vinyl Discography

An asterisk (*) indicates information the author has been unable to verify.

TITLE	LABEL	COUNTRY	RELEASE DATE
ALBUMS			
Please Please Me			
	Parlophone	United Kingdom	March 22, 1963
Introducing the Beatles			
	Vee Jay	United States	July 22, 1963
With the Beatles			
	Parlophone	United Kingdom	November 22, 1963
Meet the Beatles!			
	Capitol	United States	January 20, 1964
The Beatles' Second Album			
	Capitol	United States	April 10, 1964
A Hard Day's Night			
	United Artists	United States	June 26, 1964
	Parlophone	United Kingdom	July 10, 1964
Something New			
	Capitol	United States	July 20, 1964
The Beatles Verses the Four Seasons			
(Double Album Set)			
	Vee Jay	United States	October 1, 1964
Songs, Pictures and Stories of the Fabulous Beatles			
	Vee Jay	United States	October 12, 1964
The Beatles' Story			
(Double Record Set)			
	Capitol	United States	November 23, 1964

TITLE	LABEL	COUNTRY	RELEASE DATE
Beatles For Sale			
	Parlophone	United Kingdom	December 4, 1964
Beatles '65			
	Capitol	United States	December 15, 1964
The Early Beatles			
	Capitol	United States	March 22, 1965
Beatles VI			
	Capitol	United States	June 14, 1965
Help!			
(Original Soundtrack Album)			
	Parlophone	United Kingdom	August 6, 1965
	Capitol	United States	August 13, 1965
Rubber Soul			
	Parlophone	United Kingdom	December 3, 1965
	Capitol	United States	December 6, 1965
Yesterday and Today			
	Capitol	United States	June 20, 1966
Revolver			
	Parlophone	United Kingdom	August 5, 1966
	Capitol	United States	August 8, 1966
A Collection of Beatles Oldies			
	Parlophone	United Kingdom	December 9, 1966
Sgt. Pepper's Lonely Hearts Club Band			
	Parlophone	United Kingdom	June 1, 1967
	Capitol	United States	June 2, 1967
Magical Mystery Tour			
	Capitol	United States	November 27, 1967
The Beatles (White Album)			
	Apple	United Kingdom	November 22, 1968
	Apple	United States	November 25, 1968
Yellow Submarine			
	Apple	United States	January 13, 1969
	Apple	United Kingdom	January 17, 1969
Abbey Road			
	Apple	United Kingdom	September 26, 1969
	Apple	United States	October 1, 1969
Hey Jude (also called: The Beatles Again)			
	Apple	United States	February 26, 1970
The Beatles Circa 1960—In the Beginning			
	Polydor	United States	May 4, 1970
Let It Be			
	Apple	United Kingdom	May 8, 1970
	Apple	United States	May 18, 1970
The Beatles 1962–1966 (Red Album)			
	Apple	United States	April 2, 1973
	Parlophone	United Kingdom	April 19, 1973
The Beatles 1967–1970 (Blue Album)			
	Apple	United States	April 2, 1973
	Parlophone	United Kingdom	April 19, 1973
Rock'n'Roll Music			
	Capitol	United States	June 17, 1976

Title	Label	Country	Release Date
The Beatles at the Hollywood Bowl			
	Capitol	United States	May 4, 1977
The Beatles Live! At the Star Club in Hamburg, Germany			
	Lingasong	United Kingdom	May 25, 1977
	Lingasong	United States	June 13, 1977
Love Songs			
	Capitol	United States	October 21, 1977
	Parlophone	United Kingdom	November 19, 1977
The Beatles Collection 13 LP Boxed Set			
	Capitol	United States	December 1, 1978
Rarities			
	Capitol	United States	March 24, 1980
Reel Music			
	Capitol	United States	March 22, 1982
The Complete Silver Beatles			
	Audio Rarities	United States	September 27, 1982
20 Greatest Hits			
	Capitol	United States	October 11, 1982
Past Masters Volume 1			
	Capitol	United States	March 7, 1988
Past Masters Volume 2			
	Capitol	United States	March 7, 1988
The Beatles Live at the BBC			
	Capitol	United States	November 30, 1994
The Beatles Anthology 1			
	Capitol	United States	November 21, 1995
The Beatles Anthology 2			
	Capitol	United States	March 18, 1996
The Beatles Anthology 3			
	Capitol	United States	October 29, 1996

SINGLES

	Label	Country	Release Date
My Bonnie (Lies Over the Ocean)/The Saints (When the Saints Go Marching In)			
	Polydor	Germany	June 1961
My Bonnie/Cry for a Shadow			
	Parlophone	United States	April 23, 1962
Love Me Do (Version One)/P.S. I Love You			
	Parlophone	United Kingdom	October 5, 1962
Please Please Me/Ask Me Why			
	Parlophone	United Kingdom	January 11, 1963
	Vee Jay	United States	February 25, 1963
From Me to You/Thank You Girl			
	Parlophone	United Kingdom	April 11, 1963
	Vee Jay	United States	May 27, 1963
She Loves You/I'll Get You			
	Parlophone	United Kingdom	August 23, 1963
	Swan	United States	September 16, 1963
I Want to Hold Your Hand/This Boy			
	Parlophone	United Kingdom	November 29, 1963

TITLE	LABEL	COUNTRY	RELEASE DATE
The Beatles Christmas Record			
	Fan Club	United States	December 1963
I Want To Hold Your Hand/I Saw Her Standing There			
	Capitol	United States	December 26, 1963
Please Please Me/From Me to You			
	Vee Jay	United States	January 30, 1964
Twist and Shout/There's a Place			
	Tollie	United States	March 2, 1964
Komm, Gib Mir Deine Hand/Sie Liebt Dich			
	*	Germany	March 1964
Can't Buy Me Love/You Can't Do That			
	Capitol	United States	March 16, 1964
	Parlophone	United Kingdom	March 20, 1964
Do You Want to Know a Secret/Thank You Girl			
	Vee Jay	United States	March 23, 1964
Why/Cry for a Shadow (w/Tony Sheridan)			
	Polydor	United Kingdom	February 28, 1964
	MGM	United States	March 27, 1964
Love Me Do/P.S. I Love You			
	Tollie	United States	April 27, 1964
Sie Liebt Dich/I'll Get You			
	Swan	United States	May 21, 1964
Sweet Georgia Brown/Take Out Some Insurance on Me, Baby (w/Tony Sheridan)			
	ATCO	United States	June 1, 1964
Ain't She Sweet/Nobody's Child (w/Tony Sheridan)			
	ATCO	United States	July 6, 1964
A Hard Day's Night/Things We Said Today			
	Parlophone	United Kingdom	July 10, 1964
A Hard Day's Night/I Should Have Known Better			
	Capitol	United States	July 13, 1964
And I Love Her/If I Fell			
	Capitol	United States	July 20, 1964
I'll Cry Instead/I'm Happy Just to Dance with You			
	Capitol	United States	July 20, 1964
Do You Want to Know a Secret/Thank You Girl			
	Capitol	United States	August 1964
Matchbox/Slow Down			
	Capitol	United States	August 24, 1964
I Feel Fine/She's a Woman			
	Capitol	United States	November 23, 1964
	Parlophone	United Kingdom	November 27, 1964
Another Beatles Christmas Record			
	Fan Club	United States	December 1964
Eight Days a Week/I Don't Want to Spoil the Party			
	Capitol	United States	February 15, 1965
Ticket to Ride/Yes It Is			
	Palophone	United Kingdom	April 9, 1965
	Capitol	United States	April 19, 1965
Help!/I'm Down			
	Capitol	United States	July 19, 1965
	Parlophone	United Kingdom	July 23, 1965

TITLE	LABEL	COUNTRY	RELEASE DATE
Yesterday/Act Naturally			
	Capitol	United States	September 13, 1965
Roll Over Beethoven/Misery			
	Capitol	United States	October 11, 1965
Boys/Medley: (Kansas City/Hey-Hey-Hey-Hey)			
	Capitol	United States	October 11, 1965
We Can Work It Out/Day Tripper			
	Parlophone	United Kingdom	December 3, 1965
	Capitol	United States	December 6, 1965
The Beatles Third Christmas Record			
	Fan Club	United States	December 1965
Nowhere Man/What Goes On			
	Capitol	United States	February 21, 1966
Paperback Writer/Rain			
	Capitol	United States	May 30, 1966
	Parlophone	United Kingdom	June 10, 1966
Eleanor Rigby/Yellow Submarine			
	Parlophone	United Kingdom	August 5, 1966
	Capitol	United States	August 8, 1966
The Beatles Fourth Christmas Record			
	Fan Club	United States	December 1966
Strawberry Fields Forever/Penny Lane			
	Capitol	United States	February 13, 1967
	Parlophone	United Kingdom	February 17, 1967
All You Need Is Love/Baby, You're a Rich Man			
	Parlophone	United Kingdom	July 7, 1967
	Capitol	United States	July 17, 1967
Hello Goodbye/I Am the Walrus			
	Parlophone	United Kingdom	November 24, 1967
	Capitol	United States	November 27, 1967
Christmas Time Is Here Again			
	Fan Club	United States	December 1967
Lady Madonna/The Inner Light			
	Parlophone	United Kingdom	March 15, 1968
	Capitol	United States	March 18, 1968
Hey Jude/Revolution			
	Apple	United States	August 26, 1968
	Apple	United Kingdom	August 30, 1968
1968 Christmas Record			
	Fan Club	United States	December 1968
Get Back/Don't Let Me Down			
	Apple	United Kingdom	April 11, 1969
	Apple	United States	May 5, 1969
The Ballad of John and Yoko/Old Brown Shoe			
	Apple	United Kingdom	May 30, 1969
	Apple	United States	June 4, 1969
Something/Come Together			
	Apple	United States	October 6, 1969
	Apple	United Kingdom	October 31, 1969
The Beatles Seventh Christmas Record			
	Fan Club	United States	December 1969

TITLE	LABEL	COUNTRY	RELEASE DATE

Hey Jude/Revolution

	Apple	United States	February 1970

Let It Be/You Know My Name (Look Up the Number)

	Apple	United Kingdom	March 6, 1970
	Apple	United States	March 11, 1970

The Long and Winding Road/For You Blue

	Apple	United States	May 11, 1970

Got to Get You into My Life/Helter Skelter

	Capitol	United States	May 31, 1976

Ob-La-Di, Ob-La-Da/Julia

	Capitol	United States	November 8, 1976

Medley: Sgt. Pepper's Lonely Hearts Club Band–With a Little Help from My Friends/ A Day in the Life

	Capitol	United States	August 7, 1978
	Parlophone	United Kingdom	September 30, 1978

The Beatles Movie Medley/I'm Happy Just to Dance with You

	Capitol	United States	March 13, 1982

The Beatles CD Singles (Boxed Set)

	Parlophone/EMI	United States	November 5, 1992

Baby It's You/I'll Follow the Sun/Devil in Her Heart/Boys

	Capitol	United States	March 20, 1995

Free as a Bird/I Saw Her Standing There/This Boy/Christmas Time (Is Here Again)

	Capitol	United States	December 4, 1995

Real Love/Baby's in Black/Yellow Submarine/Here, There and Everywhere

	Capitol	United States	March 3, 1996

EPS (EXTENDED PLAY)

Twist and Shout
TWIST AND SHOUT/A TASTE OF HONEY/DO YOU WANT TO KNOW A SECRET/THERE'S A PLACE

	Parlophone	United Kingdom	July 12, 1963

The Beatles' Hits
FROM ME TO YOU/THANK YOU GIRL/PLEASE PLEASE ME/LOVE ME DO

	Parlophone	United Kingdom	September 6, 1963

The Beatles (No. 1)
I SAW HER STANDING THERE/MISERY/ANNA (GO TO HIM)/CHAINS

	Parlophone	United Kingdom	November 1, 1963

All My Loving
ALL MY LOVING/ASK ME WHY/MONEY (THAT'S WHAT I WANT)/P.S. I LOVE YOU

	Parlophone	United Kingdom	February 7, 1964

The Beatles
MISERY/A TASTE OF HONEY/ASK ME WHY/ANNA (GO TO HIM)

	Vee Jay	United States	March 23, 1964

Four by the Beatles
ROLL OVER BEETHOVEN/ALL MY LOVING/THIS BOY/PLEASE MR. POSTMAN

	Capitol	United States	May 11, 1964

Long Tall Sally
LONG TALL SALLY/I CALL YOUR NAME/SLOW DOWN/MATCHBOX

	Parlophone	United Kingdom	June 19, 1964

TITLE	LABEL	COUNTRY	RELEASE DATE

Extracts from the Film A Hard Day's Night
I SHOULD HAVE KNOWN BETTER/IF I FELL/TELL ME WHY/AND I LOVE HER

| | Parlophone | United Kingdom | November 6, 1964 |

Extracts from the Album A Hard Day's Night
ANY TIME AT ALL/I'LL CRY INSTEAD/THINGS WE SAID TODAY/WHEN I GET HOME

| | Parlophone | United Kingdom | November 6, 1964 |

4 by the Beatles
HONEY DON'T/I'M A LOSER/MR. MOONLIGHT/EVERYBODY'S TRYING TO BE MY BABY

| | Capitol | United States | February 1, 1965 |

Beatles For Sale
NO REPLY/I'M A LOSER/ROCK AND ROLL MUSIC/EIGHT DAYS A WEEK

| | Parlophone | United Kingdom | April 6, 1965 |

Beatles For Sale (No. 2)
I'LL FOLLOW THE SUN/BABY'S IN BLACK/WORDS OF LOVE/I DON'T WANT TO SPOIL THE PARTY

| | Parlophone | United Kingdom | June 4, 1965 |

The Beatles' Million Sellers
SHE LOVES YOU/I WANT TO HOLD YOUR HAND/CAN'T BUY ME LOVE/I FEEL FINE

| | Parlophone | United Kingdom | December 6, 1965 |

Yesterday
YESTERDAY/ACT NATURALLY/YOU LIKE ME TOO MUCH/IT'S ONLY LOVE

| | Parlophone | United Kingdom | March 4, 1966 |

Nowhere Man
NOWHERE MAN/DRIVE MY CAR/MICHELLE/YOU WON'T SEE ME

| | Parlophone | United Kingdom | July 8, 1966 |

BOOTLEG SINGLES

From Me to You/She Loves You/Till There Was You/Twist and Shout

| | Deccagone | United Kingdom | November 4, 1963 |

Hound Dog/Long Tall Sally

| | Heavy | United States | * |

Kansas/Hey Hey Hey/Ain't Nothin' Shakin' (Like the Leaves on a Tree)

| | Collectables | United States | * |

Like Dreamers Do/Searchin'

| | Deccagone | United Kingdom | * |

Matchbox/Red Sails in the Sunset

| | Collectables | United States | * |

Memphis/Love of the Loved

| | Deccagone | United Kingdom | * |

Money/Sure to Fall

| | Deccagone | United Kingdom | * |

September in the Rain/Sheik of Araby

| | Deccagone | United Kingdom | * |

Till There Was You/Crying, Waiting, Hoping

| | Deccagone | United Kingdom | * |

TITLE LABEL	COUNTRY	RELEASE DATE

BOOTLEG ALBUMS

TITLE LABEL	COUNTRY	RELEASE DATE
Abbey Road Revisited		
Wizardo	*	*
ABC Manchester		
Wizardo	*	*
Across the Universe		
Tobe-Milo	*	*
A Hard Day's Night		
Wizardo	*	*
Alive at Last in Alaska		
Walrus	*	*
Alpha Omega Vols. 1–3		
Audiotape ATRBH	*	*
And the Beatles Were Born		
Napolean	*	*
Apple Slices		
Beat-L	*	*
Appletrax '69 Vols. 1–2		
CBM219	*	*
Around the Beatles		
Wizardo	*	*
As It Happened: The Beatles and Murry the K		
Fairway	*	*
At the Cavern Club		
*	*	*
At the Hollywood Bowl		
TMOQ	*	*
At the Rarest		
Joker-Saar	*	*
A Way with Words		
Wizardo	*	*
Back in 1964 at the Hollywood Bowl		
Lemon	*	*
B.C. 64		
Wizardo	*	*
Beat Legged Live		
*	*	*
Beatlemania: 1963–69 Twenty Never Published Songs		
Zakatecas	*	*
Beatles—Alive in Atlanta at Last		
Walrus	*	*
The Beatles at Shea Stadium		
Idle Mind	*	*
The Beatles by Royal Command		
Vewy Qween Wecords	*	*
The Beatles Collector's Item		
Capitol	*	*
Beatles Dec. 1963		
ODD-Four	*	*

TITLE	LABEL	COUNTRY	RELEASE DATE
The Beatles Get Together			
	Beat-L	*	*
Beatles Happy Birthday			
	CBM	*	*
Beatles in Atlanta Whiskey Flat			
	TMOQ	*	*
Beatles in Italy			
	Parlophone	*	*
The Beatles "John, Paul, George and Jimmy" Copenhagen '64			
	Wizardo	*	*
The Beatles Live in Washington, D.C.			
	CBM	*	*
Beatles on Stage in Japan—The 1968 Tour			
	TAKRL	*	*
The Beatles Rarest Vols. 1–7			
	TAKRL	*	*
The Beatles Show			
	Beat-L	*	*
The Beatles—The Great Take Over			
	Wizardo	*	*
Complete Christmas Album			
	*	*	*
Complete Ed Sullivan Shows			
	CBM	*	*
Decca Audition Outtakes			
	CBM	*	*
Dr. Robert			
	Wizardo	*	*
Don't Pass Me By			
	CBM	*	*
Dylan/Beatles/Stones			
	IRC	*	*
Early Beatles Live			
	BE	*	*
ED's Really Big Beatles Blasts			
	Melvin	*	*
Elvis Meets . . . The Beatles			
	Best Seller Records	*	*

—Compiled by Vrnda Devi and Steven Galbraith

The Lost Songs

THE BALLAD OF
LENNIE AND MACCA*

Paul and I wanted to be the Goffin and King of England. This was an old story because they were writing this great stuff at the time and we decided, well, we're better than them!

—John Lennon

John and I would get together, "Oh, we gotta write one for Billy J., okay, 'The birds in the sky will be . . .'" and just knock them off. In our minds there was a very vague formula and we could do it quite easily.

—Paul McCartney

Aside from their own hefty catalogue of songs, Lennon and McCartney proved themselves prolific tunesmiths for a diverse host of artists. In the years 1963 through 1969, some twenty-two Lennon and McCartney compositions (that were neither officially recorded nor released by the Beatles) were summarily *given away* to other acts. The majority (written largely by either John *or* Paul) were penned as potential Beatles tracks, with only a handful composed specifically for others. Interestingly, fifteen of the twenty-two were requests from Brian Epstein for his vaunted NEMS "stable" of artistes.

In 1963, the two-man team was responsible for some seven compositions recorded by other acts, six of which ultimately made the charts. Never before had any songwriting team dominated the number-one position so completely. The Beatles no sooner left the top of the charts with "From Me to You" in June when in charged Billy J. Kramer covering the duo's "Do You Want to Know a Secret." The B-side of the single, the calypsoish "I'll Be On My Way,"

* "Lennie" was Paul's affectionate nickname for John and "Macca" was John's for Paul.

was a pleasant if underwhelming McCartney composition tailor-made for the emerging Liverpudlian heartthrob who had only recently been teamed with the established, and more obviously talented, Dakotas. The Manchester group picked to soup up Billy's lackluster sound was manned by Mike Maxfield (lead guitar), Robin McDonald (rhythm guitar), Ray Jones (bass), and Tony Mansfield (drums). Lennon later laughingly dismissed the tune, saying, "That's Paul through and through. Doesn't it sound like him? Tra la la la la!"

On the heels of the million-selling "Secret" came Kramer's second chart topper, "Bad to Me," released in July. It was written by Lennon during his controversial "Spanish holiday" with Brian Epstein. John recalled the song's creation: "That was a commissioned song, done strictly for Billy J."

Tony Mansfield reminisces, "John and Paul came down to Abbey Road with the lyrics scrawled on the back of a Senior Service cigarette pack. Whenever we were in the studio with them we generally had to learn their tunes on the spot. They always showed us the chord structures on acoustic guitar. Paul was a good musician with lots of energy and he always listened to you when you were talking, or *seemed* to anyway."

Happily, "Bad to Me" proved a chart topper on both sides of the Atlantic as Yank and Brit alike embraced the catchy tune sparked by Robin MacDonald's crisp guitar work.

The Lennon and McCartney touch, however, was not always golden, as proven by the July release of "Tip of My Tongue," from nineteen-year-old Tommy Quickly. The first solo artist to be signed by Epstein, Quickly was lavishly touted by the manager, who boldly predicted, "He's going to be a star, every bit as big as the Beatles!"

Quickly's raucous singing style, dubbed "half soul, half Herman's Hermits," made for a stage personality that often stole the show from fellow Merseybeat heavyweights Gerry and the Pacemakers and songstress Cilla Black. Quickly's frenetic energy, however, didn't quite translate to the more disciplined demands of the studio. "Tip of My Tongue," a melodically forgettable track, was recorded at Pye with Quickly's insipid schoolboy delivery under Les Reed's equally puerile production.

Colin Manley, lead guitarist for the Remo Four, Quickly's backing group, later noted, "Tommy could have been very big if he'd been handled correctly. He was a pro, but even with the Lennon-McCartney songwriter's tag, it didn't come over on record."

Quickly's group, the Remo Four, were Phil Rogers (bass), Roy Dyke (drums), Tony Ashton (keyboards), and Colin Manley.

Unfortunately, "Tongue," issued on Pye Records, failed to make the charts. Lennon later dismissed the song, commenting, "Another piece of Paul's garbage, not my garbage!" Quickly, clearly out of his element, soon left not only NEMS but the music business altogether, tragically becoming one of the first victims of the emerging drug culture.

Longtime Beatle associate Bill Harry recalls running into young Quickly at a local Liverpool haunt. "I remember seeing Tommy in the Blue Angel one night, crawling on the floor, howling like a dog. I was told he had a breakdown soon after and his success proved to be short-lived."

Another act in the NEMS family was the Fourmost, a quartet of scholars who impressed Brian Epstein with their politeness, sense of humor, and astounding twenty-seven G.C.E. passes among them. They were Brian O'Hara (vocals/lead guitar), Billy Hatton (bass guitar), Mike Millward (rhythm guitar), and Dave Lovelady (drums). Of all the artists who recorded a Lennon and McCartney work, this group most closely matched the Beatles' early sound. They hit the charts (landing at number ten) in August with the first of two John Lennon compositions, "Hello Little Girl."

Vocalist O'Hara remembers, "We had nothing original to offer George Martin for a single. I asked John Lennon for a song—I've still got the tape he gave me. [John] says, 'I wrote this one while I was on the toilet.'"

Cilla Black, the former Liverpool hat-check girl, known locally as the Cavern Screamer, was belting out rock songs when Brian Epstein decided to take her on as his lone female act. Noting her "magnificent singing voice suitable for recording along with a whispy, ethereal quality," he promptly had her sign with Parlophone and provided her with four songs written by Paul McCartney and produced by George Martin.

Black's initial McCartney song, her first record (released in September of 1963), was "Love of the Loved," which Paul composed as a teenager while walking home late at night across the Allerton golf course.

Cilla remembers, "I'd heard the Beatles do it many times at the Cavern. I wanted to do a group arrangement and I was ever so disappointed when I got to the studio and there was brass and everything. Les Reed did the arrangement. He was playing piano and Peter Lee Sterling was on lead guitar. I thought it was very jazzy and didn't think it would be a hit." Her notion was prophetic, as the single barely scraped the top thirty.

"I'll Keep You Satisfied" became the third McCartney song for the often petulant Billy J. George Martin comments on Kramer's well-known musical shortcomings: "I treated each of the other artists I had totally differently; it was the only way to work with so many acts at one time. I took on Billy reluctantly, because although he looked very good, his voice wasn't the best in the world, so I decided to always double-track him. I also used a wound-up piano to cover some of the bad notes."

Released on November 1, the spirited single shot to number four on the British top thirty, remaining on the charts for more than ten weeks. It was reissued the following July in the States for a bumpy seven-week run in the top one hundred.

Rounding out the Lennon-McCartney songbook for 1963 was John's second offering for the Fourmost, the romantic "I'm in Love," of which he confessed, "It sounds like me, but I don't remember a thing about it." A potential Beatles chart buster, the toe-tapping melody was patented Fab Four right down to the Harrison-like guitar work and breezy harmonies. Bassist Billy Hatton comments, "As opposed to the Beatles doing a song on an album and people saying, 'Can we have this one?' or 'Can we have that one?' before it's released, 'I'm in Love' was written by Lennon and McCartney for the Fourmost." The single, issued in November, remained in the top thirty for seven weeks, peaking at number twelve. The quartet went on to become a popular cabaret act throughout the seventies and eighties.

The year 1964 found the Lennon-McCartney bandwagon still rolling on, further establishing the team as formidable, versatile composers. It also marked the first time that artists not part of the NEMS family were awarded a coveted Maclen tune to record. Paul's lilting "World Without Love" was duly bestowed upon the harmonic Peter and Gordon. The upper-class pair who'd joined forces during their tenure at a private Westminster school had a two-month booking at London's Pickwick Club when they were brought to the attention of EMI's distinguished producer-arranger Norman Newell, who asked them to audition.

The A-side of Peter and Gordon's first record was to be their own "If I Were You." Fate, however, intervened when McCartney was introduced to Peter through his big sister, Jane Asher. As the bespectacled Asher remembers it, "Paul had already played a song for me that the Beatles didn't think was right for them. He offered it to Billy J. Kramer, but he decided not to record it. . . . That song, 'World Without Love,' was chosen to be our first single."

"World Without Love" showcased the pair's trademark ballad material superimposed over a soft rock beat. This was McCartney at his Tin Pan Alley best, grafting a humble melody with memorable lyrics and a clever musical hook. Newell delivered a top-notch arrangement that featured an effective marriage of bass, drum, and organ capped off by a superb mix. The single caught fire both in the U.K. and the U.S., holding the top position for two weeks and selling yet another global million.

"Nominally [the tunes we got through the Beatles were billed as] Lennon-McCartney, but they were actually Paul's songs," recalls Asher. "At that point in time, even if they wrote separately, they were construed as written together. Paul had done 'World Without Love,' but the Beatles didn't want to do it. I heard him sing it in passing, because we were friends and spent time together, even before we had passed our audition with EMI. I liked it a lot, but it was unfinished and didn't have a bridge. When we were picking songs for the first session, I told Paul if he could finish it, we'd like to do it. He wrote the bridge and it was one of the three or four songs we cut on our first session. That was the first single and it went to number one all over the world. We got off to a very rapid and fortunate start.

"I remained friends with Paul throughout that period and he told me a lot about his plans for Apple. He was aware I was interested in producing; indeed, I produced a couple singles after I stopped recording."

One of the few McCartney compositions to dissolve into rapid obscurity was the admittedly trite "One and One Is Two," recorded by the equally forgettable collective the Strangers with Mike Shannon. This frenzied, amateurish recording with its cluttered, intrusive drumming released May 8, 1964, on the Phonogram label didn't even make the charts and was so unimpressive that even the identity of its producer remains a mystery. Lennon summed it up by declaring quite simply, "This was a terrible one, another of Paul's bad attempts at writing a song." Nonetheless, the Beatles recorded an unreleased version later that year.

"Nobody I Know," produced by George Martin's future partner, John Burgess, was McCartney's second composition for Peter and Gordon, issued on May 29. Although it never entered the American charts, it was reasonably popular in England, remaining in the top thirty for nine weeks and rising to number nine for a fortnight. Burgess wisely stuck with the similar bass lines and guitar runs that had scored on the pair's first hit. With the Lennon-McCartney touch, this one, too, provided yet another gold disc for the affable British duo.

The next single to achieve top-thirty status was the upbeat "Like Dreamers Do" for the Applejacks. This second of three modest hits for the band (who hailed from Solihull, Warwickshire, in the West Midlands) was once again composed by McCartney. The former Sunday-school skiffle group was spotted by Decca's A&R man Mike Smith.

In conjunction with the record's June 5 release, McCartney commented on his inspiration: "As I see it now, we all have a great opportunity for a fantastically lucky life. We don't have to have schedules. We're the way everybody could be if they could afford it."

Predictably, after their brief, orchestrated flirt with fame, the Applejacks fell back into obscurity on the local Birmingham beat scene and then disbanded.

"From a Window," the final Lennon-McCartney gift to Billy J. Kramer's hit parade, was written largely by Paul. George Martin maintained a streamlined vocal arrangement for Kramer's narrow range while relying on both the strength of the material and the talented musicianship of the Dakotas to deliver a delicate, tuneful punch. Although the song was the least successful of the group's hits, reaching only number thirteen and twenty-three in the U.K. and America respectively, Kramer dubbed it "the best of all the Lennon and McCartney songs I recorded."

"It's for You," another solo McCartney composition, provided a fourth hit for Cilla Black. With its dominating piano and sweeping cymbals, the tune (in ¾ time) featured the flashy orchestral style popularized by Burt Bacharach.

Black's vocal, in kind, greatly resembled her old showbiz rival, Dusty Springfield. "Paul sounded great on the demo," Black reveals, "but once we got into the studio I was, again, a bit disappointed with the arrangement. It was done as a jazz waltz, but I appreciate now that it was fabulous for its time."

Released on July 31, "It's for You" remained in the top thirty for a respectable seven weeks, peaking at number eight.

In a curious turn, just as Peter and Gordon's "Nobody I Know" failed to register with America's youth, their third McCartney song, "I Don't Want to See You Again," was notoriously unpopular with British listeners. Ironically, the duo was riding high in the United States, where they were perceived as very British, unlike many other U.K. invaders who were frantically trying to discard their accents and emulate their American heroes. Issued September 21 on Columbia Records, the song remained on the *Billboard* charts for nine weeks, rising to only number sixteen.

By the mid-sixties, the demand for Lennon and McCartney songs for Epstein's clients came to an abrupt end. As the golden era of Merseymania was tailing off, Epstein's misguided zeal to acquire new talent left his already established artists in a sorry state of neglect.

Over the next five years, only six of John and Paul's tunes were given to other artists. American turned Londoner P. J. "Jim" Proby was perhaps the most unlikely recipient of a McCartney tune. Touring with Cilla Black, Britain's reigning bad boy was renowned for his infamous maniacal live performances. With his frilled shirts, Revolutionary War hairdo, and skintight pants, Proby was a prehistoric forerunner of the punk scene. "That Means a Lot," written by McCartney and released on September 17, 1965, on the United Artists label, was one of Proby's seven U.K. hits. In contrast to his wild onstage persona, the single, produced by Ron Richards, was reminiscent of the "Town Without Pity" style of Gene Pitney. As for Proby (who once cut demos for Elvis Presley and did some bit parts in B westerns), his scattered career, which flitted from R&B to show tunes, lacked direction and he never achieved his promising potential.

The lone non-Beatles hit for 1966 was Paul McCartney's final offering to Peter and Gordon, "Woman," of which McCartney cut a demo some two years earlier. The songwriting credit, however, appeared as the mysterious Bernard Webb, who was said to be an aspiring songwriter and student in Paris.

Bowing to the inevitable pressure, Paul later revealed that the composer was none other than himself. "It was kind of an experiment, really," he explained. "I was curious to see whether a Lennon and McCartney song would still sell records under a pseudonym."

Although the tune was a minor hit in England, reaching number twenty-two, it suffered from an outrageously overblown production. John Burgess, inexplicably abandoning the duo's understated trademark, instead buried the song beneath a lush orchestration with an over-the-top violin section.

The following year, 1967, was unremarkable too, noted only for McCartney's brief foray into the jazz arena with his steamy instrumental "Catcall," recorded by the Chris Barber Band. Originally entitled "Cat's Walk," the number was performed by the Beatles way back in 1961. Barber, an old mate of McCartney's from the Cavern, appeared on the bill with the Beatles at the Royal Albert Hall in 1963 and later, the five-piece band became the first U.K. combo to appear on *The Ed Sullivan Show*.

Trombonist Barber and his band scored three hits during the trad fad, with the biggest, "Petite Fleur," soaring all the way to number three in 1959.

"Catcall," produced by Barber, Giorgio Gomelsky, and Reggie King, offers a lively four-to-the-bar Dixieland romp that vividly evokes images of an alley cat out on a midnight prowl. The tune concludes with a provocative striptease through which McCartney can be heard catcalling "More, more!" Recorded at Pye Studios and released on the Marmalade label on October 20, 1967, the lively instrumental, unfortunately, did not make the charts.

The year 1968 was noted for two more McCartney compositions, written as theme songs for television programs. In March, Cilla Black again teamed up with McCartney and Martin for "Step Inside Love," composed specifically for the singer's popular BBC offering, *Cilla*.

Black remembers, "Paul said, 'What are you going to open your new TV series with?' and I said, 'I don't know.' It was a problem, because variety shows like *The Billy Cotten Show* had big openings, usually with band arrangements.

"He said, 'I think you should have a friendly song, a more intimate thing, I'll write you one.' Paul wrote 'Step Inside Love' and he also had the idea of beginning the show with opening doors. When I first sang it live on telly I forgot the words because I was nervous. I made up the lyrics as I went along and Paul, who was watching the show, was upset because he thought the producers had been at me to change the words."

The verse opens with a soft bossa nova run backed by classical guitar and slowly builds to a driving gospel crescendo. McCartney plays guitar on the track and can also be seen in the song's promotional film clip.

The second McCartney theme was written for the London Weekend Television comedy *Thingamybob,* and performed by the John Foster and Sons Ltd. Black Dyke Mills Brass Band. Founded in the forties by the Yorkshire firm, the band was comprised of thirty-nine men between the ages of sixteen and sixty. The outfit won the National Brass Band Championship of Great Britain an unprecedented ten times. McCartney was commissioned by the band's conductor, Geoffrey Brand, to compose the number as well as arrange and produce it.

On April 30, 1968, Paul (and his justly famous sheepdog, Martha) traveled to Bradford to record the disc on a quiet Sunday afternoon. The result was a rousing theme song (released on September 6) that helped launched the new Apple label, becoming the company's first non-Beatles single. An omen of things to come, the record failed to click with the public and didn't even register on the charts.

The Black Dyke boys, though, also recorded an instrumental version of "Yellow Submarine"—produced by McCartney—for the record's flip side. Interestingly, this became the A-side when the disc was issued in America. Although the group never recorded for the label again, McCartney was to feature them on the 1979 Wings album, *Back to the Egg,* on the sultry "Winter Rose/Love Awake."

Nineteen sixty-nine was the year comely Welsh girl-next-door Mary Hopkin scored a megahit with the McCartney-written and -produced "Goodbye." Hopkin, who has long since given up showbiz, remembers her first big break. "I suppose it was taken for granted that I was going to be signed. They had more trouble with my father than anything else, because he was very cautious about contracts and things. But they immediately signed me up.

"It was very interesting to see the whole setup at Apple. It was like one big party, or one big happy family. I didn't know what was going on behind the scenes because the business side wasn't as pleasant as it seemed to be.

"People like Derek Taylor always seemed to be in control, but there appeared to be a lot of hangers-on. The money spent was astounding. Booze coming in every day, and God knows what else."

Two years earlier, supermodel Twiggy had spotted the seventeen-year-old blonde performing on a TV talent show, *Opportunity Knocks,* and brought her to the attention of McCartney, who was then searching for fresh talent to develop for Apple.

"I knew she was great," Paul enthused. "She seemed to mean what she sang. Most impressive. But at the same time I thought she was very Joan Baez, a lot of her influence showed. Mary, however, said she could do other things and I agreed that there was no limit to her possibilities."

"Goodbye" was, of course, the follow-up to the five-million-seller "Those Were the Days," also produced by McCartney. "Goodbye" (on which Paul himself performed) was perfectly suited for Hopkin's wistful, affecting soprano. The single, released on March 28, spent eleven weeks in the British top thirty, peaking at an impressive number two, while lingering some seven weeks on America's *Billboard* charts.

The year also took on a foreign flavor. While McCartney was on holiday in Portugal, he wrote a piece called "Penina," after the hotel where he was staying. As it happened, Latin singer Carlos Mendes heard Paul's demo and liked it so much that McCartney allowed him to do the song. Recorded at EMI Studios in Portugal, the ballad suffered from a weak, garbled vocal, strident brass section, and sadly clichéd lyrics. It was subsequently released on July 18 on Parlophone, in Portugal only.

The following year, when the Dutch group Jotte Herre recorded the tune, McCartney forgot to inform Northern Songs that he'd allowed the group to record it. So much for that one!

Closing out 1969 was the catchy McCartney composition "Come and Get It," by Apple's most successful group, Badfinger. The four-man Swansea powerhouse (formerly known as the Iveys), consisting of Tom Evans (guitar, piano, and bass), Joey Molland (guitar, piano, and bass), Mike Gibbons (drums and guitar), and Pete Ham (keyboards and guitar), was introduced to Apple by their manager, jazz band leader Bill Collins, through his friendship with Paul's father, Jim.

Following their first Apple release, *Maybe Tomorrow,* a critically acclaimed LP that caused only minor ripples with fans, the Iveys' fortunes changed when Neil Aspinall renamed the group Badfinger, and they were commissioned by Commonwealth United Films to compose and perform the score for the zany, antiestablishment spoof *The Magic Christian,* which starred Ringo Starr and Peter Sellers. Although the soundtrack was basically a rehash of their debut LP, it was McCartney's contribution to the movie, "Come and Get It," that jump-started the talented foursome's careers. In August 1969 he took the group into the studio to produce the record.

Reveals McCartney, "I often find my demos turn out better than the finished recording. I did a demo for 'Come and Get It' which took about twenty minutes—it was before a Beatles session. Throwaways are a great thing. I did two demos I was very pleased with. That one and 'Goodbye' for Mary Hopkin, they were nice. I said to Badfinger, 'Look, lads, don't vary, this is good, just copy this down to the letter. It's perhaps a little bit undignified, a little bit lacking in integrity to have to copy someone's work that rigidly, but this is a hit sound. Do it like this and we're all right, we've got a hit. No one will know anyway. And if they do say anything say, "Yes, Paul did the arrangement," big deal, it's not unheard of.' "

The poppy rocker with its strong harmonies and infectious, repetitious lyrics soon bounded to the number-three spot on both sides of the Atlantic. Badfinger's derivative style, down to McCartney lookalike, guitarist Joey Molland, drew fans hungry for the Beatles following their breakup and accounted for several more hits after Badfinger left Apple. The imitative approach, however, distressed the talented Pete Ham–Tom Evans writing team and when Ham committed suicide in 1975 the promising group disbanded.

Of the twenty-two Lennon and McCartney giveaways, some nineteen by the original artists appear on an obscure 1979 compilation entitled *The Songs Lennon and McCartney Gave Away*. Released on EMI (Nut 18) with liner notes by former Beatles press officer Tony Barrow, the album bears witness to the most brilliant songwriting team of the century and the impossible, long-ago days that spawned them.

The Commercially Unreleased Songs*

*T*hese pieces represent the more finished rehearsals, warmups, and early version of completed songs, and are legitimate unreleased compositions by Lennon and McCartney. This list includes the best available information as to the date of recording and the specific composer.

"12-Bar Original." Recorded November 11, 1965; *written by John Lennon and Paul McCartney.*

"A Rare Cheese." Recorded November 25, 1966; *written by John Lennon and Paul McCartney.**

"All Together on the Wireless Machine." Recorded 196?; *written primarily by John Lennon.*

"Always and Only." Recorded October 1964; *written primarily by Paul McCartney.*

"Another Beatles Christmas Record." Recorded October 26, 1964; *written by John Lennon and Paul McCartney.*

"Annie." Recorded 1967; *written by Paul McCartney.*

"Anything." Recorded February 22, 1967; *specific composer unknown.*

"Aunt Jessie's Dream." Recorded 1967; *written by John Lennon and Paul McCartney.**

"Baby Jane, I'm Sorry." Recorded 196?; *specific composer unknown.*

"Bad Penny Blues." Recorded March 1969; *specific composer unknown.*

"The Beatles' Christmas Record." Recorded October 17, 1963; *specific composer unknown.**

"The Beatles' Third Christmas Record." Recorded November 8, 1965; *specific composer unknown.**

"Billy's Song (I and II)." Recorded January 28, 1969; *specific composer unknown.*

*Compositions may have been released on a solo Beatles project or as a Beatles recording in limited release. This list does not include any of the songs Lennon and McCartney wrote for other artists as they have been discussed elsewhere in the book.

"Blues." Recorded January 23, 1969; *specific composer unknown.*

"Bound by Love." Recorded 196?; *written primarily by Paul McCartney.*

"Christmas Time (Is Here Again)." Recorded November 28, 1967; *written primarily by Paul McCartney.**

"Colliding Circles." Recorded mid-1966; *written primarily by John Lennon.*

"Commonwealth." Recorded January 1969; *written by Paul McCartney.*

"Domino." Recorded January 1969; *written by John Lennon and Paul McCartney.*

"Don't Dig No Pakistanis." Recorded January 1969; *written by Paul McCartney.*

"Echoes of the Mersey Side." Recorded 196?; *specific composer unknown.*

"Etcetera." Recorded August 20, 1968; *written by Paul McCartney.*

"Everybody Needs Someone." Recorded 196?; *specific composer unknown.*

"Everybody's Rockin' Tonight." Recorded 196?; *specific composer unknown.*

"The Feast." Recorded November 25, 1966; *written by John Lennon and Paul McCartney.**

"Felpin Mansions: Part One." Recorded November 25, 1966; *written by John Lennon and Paul McCartney.**

"Felpin Mansions: Part Two." Recorded November 25, 1966; *written by John Lennon and Paul McCartney.**

"Four Nights in Moscow." Recorded 1969; *written by Paul McCartney.*

"From Us to You." Recorded 196?; *written by John Lennon and Paul McCartney.**

"Gimme Some Truth." Recorded 196?; *written by John Lennon.**

"Harry Pinsker." Recorded January 1969; *written by Paul McCartney.*

"Heather." Recorded 1969; *written by Paul McCartney.*

"Hitch Hike." Recorded 196?; *specific composer unknown.*

"Hole in the Head (Negro in Reserve)." Recording date unknown; *written by John Lennon.*

"Home." Recorded 196?; *specific composer unknown.*

"Hot as Sun." Recorded 1969; *written by Paul McCartney.**

"I Don't Want to See You Again." Recorded 196?; *specific composer unknown.*

"I Need You." (not the version from the movie *A Hard Day's Night*). Recorded 196?; *written primarily by John Lennon.*

"I'll Be On My Way." Recorded 196?; *specific composer unknown.*

"I'm in Love." Recorded 196?; *written by John Lennon and Paul McCartney.*

"If You've Got Trouble." Recorded February 18, 1965; *written by John Lennon and Paul McCartney.*

"In Spite of All Danger." Recorded 1958; *specific composer unknown.*

"Indian Rope Trick." Recorded March 15, 1968; *written by John Lennon and Paul McCartney.*

"Isolation." Recorded 196?; *written by John Lennon.**

"It's Only Make Believe." Recorded 196?; *specific composer unknown.*

"Jubilee" (also known as "Junk"). Recorded March 1969; *written by Paul McCartney.**

"Just Dancing Around." Recorded March 1969; *specific composer unknown.*

"Keep Looking That Way." Recorded 196?; *specific composer unknown.*

"Little Eddie." Recorded March 1969; *written primarily by John Lennon.*

"Look at Me." Recorded 1969; *written by John Lennon.**

"Looking Glass." Recorded 1962; *written primarily by John Lennon.*

"Love of the Loved." Recorded 196?; *specific composer unknown.*

"The Loyal Toast." Recorded November 25, 1966; *written primarily by John Lennon and Paul McCartney.**

"Lullaby for a Lazy Day." Recorded 19??; *written by John Lennon.*

"Maisy Jones." Recorded 196?; *written primarily by Paul McCartney.*

"Moonglow." Reccorded 196?; *written primarily by Paul McCartney.*

"My Kind of Girl." Recorded March 1969; *specific composer unknown.*

"Nobody I Know." Recorded 196?; *specific composer unknown.*

"Oh My Love." Recorded 196?; *written by John Lennon.*

"On Me." Recorded January 26, 1969; *specific composer unknown.*

"One and One Is Two." Recorded 1964; *written primarily by Paul McCartney.*

"The One and Only." Recorded 196?; *specific composer unknown.*

"Orowayna" (Corsican Choir and Small Choir). Recorded November 25, 1966; *written by John Lennon and Paul McCartney.**

"Pantomime: Everywhere It's Christmas." Recorded November 25, 1966; *written by John Lennon and Paul McCartney.**

"Peace of Mind." Recorded 1967; *written by John Lennon.*

"Piano Boogie." Recorded 196?; *written by Paul McCartney.*

"Piano Theme." Recorded 196?; *written by Paul McCartney.*

"Please Don't Bring Your Banjo Back." Recorded November 25, 1966; *written primarily by Paul McCartney.**

"Plenty of Jam Jars." Recorded November 28, 1967; *specific composer unknown.*

"Podgy the Bear and Jasper." Recorded November 25, 1966; *written by John Lennon and Paul McCartney.**

"Portraits of My Love." Recorded 1969; *written primarily by Paul McCartney.*

"Proud as You Are." Recorded March 1969; *specific composer unknown.*

"Rocker." Recorded January 22, 1969; *specific composer unknown.*

"Rubber Soul." Recorded 196?; *written by John Lennon and Paul McCartney.*

"Shakin' in the Sixties." Recorded 196?; *written primarily by John Lennon.*

"Shirley's Wild Accordion." Recorded October 12, 1967; *written by John Lennon and Paul McCartney.**

"Suicide." Recorded March 1969; *written by Paul McCartney.**

"Swinging Days." Recorded March 196?; *specific composer unknown.*

"Teddy Boy." Recorded January 24, 25, and 29, 1969; *written by Paul McCartney.* *

"Thinking of Linking." Recorded 1962; *written primarily by Paul McCartney.*

"Tip of My Tongue." Recorded 1963; *specific composer unknown.*

"Too Bad About Sorrows." Recorded 196?; *specific composer unknown.*

"Untitled Pieces." Recorded January 5, 1967, May 9, 1967, June 1 and 2, 1967, November 1, 1967, July 24, 1968, and January 25, 1969; *specific composer unknown.*

"Watching Rainbows." Recorded January 1969; *written by John Lennon.*

"What a Shame, Mary Jane Had a Pain at the Party." Recorded 1967; *written by John Lennon.*

"White Power." Recorded January 1969; *written by Paul McCartney.*

"Winston's Walk." Recorded 1962; *written by John Lennon.*

"The Years Roll Along." Recorded 1962; *specific composer unknown.*

"You Win Again." Recorded January 1969; *specific composer unknown.*

"Zero Is Just Another Even Number." Recorded March 1969; *written primarily by John Lennon.*

John Lennon's Family Tree

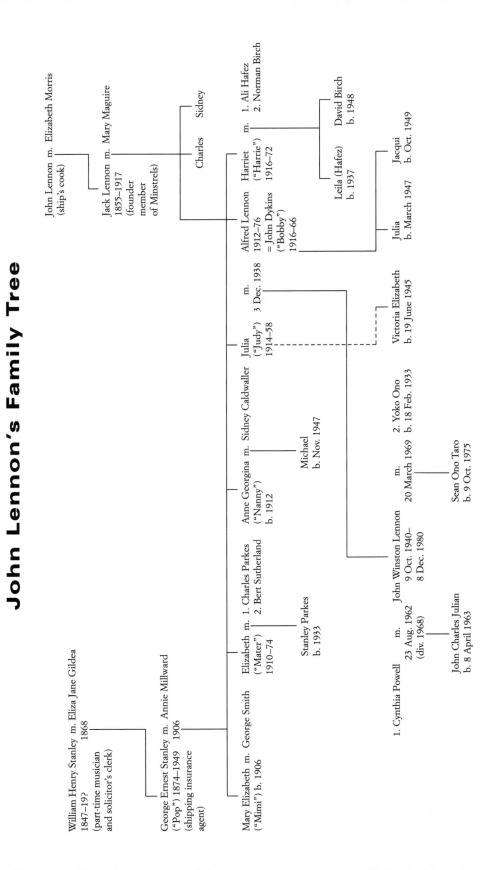

Paul McCartney's Family Tree

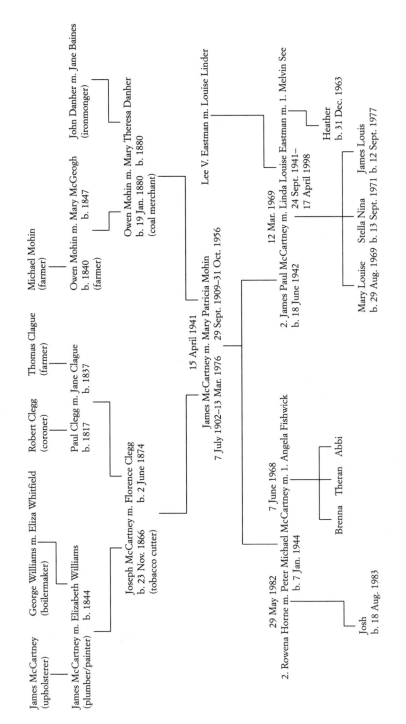

BOOKS

Aldridge, Alan, ed. *The Beatles Illustrated Lyrics.* New York: Delacorte Press, 1969.

Baird, Julia, and Geoffrey Giuliano. *John Lennon: My Brother.* New York: Henry Holt and Company, 1988.

Benson, Ross. *Paul McCartney: Behind the Myth.* London: Gollancz, 1992.

Brown, Peter, and Steven Gaines. *The Love You Make: An Insider's Story of the Beatles.* New York: McGraw-Hill Book Company, 1983.

Carr, Roy, and Tony Tyler. *The Beatles: An Illustrated Record.* London: New English Library, 1978.

Cepican, Bob, and Waleed Ali. *Yesterday . . . Came Suddenly: The Definitive History of the Beatles.* New York: Arbor House Publishing Company, 1985.

Coleman, Ray. *John Winston Lennon, Volume 1: 1940–1966.* London: Sidgwick & Jackson Limited, 1984.

———. *John Winston Lennon, Volume 2: 1967–1980.* London: Sidgwick & Jackson Limited, 1984.

———. *The Man Who Made the Beatles: An Intimate Portrait of Brian Epstein.* New York: McGraw-Hill Book Company, 1989.

Cott, Jonathan, and Christine Doudna, eds. *The Ballad of John and Yoko.* New York: Rolling Stone Press, 1982.

Davies, Hunter. *The Beatles: The Authorized Biography.* New York: McGraw-Hill Book Company, 1968.

Doney, Malcolm. *Lennon and McCartney.* New York: Hippocrene Books, 1981.

Dowlding, William J. *Beatlesongs.* New York: Fireside, 1989.

Epstein, Brian. *A Cellarful of Noise.* London: Souvenir Press, 1964.

Fawcett, Anthony. *John Lennon: One Day at a Time.* New York: Grove Press, 1981.

Flippo, Chet. *Yesterday: The Unauthorized Biography of Paul McCartney.* New York: Doubleday, 1988.

Gambaccini, Paul. *Paul McCartney: In His Own Words.* New York and London: Flash Books, 1976.

Giuliano, Geoffrey. *The Beatles: A Celebration.* New York: St. Martin's Press, 1986.

———. *Blackbird: The Life and Times of Paul McCartney.* New York: Dutton, 1991.

———. *Dark Horse: The Life and Art of George Harrison.* New York: Dutton, 1990.

Goldman, Albert. *The Lives of John Lennon.* New York: William Morrow and Company, 1988.

Harry, Bill. *The Ultimate Beatles Encyclopedia.* London: Virgin, 1993.

Lennon, Cynthia. *A Twist of Lennon.* London: W. H. Allen & Co. (Star Books), 1978.

Lennon, John. *In His Own Write.* London: Jonathan Cape, 1964.

———. *A Spaniard in the Works.* London: Jonathan Cape, 1965.

Lewisohn, Mark. *The Beatles: Recording Sessions.* New York: Harmony Books, 1988.

Martin, George, with Jeremy Hornsby. *All You Need Is Ears.* New York: St. Martin's Press, 1979.

Miles, Barry. *Paul McCartney: Many Years from Now.* London: Secker & Warburg, 1997.

Miles, Barry, comp. *The Beatles: In Their Own Words.* New York and London: Omnibus Press, 1978.

———. *John Lennon: In His Own Words.* New York: Quick Fox, 1981.

Norman, Philip. *Shout! The True Story of the Beatles.* London: Hamish Hamilton (Elm Tree Books), 1981.

Russell, J. P. *The Beatles On Record.* New York: Charles Scribner's Sons, 1982.

Sauceda, Dr. James. *The Literary Lennon: A Comedy of Letters.* Michigan: The Pierian Press, 1983.

Schaffner, Nicholas. *The Beatles Forever.* New York: Cameron House, 1977.

Schaumburg, Ron. *Growing Up with the Beatles.* New York: Pyramid Books, 1976.

Seaman, Frederic. *The Last Days of John Lennon.* New York: Carol Publishing, 1991.

Sheff, David. *The Playboy Interviews with John Lennon and Yoko Ono.* New York: Playboy Press, 1980–1.

Shevey, Sandra. *The Other Side of Lennon.* London: Sidgwick & Jackson, 1990.

Shotton, Pete, and Nicholas Schaffner. *John Lennon: In My Life.* New York: Stein and Day, 1983.

Taylor, Derek. *As Time Goes By.* San Francisco: Straight Arrow Books, 1973.

———. *It Was Twenty Years Ago Today.* New York: Fireside, 1987.

Thomson, Elizabeth, and David Gutman, eds. *The Lennon Companion: Twenty-five Years of Comment.* New York: Schirmer Books, 1987.

Tremlett, George. *The Paul McCartney Story.* London: Futura Books, 1975.

Wenner, Jann. *Lennon Remembers.* San Francisco: Straight Arrow Books, 1971.

PERIODICALS

Book Week, May 3, 1964.

Crawdaddy, May 1975, June 1976, February 1977, March 1978.

Digital, December 1985.

Gramaphone, October 1966.

Guitar, November 1987.

Hit Parader, April 1972.

Jammin', June 1982.

The Times (London), November 22, 1968.

Melody Maker, n.d.

Musician, February 1985, October 1986, June 1987, July 1987, February 1988, April 1988, June 1988.

New Musical Express, May 1970.

Paul McCartney World Tour (program/magazine).

Playboy, September 1980, January 1981, December 1984.

Rolling Stone, November 1968; January 1971; January 31, 1974; April 30, 1981; Febraury 16, 1984; September 11, 1986; December 10, 1987.

The Village Voice, August 27, 1964.

The Washington Post, February 1985.